Scott, Foresman

Texas Edition

Discover SCIENCE

Authors	**Dr. Michael R. Cohen** Professor of Science and Environmental Education School of Education Indiana University Indianapolis, Indiana
	Dr. Timothy M. Cooney Chairperson K-12 Science Program Malcolm Price Laboratory School University of Northern Iowa Cedar Falls, Iowa
	Cheryl M. Hawthorne Science Curriculum Specialist Mathematics, Engineering, Science Achievement Program (MESA) Stanford University Stanford, California
	Dr. Alan J. McCormack Professor of Science Education San Diego State University San Diego, California
	Dr. Jay M. Pasachoff Director, Hopkins Observatory Williams College Williamstown, Massachusetts
	Dr. Naomi Pasachoff Research Associate Williams College Williamstown, Massachusetts
	Karin L. Rhines Science/Educational Consultant Valhalla, New York
	Dr. Irwin L. Slesnick Professor of Biology Western Washington University Bellingham, Washington

Scott, Foresman and Company
Editorial Offices: Glenview, Illinois

Regional Offices: Sunnyvale, California • Tucker, Georgia •
Glenview, Illinois • Oakland, New Jersey • Dallas, Texas

Consultants

Special Content Consultant

Dr. Abraham S. Flexer
Science Education Consultant
Boulder, Colorado

Health Consultant

Dr. Julius B. Richmond
John D. MacArthur Professor of
  Health Policy
Director, Division of Health Policy
  Research and Education
Harvard University
Advisor on Child Health Policy
Children's Hospital of Boston
Boston, Massachusetts

Safety Consultant

Dr. Jack A. Gerlovich
Science Education Safety
  Consultant/Author
Des Moines, Iowa

Process Skills Consultant

Dr. Alfred DeVito
Professor Emeritus Science
  Education
Purdue University
West Lafayette, Indiana

Activity Consultants

Edward Al Pankow
Teacher
Petaluma City Schools
Petaluma, California

Valerie Pankow
Teacher and Writer
Petaluma City Schools
Petaluma, California

Science and Technology Consultant

Dr. David E. Newton
Adjunct Professor—Science and
  Social Issues
University of San Francisco
College of Professional Studies
San Francisco, California

Cooperative Learning Consultant

Dr. Robert E. Slavin
Director, Elementary School Program
Center for Research on Elementary
  and Middle Schools
Johns Hopkins University
Baltimore, Maryland

Gifted Education Consultants

Hilda P. Hobson
Teacher of the Gifted
W.B. Wicker School
Sanford, North Carolina

Christine Kuehn
Assistant Professor of Education
University of South Carolina
Columbia, South Carolina

Nancy Linkel York
Teacher of the Gifted
W.B. Wicker School
Sanford, North Carolina

Special Education Consultants

Susan E. Affleck
Classroom Teacher
Salt Creek Elementary School
Elk Grove Village, Illinois

Dr. Dale R. Jordan
Director
Jordan Diagnostic Center
Oklahoma City, Oklahoma

Dr. Shirley T. King
Learning Disabilities Teacher
Helfrich Park Middle School
Evansville, Indiana

Jeannie Rae McCoun
Learning Disabilities Teacher
Mary M. McClelland Elementary
  School
Indianapolis, Indiana

Thinking Skills Consultant

Dr. Joseph P. Riley II
Professor of Science Education
University of Georgia
Athens, Georgia

Reading Consultants

Patricia T. Hinske
Reading Specialist
Cardinal Stritch College
Milwaukee, Wisconsin

Dr. Robert A. Pavlik
Professor and Chairperson of
  Reading/Language Arts
  Department
Cardinal Stritch College

Dr. Alfredo Schifini
Reading Consultant
Downey, California

Cover painting commissioned by Scott, Foresman
Artist: Ralph Giguere

ISBN: 0-673-42492-8
Copyright © 1991
Scott, Foresman and Company, Glenview, Illinois
All Rights Reserved. Printed in the United States of America.

Reviewers and Content Specialists

Dr. Ramona J. Anshutz
Science Specialist
Kansas State Department of Education
Topeka, Kansas

Teresa M. Auldridge
Science Education Consultant
Amelia, Virginia

Annette M. Barzal
Classroom Teacher
Willetts Middle School
Brunswick, Ohio

James Haggard Brannon
Classroom Teacher
Ames Community Schools
Ames, Iowa

Priscilla L. Callison
Science Teacher
Topeka Adventure Center
Topeka, Kansas

Rochelle F. Cohen
Education Coordinator
Indianapolis Head Start
Indianapolis, Indiana

Linda Lewis Cundiff
Classroom Teacher
R. F. Bayless Elementary School
Lubbock, Texas

Dr. Patricia Dahl
Classroom Teacher
Bloomington Oak Grove Intermediate
   School
Bloomington, Minnesota

Audrey J. Dick
Supervisor, Elementary Education
Cincinnati Public Schools
Cincinnati, Ohio

Nancy B. Drabik
Reading Specialist
George Washington School
Wyckoff, New Jersey

Bennie Y. Fleming
Science Supervisor
Providence School District
Providence, Rhode Island

Mike Graf
Classroom Teacher
Branch Elementary School
Arroyo Grande, California

Thelma Robinson Graham
Classroom Teacher
Pearl Spann Elementary School
Jackson, Mississippi

Robert G. Guy
Classroom Teacher
Big Lake Elementary School
Sedro-Woolley, Washington

Dr. Claude A. Hanson
Science Supervisor
Boise Public Schools
Boise, Idaho

Dr. Jean D. Harlan
Psychologist, Early Childhood Consultant
Lighthouse Counseling Associates
Racine, Wisconsin

Dr. Rebecca P. Harlin
Assistant Professor of Reading
State University of New York—Geneseo
Geneseo, New York

Richard L. Ingraham
Professor of Biology
San José State University
San José, California

Ron Jones
Science Coordinator
Salem Keizer Public Schools
Salem, Oregon

Sara A. Jones
Classroom Teacher
Burroughs-Molette Elementary School
Brunswick, Georgia

Dr. Judy LaCavera
Director of Curriculum and Instruction
Learning Alternatives
Vienna, Ohio

Jack Laubisch
K-12 Science, Health, and Outdoor
   Education Coordinator
West Clermont Local School District
Amelia, Ohio

Douglas M. McPhee
Classroom Teacher/Consultant
Del Mar Hills Elementary School
Del Mar, California

Larry Miller
Classroom Teacher
Caldwell Elementary School
Caldwell, Kansas

Dr. Robert J. Miller
Professor of Science Education
Eastern Kentucky University
Richmond, Kentucky

Jan Murphy
Classroom Teacher
Rosemeade Elementary School
Carrollton, Texas

Sam Murr
Teacher—Elementary Gifted Science
Academic Center for Enrichment—Mid Del
   Schools
Midwest City—Del City, Oklahoma

Janet Nakai
Classroom Teacher
Community Consolidated School District
   #65
Evanston, Illinois

Patricia Osborne
Classroom Teacher
Valley Heights Elementary School
Waterville, Kansas

Elisa Pinzón-Umaña
Classroom Teacher
Coronado Academy
Albuquerque, New Mexico

Dr. Jeanne Phillips
Director of Curriculum and Instruction
Meridian Municipal School District
Meridian, Mississippi

Maria Guadalupe Ramos
Classroom Teacher
Metz Elementary School
Austin, Texas

Elissa Richards
Math/Science Teacher Leader
Granite School District
Salt Lake City, Utah

Mary Jane Roscoe
Teacher and Team Coordinator
Fairwood Alternative Elementary School of
   Individually Guided Education
Columbus, Ohio

**Sister Mary Christelle Sawicki,
   C. S. S. F.**
Science Curriculum Coordinator
Department of Catholic Education Diocese
   of Buffalo
Buffalo, New York

Linda Shepard
Classroom Teacher
Oscar Hinger School
Canyon, Texas

Ray E. Smalley
Classroom Teacher/Science Specialist
Cleveland School of Science
Cleveland, Ohio

Anita Snell
Elementary Coordinator for Early
   Childhood Education
Spring Branch Independent School District
Houston, Texas

Norman Sperling
Chabot Observatory
Oakland, California

Sheri L. Thomas
Classroom Teacher
McLouth Unified School District #342
McLouth, Kansas

Lisa D. Torres
Science Coordinator
Lebanon School District
Lebanon, New Hampshire

Alice C. Webb
Early Childhood Resource Teacher
Primary Education Office
Rockledge, Florida

v

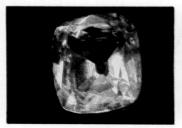

Human Body

Chapter 14

Your Body's Health Needs   292

Scientific Methods

Discovering Science

The instruments in an orchestra make many different sounds. Some instruments make loud, sharp sounds. Some make soft, low sounds. Others make sounds in between. How do the instruments make the sounds? You can use a **scientific method** to find the answer to this question.

Scientists use scientific methods to study problems. These methods have certain steps. The order of the steps might change depending on the problem. Read on to see how you can use these steps to answer some of your own questions.

Identify Problem

The problem is the question you want to answer.

Nicole had a question about the flute. She wondered how the many different sounds of the flute were made. Her problem was: How does the flute make different sounds?

Make Observations

Observations are anything you notice about the problem.

The first step in finding the answer to the problem is to make observations. Nicole noticed that a flute has several holes. A flute player blows across the mouthpiece of the flute. Each time the player opens a hole the flute makes a different sound. Nicole wrote down what she observed.

1

State Hypothesis

A hypothesis is a possible answer to the problem.

Nicole thought about her problem and her observations. She knows that there is air in the flute. You change the amount of air inside the flute when you open different holes. Nicole thought of a hypothesis. Her hypothesis was that changing the amount of air inside a flute causes different sounds.

Test Hypothesis

You can test a hypothesis by doing an experiment.

Nicole thought about how she could do an experiment to test her hypothesis. She decided to use four straws. Nicole cut three of the straws. One straw she made 14 centimeters long. Another straw she made 10 centimeters long. Nicole made the third straw 6 centimeters long. So each straw had a different amount of air inside. Then Nicole blew across the top of each straw to find out if the sound changed. She started with the longest straw.

Anything in an experiment that can be changed is a **variable.** The variable Nicole changed was the length of the straws. Would it matter if she blew harder across each straw? Yes, because then she would be changing two variables. She would not know which variable caused the different sounds.

If possible, an experiment should have a **control.** The control is the part of the experiment that does not change. In Nicole's experiment, the uncut straw is the control.

Collect Data

Data are observations from the experiment.

To collect her data, Nicole blew across the top of each straw. She noticed the sound each straw made.

Study Data

Decide what the information means.

Nicole looked at her data and thought about what it meant. To help study the data, she put some of it into a chart. Then she could quickly see what the experiment showed.

Length of Straw	Sound
whole	Very Low
14 cm	Low
10 cm	Higher
6 cm	Highest

Make Conclusions

Decide if your hypothesis is correct.

Nicole decided that changing the amount of air inside a flute causes different sounds. Notice how her conclusion is like her hypothesis.

3

Applying Science

Synthesizers

Scientists discovered new ways to make musical sounds.

Some sounds from musical instruments are made by plucking or rubbing strings. Other sounds are made by blowing into a tube or hitting the instrument. Today, some musicians use a new kind of instrument called a synthesizer (sin′ thə sī′ zər).

A scientist named Robert Moog invented the synthesizer in 1964. This instrument uses electric current to make sounds.

A synthesizer has a keyboard and many switches and dials. Some musicians use synthesizers because they can sound like different instruments. By flipping the right switch or turning the right dial, a synthesizer can sound like a trumpet, a drum, a piano, or a violin. It can also make sounds like wind, rainfall, and thunder. Most musicians use synthesizers because they can make sounds that no other instrument can make.

Today, synthesizers use computers to put together the sounds of many instruments. From this one machine, you can get the sounds of a whole orchestra!

Life Science

These zebras stay together most of the time. Together, they look for food and water. Zebras usually live in places where tall grass grows.

Many other living things live in groups. In this unit, you will learn about living things. You will discover ways living things affect each other.

SCIENCE IN THE NEWS During the next few weeks, look in newspapers or magazines for stories about plants and animals. Also look for news about places, such as parks or forests, where plants and animals live. Share the news with your class.

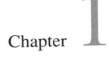

Plant Growth

Have you seen plants like some of the ones in this garden? Notice how the plants look different from each other. Yet all these plants are alike in some ways.

Introducing the Chapter

In this chapter, you will learn about the parts of a plant. You also will learn how plants live and grow. The activity below will help you learn how leaves of some plants look different.

Observing Leaves

DISCOVER!

You probably have seen leaves with many shapes and sizes. A maple leaf is about the size and shape of your hand. An oak leaf can be long and thin. A horse chestnut leaf has more than one part. You can make a leaf collection to compare the sizes and shapes of leaves.

Make leaf rubbings to record the sizes and shapes of your leaves. First, cover your desk with heavy paper. Place a leaf on the paper with the rough side facing up. Next, place a sheet of white paper on top of the leaf. Then rub the paper lightly with a pencil or crayon.

Compare your leaf rubbings with the leaves in the picture. Notice how some of your leaves look alike. Group your leaves in two different ways, such as by color and size.

Talk About It
1. Describe the sizes and shapes of the leaves you found.
2. How did you group your leaves?

9

1 How Are Roots, Stems, and Leaves Important?

LESSON GOALS

You will learn
- how plant roots help plants live and grow.
- how plant stems are important to plants.
- how green leaves make food for plants.

---

mineral (min′ər əl), a material that was never alive and that can be found in soil.

Your body has many parts. Each part of your body helps you in a different way. Plants also have many parts. Each part of a plant helps the plant in a different way.

How Roots Are Important

Imagine trying to pull a weed like this one out of the ground. You might find that the weed does not come out easily. Compare the pictures of plant roots. Notice that the weed has a long, thick root that grows deep into the soil. The grass plant has thin roots that spread out under the plant. Both kinds of roots hold plants tightly in soil.

Roots take in water and **minerals**— materials in the soil that were never alive. Plants need water and minerals to live.

How Stems Are Important

The stems of most plants hold up the leaves and other plant parts that grow above the ground. Look at the different kinds of stems in the picture. Find the plants with thin stems growing along the ground. Which plant has thick, woody stems that hold up many leaves?

Stems have tiny tubes. These tubes carry water and minerals from the roots to the other parts of a plant. The tubes also carry food from the leaves to the roots.

How Leaves Are Important

Think about different kinds of leaves you have seen. The leaves of green plants make most of the food a plant needs. This food is sugar.

Look at the picture as you read about the way a plant makes sugar. Find the arrow that goes from the soil to the leaves. This arrow shows that water goes from the soil through the roots and stems to the leaves. Now find the arrows that point to the leaf. A gas from the air, called **carbon dioxide,** goes into the plant through tiny openings in the leaves. Green leaves use sunlight to change water and carbon dioxide to sugar and **oxygen.** Oxygen is a gas in the air that living things need to stay alive. The oxygen from the plant goes into the air. Plants use the sugar to live and grow.

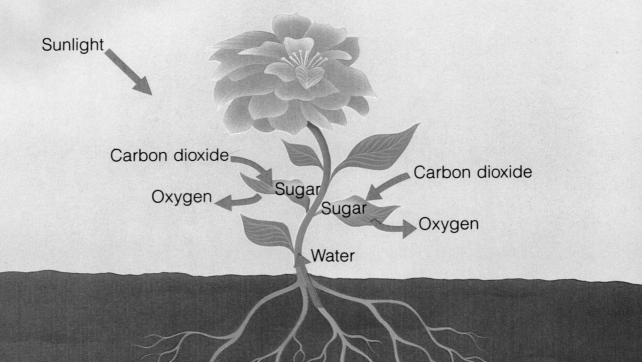

Sunlight

Carbon dioxide

Oxygen

Sugar

Carbon dioxide

Sugar

Oxygen

Water

Spring   Summer   Autumn   Winter

Most plants store some of the sugar they make in their stems and roots. Plants use stored food when the leaves cannot make enough food for the plant.

Notice how this tree changes from season to season. How do leaves help the tree in the summer? What happens to the leaves in the autumn? You can see that the tree has no leaves in the winter. Then the tree uses stored food. The tree also uses stored food to make new leaves in the spring.

SCIENCE IN YOUR LIFE

People eat some plant roots and stems that store food. You eat roots when you eat carrots, radishes, or beets. You eat stems when you eat potatoes or asparagus.

Lesson Review

1. How do roots help plants?
2. How are stems important to plants?
3. How do green leaves make food for plants?
4. **Challenge!** What makes this tree need more water in the summer than in the winter?

Study on your own, pages 316–317.

Look in a book about plants to find out what chemical makes some plants green. Write a few sentences explaining how this chemical helps plants make food.

PHYSICAL SCIENCE
FIND OUT ON YOUR OWN
CONNECTION

ACTIVITY

Observing the Movement of Water in Plants

Purpose
Observe the movement of water up through celery.

Gather These Materials
• cup containing red food coloring in water • celery stalk • scissors

Follow This Procedure
1. Use a chart like the one shown to record your observations.
2. Using scissors, cut a small piece off the bottom of the celery. *CAUTION: Use scissors carefully.*
3. Put the cut end of the celery into the cup of food coloring like you see in the picture.
4. Record what you think will happen to the celery.
5. After 30 minutes, remove the celery from the cup.
6. Use a pair of scissors to cut the celery in half.

7. Notice any color changes in the cut ends of the celery. If you see color in both ends, cut the celery higher to see where the color stops. If you do not see color in the ends, cut lower to find the color.
8. Put the pieces of celery back in order. Measure how far the food coloring went up the celery.

Record Your Results

What you think might happen	What happened	Distance the color moved

State Your Conclusion
1. Explain the color changes you saw in the celery stalk.
2. Suppose you left the celery in the food coloring for two more hours. How would you expect the color to change in the celery? Explain your answer.

Use What You Learned
Suppose the stem of a green plant was broken. What might happen to the plant?

Helping Roots Do Their Jobs

Roots have many jobs. One of these jobs is to hold a plant in the soil. Another job is to hold the soil in its place. Roots help keep soil from being washed away. When a forest is cut down, the tree roots no longer hold the soil. The soil washes away. New plants have trouble growing on the bare land. Without plants, animals leave the area to find food or hiding places.

The same problem can happen in oceans. The water can become polluted—filled with harmful materials. This can kill sea grasses that grow on the ocean floor. Then the sea grass roots do not hold down the sand. The ocean floor can get stirred up, making the water muddy. Fish and other animals leave the area when the plants are gone.

Dr. Anitra Thorhaug is working to help protect the oceans. She finds places where polluted water has killed the sea grasses. Then, she plants new grasses. They spread out and cover the bare area. The grasses then hold down the sand.

If the polluted water has been cleaned up, Dr. Thorhaug plants the same kind of grasses that were there before. If the water is still polluted, she plants other grasses. These other grasses are tough. They can live even if the

Dr. Anitra Thorhaug

area is still polluted.

To do her job, Dr. Thorhaug has to swim in rough water. Sometimes the water is muddy and dark. In the picture, you can see her working at her difficult job. She also teaches other people how to plant sea grasses. Dr. Thorhaug goes all over the world to help protect the oceans and their plants.

What Do You Think?
1. How do sea grasses help protect the ocean floor?
2. Why do you think Dr. Thorhaug does not plant the same kind of grasses in areas that still have a pollution problem?

15

2 How Are Flowers and Cones Important?

LESSON GOALS

You will learn
- how plants with flowers form seeds.
- two ways pollen is scattered.
- how plants with cones form seeds.

petal (pet′l), the outside parts of a flower that often are colored.

You might have seen flowers like the ones in the picture. Flowers look different from each other. Some plants have only one flower on a stem. Other plants have many flowers on one stem. Seeds grow inside each flower. These seeds can grow into new plants.

How Flowers Form Seeds

Look at the different colors of these flowers. **Petals** are the outside parts of the flower that often are colored. Some flowers have more petals than other flowers. Notice the sizes and shapes of these petals. What are the colors of these flower petals?

Seeds grow inside flowers.

16

Look inside the flower petals in the picture below. The center part of the flower makes seeds. A yellow powder called **pollen** must move to the center part of the flower before seeds can form.

The picture in the margin shows what happens after pollen reaches the center part of the flower. This part of the flower swells and changes into a fruit. Then the flower petals dry up and fall off the plant.

You can see seeds inside fruit. Find the seeds in the picture. The fruit helps protect the seeds as they grow. Many foods people eat are fruits. You probably have seen seeds inside apples and oranges. What other kinds of fruit can you name?

You might have seen peas growing in a long, thin cover called a pod. The peas people eat are seeds. The pod is the fruit of the pea plant.

pollen (pol′ən), a fine yellowish powder in a flower.

Fruit with seeds

The parts of a flower

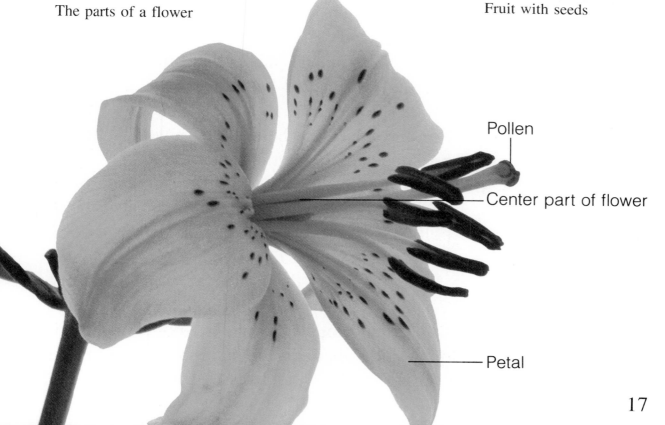

Pollen

Center part of flower

Petal

17

Pollen sticks to a bee's body.

A moth pollinates a flower.

How Pollen Is Scattered

pollinate (pol′ə nāt), to carry pollen to the center part of a flower.

You might have seen bees buzzing near flowers. Bees help flowers form seeds by moving pollen from one flower to another.

A bee lands on a flower and brushes against pollen. The picture shows that pollen sticks to a bee's body. The bee carries the pollen to another flower. Some of the pollen falls off the bee and sticks to the second flower. When a bee moves pollen to the center part of a flower, it **pollinates** the flower. Other animals, such as butterflies and hummingbirds, also help pollinate flowers. Look at the picture of the moth pollinating a flower.

Wind scatters the pollen of some flowers. Wind can blow pollen off a flower and carry the pollen through the air. The pollen can land on the flower of another plant. Wind pollinates corn and many other grasses and trees.

How Cones Form Seeds

You might have seen small objects called cones growing on a tree. Look at the cones on this pine branch. Some cones have pollen. Wind blows the pollen into the air. Some of the pollen reaches other cones. Then new seeds grow inside these cones.

Most trees with cones have leaves shaped like needles. These trees usually keep their leaves all year. Pine trees, spruce trees, and fir trees are trees with cones.

Cones on a pine tree

Lesson Review

1. How do plants with flowers form seeds?
2. What are two ways pollen is scattered?
3. How do cones form seeds?
4. **Challenge!** What might happen to a plant if you cut off all the flowers?

Study on your own, pages 316–317.

Ferns and mosses live mainly in wet places on earth. Use library books to find out how these plants are different from other kinds of plants. Also find out why water is especially important to them.

EARTH SCIENCE

**FIND OUT
ON YOUR OWN**

CONNECTION

Fern

Moss

3 How Do Plants Grow from Seeds?

LESSON GOALS

You will learn
- the parts of a seed.
- different ways seeds are scattered.
- how a seed produces a new plant.

seed leaf (sēd lēf), a part that looks like a leaf and is inside each seed.

seed coat (sēd kōt), the outside covering of a seed.

Think about different seeds you have seen. The seeds in the picture are different sizes and shapes, but they are alike in one way. These seeds can grow into new plants.

Parts of a Seed

The drawings show that a tiny new plant grows inside each seed. This new plant uses stored food to grow.

Find the **seed leaf** in each seed. Some seeds, such as the bean seed, have two seed leaves. Food is stored in these seed leaves. Other seeds, such as corn, have only one seed leaf. Notice that food is stored outside of this seed leaf. A hard covering, called the **seed coat,** protects the seed. Find the seed coat of each of these seeds.

Parts of a seed

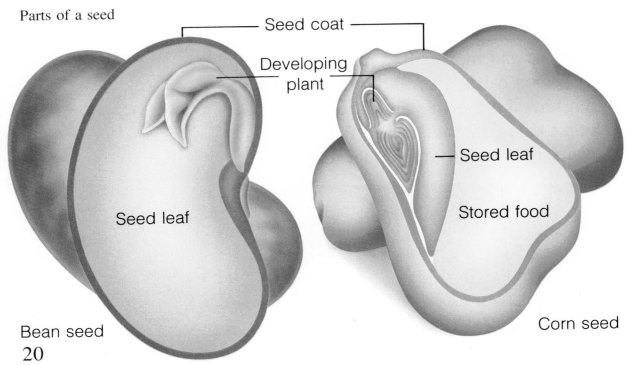

Seed coat

Developing plant

Seed leaf

Seed leaf

Stored food

Bean seed

Corn seed

20

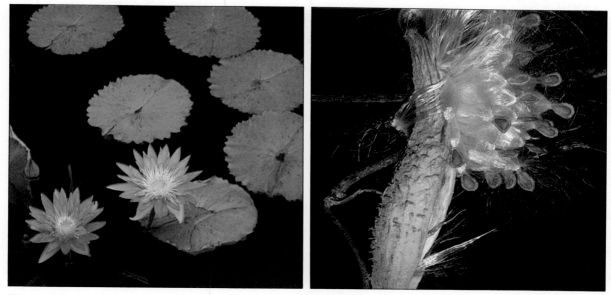

Water lily

Milkweed plant

How Seeds Are Scattered

Suppose you planted seeds in a garden. You probably would spread out the seeds in the soil. Scattering seeds helps each plant get enough water and sunlight to grow.

Animals can help scatter seeds. Some fruits can stick to an animal's fur or a bird's feathers. Some of the fruits fall to the ground as the animals move from place to place.

Water and wind also help scatter seeds. The fruits of this water lily can float long distances on water. How can wind help scatter the seeds of this milkweed plant?

How a Seed Grows into a New Plant

Many seeds grow into new plants. A seed **germinates** when the small plant inside begins to grow. A seed germinates only when it gets enough air and water. A seed also needs the proper temperature to germinate.

INVESTIGATE!

Find out if plant stems grow toward light. Write a hypothesis and test your hypothesis with an experiment. You might observe a house plant sitting on a window ledge for several days and a similar plant elsewhere in the room.

germinate (jėr′mə nāt), begin to grow and develop.

21

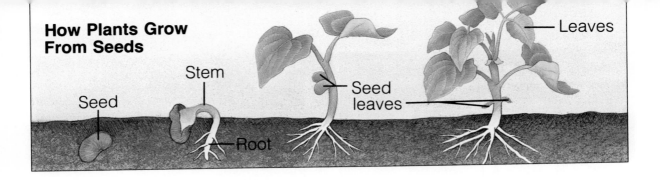

How Plants Grow From Seeds

Leaves

Seed leaves

Seed

Stem

Root

seedling (sēd′ling), a young plant that grows from a seed.

life cycle (sī′kəl), the stages in the life of a plant or animal.

The pictures show how a bean plant grows from a seed. The root pushes through the seed coat and into the soil. Then the young plant, or **seedling,** grows out of the ground. The seedling uses the stored food in the seed leaves. Finally, the seed leaves fall off and the new plant begins to make its own food.

All the stages in the life of a plant make up the **life cycle** of a plant. A seed grows into a new plant that forms seeds. Then the new seeds repeat the life cycle.

Lesson Review

1. What are the parts of a seed?
2. What are three ways seeds are scattered?
3. How does a seed grow into a new plant?
4. **Challenge!** Explain why some seeds people plant might not germinate.

Study on your own, pages 316–317.

LIFE SCIENCE

FIND OUT ON YOUR OWN

Look in a book about flowers to find out how plants grow from bulbs. Draw a picture of a bulb. Under your picture, write a few sentences telling about bulbs.

Observing How Seeds Germinate and Grow Without Light

Purpose
Observe how seeds germinate and grow without light.

Gather These Materials
- 2 cups • potting soil • pencil
- 4 radish seeds • spoon

Follow This Procedure
1. Use a chart like the one shown to record your observations.
2. Fill your cups almost full with potting soil as shown.
3. Poke about 4 centimeters of the pencil into the soil in each cup.
4. Plant 2 seeds in each cup.
5. Cover the seeds with soil. Pour 2 spoonfuls of water over the seeds in each cup.
6. Put your name on each cup. Label one cup *light*. Put this cup in a well-lighted place.

Label the second cup *no light.* Place this cup in a dark place.
7. Give both of your plants a little water every few days.
8. When the plants in one cup are about 6–8 centimeters tall, put both cups on your desk.
9. Draw a picture of each plant. Describe the way each plant appears.

Record Your Results

	Drawing	Description
Plant in light		
Plant in dark		

State Your Conclusion
1. How do the plants grown in the dark look different from the plants grown in the light?
2. If you kept your plants in the dark for several weeks, what would happen to the plants? Explain your answer.

Use What You Learned
Sometimes people use special lights to shine on plants all the time. How would you expect such plants to appear?

23

Skills for Solving Problems

Using Thermometers and Bar Graphs

Problem: How does temperature affect the number of seeds that germinate?

Part A. Using Thermometers to Collect Information

1. The thermometers in the picture measure temperature in degrees Celsius. Notice that the heating lamp is 20 cm away from Tray A and 100 cm away from Tray

B. Tray C is outdoors in February. Twenty seeds were planted in each tray. What is the temperature of Tray A? How many seeds have germinated in the tray?

2. What is the temperature of Tray B? of Tray C? How many plants have germinated in Tray B? in Tray C?

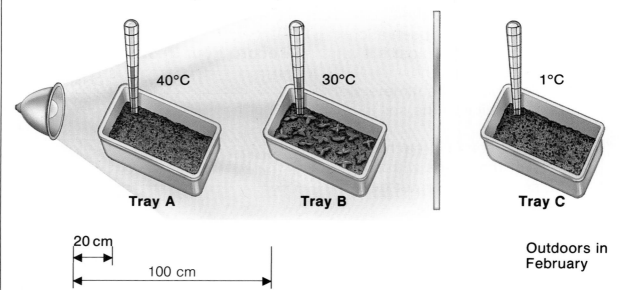

Tray A   40°C

Tray B   30°C

Tray C   1°C

Outdoors in February

20 cm

100 cm

Part B. Using Bar Graphs to Organize and Interpret Information

3. The bar graph contains the information you collected about thermometer readings for each tray in Part A. Look at the scale on the left side of the graph. What does each line on the scale stand for?

4. Look at the first bar. It shows the temperature of Tray A. With your finger, follow across from the top of this bar to the left side of the graph. What is the temperature of Tray A?

How many seeds germinated in Tray A?

5. What is the temperature of Tray B? Tray C? How many seeds germinated in Tray B? in Tray C?

6. Which temperature seemed best for seeds to germinate?

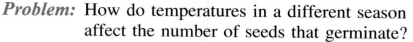

	Tray A	Tray B	Tray C
	0 seeds germinated	15 seeds germinated	0 seeds germinated

Part C. Using Thermometers and Bar Graphs to Solve a Problem

Problem: How do temperatures in a different season affect the number of seeds that germinate?

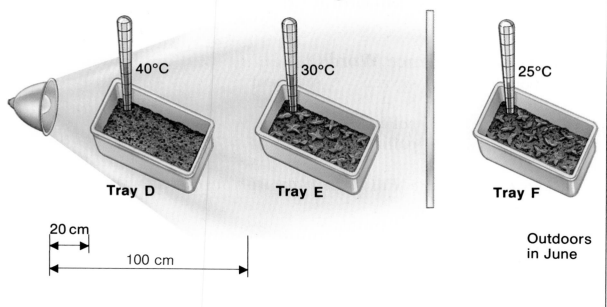

40°C   Tray D

30°C   Tray E

25°C   Tray F

20 cm
100 cm

Outdoors in June

7. Use the thermometers to collect the information you need to solve the problem. Make a bar graph similar to the one shown in Part B to organize your information.

8. Look at your bar graph. Compare it to the bar graph in Part B. How does the temperature in a different season affect how many seeds germinate?

9. You might want to do this experiment in another season and use your results to make a bar graph.

Chapter 1 Review

☑ Chapter Main Ideas

Lesson 1 • Roots hold plants in soil and take in water and minerals the plants need. • Stems hold up plant parts that grow above the ground and carry water and minerals through the plants. • Leaves make the food a plant needs.

Lesson 2 • Plants with flowers form seeds when pollen reaches the center part of the flower. • Animals and wind help pollinate flowers. • Seeds form inside a cone when pollen reaches the cone.

Lesson 3 • A seed has a small plant, at least one seed leaf, and stored food. • Animals, wind, and water help scatter seeds. • A seed can germinate and grow into a new plant that forms seeds.

☑ Reviewing Science Words

carbon dioxide	oxygen	seed coat
germinates	petal	seed leaf
life cycle	pollen	seedling
minerals	pollinate	

Copy each sentence. Fill in the blank with the correct word from the list.

1. The _____ protects a seed.
2. All the stages in the life of a plant make up the _____ of the plant.
3. A _____ is an outside part of a flower that often is colored.
4. A bee can help _____ a flower.
5. The _____ of a bean seed has stored food.
6. Green leaves make sugar and _____.
7. Roots take in water and _____ from the soil.
8. Seeds often form when _____ reaches the center part of a flower.
9. Plants need _____ from the air to make food.
10. A seed _____ when the small plant inside starts to grow.
11. A young plant is a _____.

✓ Reviewing What You Learned

Write the letter of the best answer.
1. The part of a plant that forms seeds is the
   (a) stem.   (b) root.   (c) leaf.   (d) flower.
2. A seedling uses stored food from the
   (a) petals.   (b) seed leaf.   (c) pollen.   (d) seed coat.
3. What helps protect seeds?
   (a) fruit   (b) seed leaf   (c) bees   (d) wind
4. What part holds a plant tightly in the soil?
   (a) stem   (b) root   (c) leaf   (d) flower
5. Leaves use sunlight to make
   (a) carbon dioxide.   (b) cones.   (c) water.   (d) sugar.
6. The seeds of a pine tree form in the
   (a) flowers.   (b) leaves.   (c) cones.   (d) trunk.
7. What is the number of seed leaves in a bean seed?
   (a) two   (b) three   (c) one   (d) zero
8. When a bee lands on a flower, it brushes against
   (a) seeds.   (b) cones.   (c) pollen.   (d) fruits.

✓ Interpreting What You Learned

Write a short answer for each question or statement.
1. How can animals help scatter seeds?
2. How do trees live without leaves in winter?
3. Describe two kinds of plant roots.
4. How do a bean seed and a corn seed differ?
5. How can you tell that a tomato is a fruit?

✓ Extending Your Thinking

Write a paragraph to answer each question or statement.
1. Can a seed germinate without sunlight? Explain your answer.
2. Suppose you took off all the petals of a flower. Could the flower form seeds? Explain your answer.

 To explore scientific methods, see Experiment Skills on pages 348–349.

Chapter 2

How Animals Grow and Change

A mother cheetah feeds her babies and keeps them safe. This mother takes care of her cubs. The cubs will stay with their mother until they can take care of themselves.

Introducing the Chapter

You probably have seen many animals that look different from each other. Different animals live and grow in different ways. In this chapter, you will learn how scientists group animals. The activity below will help you learn about some ways to group animals.

Classifying Animals

DISCOVER!

Think about how you might describe the animals in the picture. You might tell about the sizes or colors of the animals. You also might tell how the animals move from one place to another.

On a piece of paper, draw a picture of an imaginary animal. Your animal can be any size, shape, or color. It can walk on land, swim in the water, or fly in the air. Now exchange papers with one of your classmates.

Talk About It
1. How does each animal in this picture move from one place to another?
2. How can you tell whether the animal in your classmate's drawing walked, swam, or flew?

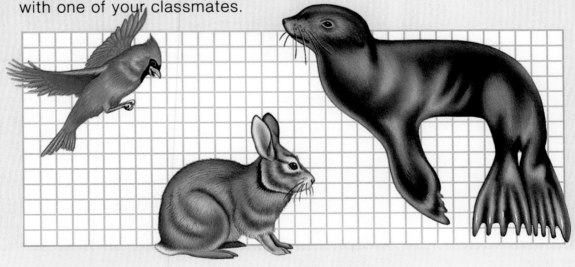

1 How Can Animals Be Grouped?

LESSON GOALS

You will learn
- that animals with backbones make up one main group of animals.
- that animals without backbones make up the other main group of animals.

Think about groups of animals at the zoo. You might find all the bears in one part of the zoo and the sea lions in another part of the zoo.

Scientists group animals in a different way. The main groups of animals are animals with backbones and animals without backbones.

Animals with Backbones

Feel the backbone in the middle of your back. Your backbone helps you stand straight. Your backbone also helps you bend and move.

You probably have seen many animals with backbones. Bears and sea lions are animals with backbones. Birds, fish, and turtles also have backbones. Look at the animals with backbones in the pictures.

Swan

Tree frog

Whitetail buck

Ladybird beetles

Starfish on purple coral

Praying mantis

Animals Without Backbones

Suppose you were having a picnic. You might notice bees or ants. A spider might crawl near you. You might see a worm in the dirt. Bees, ants, spiders, and worms are animals without backbones. Other animals without backbones are in the pictures.

Lesson Review

1. What are three animals with backbones?
2. What are three animals without backbones?
3. **Challenge!** Could a dog sit if it did not have a backbone? Explain your answer.

Study on your own, pages 318–319.

SCIENCE IN YOUR LIFE

You might have seen different kinds of seashells on a beach. Seashells come from animals without backbones, such as clams. Most of the time, these shells are empty by the time you find them. The animals have been eaten by other sea animals or birds.

Use pictures from magazines to make a poster that shows three animals with backbones and three animals without backbones. List the animals you chose from each group.

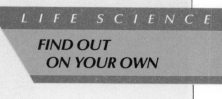

L I F E   S C I E N C E

**FIND OUT
ON YOUR OWN**

31

2 How Do Some Animals With Backbones Grow and Change?

LESSON GOALS

You will learn
- how birds, reptiles, and fish live and take care of their young.
- how a frog grows and changes.
- how mammals are different from other animals.

warm-blooded (wôrm´-blud´id), animals that have about the same body temperature even when the air or water temperature around them changes.

A robin takes care of its young.

Think about sizes and shapes of some animals with backbones. These animals often look very different from each other. Animals with backbones live and grow in different ways.

How Birds, Reptiles, and Fish Live

Imagine a bird flying high in the air. Most birds use their wings and feathers to fly. Birds also have feet and breathe with lungs.

Baby birds hatch from eggs. The parents usually protect and care for young birds. Notice how this bird feeds its young. The nest keeps the young birds warm.

Feathers also help keep birds warm. Birds are **warm-blooded** animals because they keep about the same body temperature when the temperature of the air around them changes.

Scarlet milk snake

Angelfish

You might have seen animals like those in the pictures. Snakes, turtles, lizards, and alligators are **reptiles.** These animals are **cold-blooded** because their body temperatures change with the temperature of the air around them. How does heat from sunlight change the body temperature of this snake?

Reptiles have scales and breathe with lungs. Many reptiles live on land, but some reptiles spend most of their lives in water. Young reptiles hatch from eggs. Most young reptiles can take care of themselves right away.

Which animal in the picture lives in water all its life? Find the fins a fish uses for swimming. Fish also have parts called **gills** that take in oxygen from the air in water. Fish are cold-blooded animals with scales. Fish lay eggs in the water. Young fish can care for themselves as soon as they hatch.

reptile (rep′təl), a cold-blooded animal that has a backbone, has scales, and breathes with lungs.

cold-blooded (kōld′-blud′id), an animal with a body temperature that changes with the temperature of the air or water around it.

gills (gils), the parts of fish that are used to take in oxygen from the water.

33

tadpole (tad′pōl′), a young frog.

How a Frog Changes as It Grows

Some young animals look very different from their parents. Look at the pictures of the frog. A young frog is a **tadpole.** How does the tadpole look different from its parents?

A frog is an **amphibian**—a cold-blooded animal with a backbone that lives part of its life in water and part on land. Young frogs hatch from eggs. A tadpole has gills and swims in the water. A fully grown frog breathes with lungs. An adult frog can live on land or swim in water.

Frogs have smooth, wet skin. They eat such animals as flies, mosquitoes, and moths.

Tadpole

amphibian
(am fib′ē ən), a cold-blooded animal with a backbone that lives part of its life in water and part on land.

Adult frog

34

Bat

Whale

Jaguar

How Mammals Live

Imagine touching a puppy's fur. What other animals have fur? Animals that have backbones and have hair or fur are **mammals**. This covering helps keep mammals warm. Dogs have a great deal of hair. Other mammals, such as dolphins, have very little hair.

The pictures show different kinds of mammals. All mammals breathe with lungs. Whales and dolphins are mammals that live in water. Notice how the whale comes out of the water for air. Many mammals live on land. Look at the pictures. Find a mammal that climbs trees. Name a mammal that can fly.

mammal (mam/əl), an animal that has a backbone and has hair.

35

A mother lion feeds her cubs.

Most young mammals grow inside their mothers' bodies until they are born. Young mammals get milk from their mothers. Notice how this lion feeds her cubs. Baby mammals need care for a long time from their parents. People are mammals. What kinds of care did you need when you were a baby?

Lesson Review

1. How do birds, reptiles, and fish take care of their young?
2. Explain how a frog changes as it grows.
3. How is a mammal different from other animals?
4. **Challenge!** Why do most reptiles live in places that have warm weather?

Study on your own, pages 318–319.

LIFE SCIENCE

FIND OUT ON YOUR OWN

Animals with backbones protect themselves in different ways. Use library books to find out about frogs, turtles, and porcupines. Write sentences telling how each animal can protect itself.

Observing Bones and Feathers of a Bird

Purpose
Observe that a bird's bones and feathers are light, have hollow parts, and enable a bird to fly.

Gather These Materials
• bird feather • scissors • hand lens • chicken bone • pliers • beef bone

Follow This Procedure
1. Use a chart like the one shown to record your observations.
2. Use scissors to cut the feather in half as shown in the picture. *CAUTION: Be careful with the scissors.*
3. Use a hand lens to look at the cut ends of the feather. On the chart, record what the inside of the feather looks like.
4. Use pliers to break the chicken bone into two pieces. *CAUTION: Be careful with the pliers.*
5. Use a hand lens to look at the cut ends of the chicken bone. On the chart, record what the bone looks like.
6. Look at the surface and the ends of the beef bone. On the chart, describe what you see.

Record Your Results

Bird feather	
Chicken bone	
Beef bone	

State Your Conclusion
1. Describe the bird feather and the chicken bone.
2. What makes a chicken bone more suitable for flying than a beef bone?

Use What You Learned
Suppose you wanted to make a kite. Which material would you use, a thin tube of paper or a thick block of wood? Explain your answer.

3 How Do Some Animals Without Backbones Live and Grow?

LESSON GOALS

You will learn
- how worms, snails, spiders, and insects are different from each other and from other animals.
- how a butterfly changes as it grows.

You probably have seen many animals without backbones. Most of these animals can take care of themselves as soon as they hatch from eggs. Most of the animals in the world have no backbones. Different animals without backbones live and grow in different ways.

How Some Animals Without Backbones Live

A worm has a thin, soft body and no legs. Some worms live in water. Others live on land. You might have seen an earthworm like this one. Earthworms make tunnels in the soil. Air and water can move through the tunnels. Plants need this air and water to live and grow.

An earthworm digs through the soil.

Snail

Treehopper

The snail in the picture lives on land. Other snails live in water. Look at the snail's soft body and hard shell. How does a shell help protect a snail?

Think about how a spider looks. A spider has two main body parts and eight legs. Most spiders live on land. A spider spins a web out of silk that it makes inside its body. Flies and other insects get caught in spider webs. The spider uses these insects for food.

Insects are the largest group of animals without backbones. Insects have three main body parts and six legs. Many insects also have wings. Most insects lay eggs. Some young insects, like this treehopper, look like their parents. Other young insects, such as caterpillars, look very different from their parents.

SCIENCE IN YOUR LIFE

Many insects are useful to people. For example, bees carry pollen from plant to plant. Then the plants can form seeds. People eat many of these plants. Some bees also make honey that people use for food.

How a Butterfly Grows and Changes

larva (lär′və), the young of an animal that is different from the adult. [Plural: **larvae** (lär′vē)]

pupa (pyü′pə), stage in the insect life cycle between larva and adult. [Plural: **pupae** (pyü′pē)]

All the stages in the life of an animal make up the animal's life cycle. The pictures show the stages in the life cycle of the butterfly.

The egg is the first stage of the life cycle. Butterflies often lay eggs on leaves the insects can eat after they hatch.

Find the picture of the caterpillar that hatches from the egg. The caterpillar is the second stage—or **larva**—of the butterfly. The larva looks different from the adult. A larva eats all the time and grows very quickly.

The insect is called a **pupa** when the larva makes a hard covering for itself. Inside this covering, the pupa changes.

Finally, the hard case around the pupa splits open. A butterfly like the one in the picture comes out. An adult is the fourth stage of the butterfly's life cycle.

The Life Cycle of a Butterfly

Egg

Larva

Adult

Pupa

An adult butterfly

A new adult butterfly has damp wings when it comes out of its case. When the butterfly's wings dry out, the insect will fly away.

Lesson Review

1. How are worms, snails, spiders, and insects different from each other?
2. What are the four stages of a butterfly's life cycle?
3. **Challenge!** How can the larva of the butterfly be harmful to plants?

Study on your own, pages 318–319.

Ants live in nests that have many tunnels. Some ants bring food back to the nest. These ants collect seeds and carry them underground. Look in a book about insects to find out what other work ants do. Write a few sentences describing the work.

PHYSICAL SCIENCE
**FIND OUT
ON YOUR OWN**
CONNECTION

41

Making Models of Spiders and Insects

Purpose
Make and use models of spiders and insects.

Gather These Materials
- photograph of a spider
- photograph of an insect • clay
- tooth picks • pipe cleaners
- photograph of daddy long-legs

Follow This Procedure
1. Use a chart like the one shown to record your observations.
2. Look at the photograph of the spider.
3. Make a spider body out of clay. Use toothpicks to join the body parts as in picture A.
4. Use pipe cleaners to make legs for your spider. Attach the legs to the correct body part.
5. Look at the photograph of the insect.
6. Make an insect body using clay. Use toothpicks to join the body parts.
7. Use pipe cleaners to make legs for your insect. Attach the legs to the correct body part as shown in picture B.
8. Look again at the photographs. Are there any other body parts you can add to your models?
9. In the chart, draw pictures of your spider model and your insect model. Label the parts of each animal.

Record Your Results

Spider	Insect

State Your Conclusion
1. How many body parts and legs does a spider have?
2. How does an insect differ from a spider?

Use What You Learned
Look carefully at the daddy long-legs shown in the picture. Is a daddy long-legs an insect? Explain your answer.

A

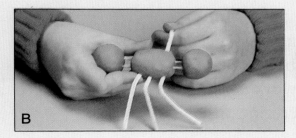

B

Seeing How Insects Behave

The bee in the picture flies back and forth between its hive and the yellow flower. How does it find its way? Can it tell apart the colors of flowers? More than a hundred years ago, Dr. Charles Henry Turner wondered about questions like these. As a boy, he watched bees, wasps, ants, and other insects. Later, as a scientist, he made up experiments to find out how insects behave.

Dr. Turner discovered that bees and wasps find their way by remembering how their surroundings look. When Dr. Turner changed the surroundings, the insects became confused. In another experiment, Dr. Turner studied bees and color. He used colored circles of paper and colored boxes filled with honey. He discovered that bees use color as well as smell to help them find flowers. Dr. Turner found that bees can even tell colors apart when they are far away.

In other experiments, Dr. Turner studied how wasps get food for their young. He also found out how insects act when light is shined on them. His work has helped people understand how insects behave. Also, his experiments showed other scientists ways to make discoveries of their own.

Bee pollinating flower

Dr. Charles Henry Turner

What Do You Think?

1. If you moved a beehive, what do you think would happen to the bees? Why?
2. Pretend you are Dr. Turner. Then, choose an insect. Think of a question you might ask about how that insect behaves.

Skills for Solving Problems

Using Calendars and Pictographs

Problem: Does how long a bird stays in its egg affect whether the bird is active as soon as it hatches?

Part A. Using Calendars to Collect Information

1. A calendar is divided into squares. Each month is divided into days. How many days are in a week? a month?
2. Look at the first calendar. How long does a chicken stay in its egg? Is a newly hatched chicken active?
3. How long does the killdeer stay in its egg? the meadowlark? Is a newly hatched killdeer active? a newly hatched meadowlark?

Time a chicken stays in its egg in days (28)

Active at birth

Time a killdeer stays in its egg in days (26)

Active at birth

Time a meadowlark stays in its egg in days (14)

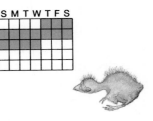

Helpless at birth

Part B. Using a Pictograph to Organize and Interpret Information.

4. This pictograph contains the information you collected about how long each chick stays in its egg. How many days was the chicken in its egg? the killdeer? the meadowlark?

5. A bird that is active and can look for food as soon as it hatches is more likely to stay alive. Compare how active these three birds are when they hatch. How do you think the amount of time spent in the egg affects how active the bird is as soon as it hatches?

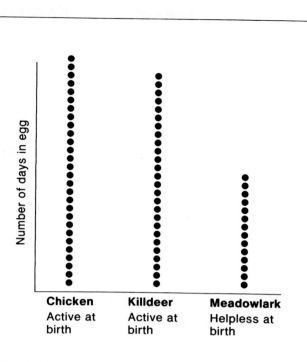

Number of days in egg

Chicken	Killdeer	Meadowlark
Active at birth	Active at birth	Helpless at birth

Part C. Using Calendars and Pictographs to Solve a Problem

Problem: Does the size of the egg affect how long the bird stays in the egg?

Chicken egg

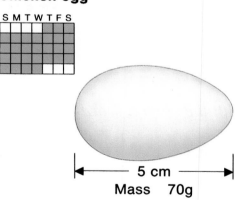

S M T W T F S

|←——— 5 cm ———→|
Mass   70g

Killdeer egg

S M T W T F S

|←— 3.5 cm —→|
Mass   35g

Meadowlark egg

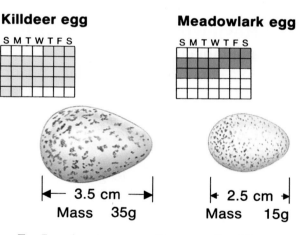

S M T W T F S

|← 2.5 cm →|
Mass   15g

6. Use the calendars to collect the information you need to solve the problem. The calendars show how many days each bird stays in its egg. Make a pictograph like the one shown in Part B to organize your information.

7. Look at your pictograph. How does the size of an egg affect how long the bird stays in the egg? What might your pictograph look like if you used the mass of an egg instead of its size?

Chapter 2 Review

☑ Chapter Main Ideas

Lesson 1 • Animals with backbones make up one main group of animals. • Animals without backbones make up the other main group of animals.

Lesson 2 • Birds are warm-blooded animals with backbones, feathers, and wings. Reptiles are cold-blooded and have backbones. Fish are cold-blooded, have backbones, and live in water. • Amphibians live part of their lives on land and part in water. • Mammals have backbones and hair and feed their young with mother's milk.

Lesson 3 • Worms have thin, soft bodies and no backbones or legs. Snails have soft bodies, shells, and no backbones. Spiders have two main body parts, eight legs, and no backbones. Insects have three main body parts, six legs, and no backbones. • Egg, larva, pupa, and adult are the four stages in the life cycle of a butterfly.

☑ Reviewing Science Words

amphibian	larva	reptile
cold-blooded	mammal	tadpole
gills	pupa	warm-blooded

Copy each sentence. Fill in the blank with the correct word from the list.

1. Fish use ____ to get oxygen from the water.
2. A hard case forms around the ____ of the butterfly.
3. A ____ is a young frog.
4. A ____ animal has a body temperature that changes with the temperature of the air around it.
5. The ____ of a butterfly eats all the time.
6. A ____ animal keeps about the same body temperature even when the air temperature around it changes.
7. A ____ is a cold-blooded animal that has scales and breathes with lungs.
8. An animal that has a backbone and has hair is a ____.
9. A frog is an ____.

46

☑ Reviewing What You Learned

Write the letter of the best answer.

1. Young animals that can care for themselves as soon as they hatch are
   (a) birds.   (b) fish.   (c) dogs.   (d) lions.
2. What is the third stage of a butterfly's life cycle?
   (a) larva   (b) tadpole   (c) egg   (d) pupa
3. One animal with a backbone is a
   (a) fish.   (b) grasshopper.   (c) spider.   (d) worm.
4. An animal with two main body parts and eight legs is a
   (a) insect.   (b) spider.   (c) larva.   (d) reptile.
5. What part of a snail helps protect its body?
   (a) gills   (b) scales   (c) shell   (d) pupa
6. One young animal that gets milk from its mother is a
   (a) turtle.   (b) whale.   (c) bee.   (d) frog.
7. How many legs do insects have?
   (a) four   (b) eight   (c) ten   (d) six
8. One animal that is warm-blooded is a
   (a) snake.   (b) fish.   (c) frog.   (d) bird.

☑ Interpreting What You Learned

Write a short answer for each question or statement.

1. How does a tadpole get oxygen from the water?
2. How do birds keep warm?
3. List two young animals that need care from their parents.
4. What are the two main groups of animals?
5. List three kinds of reptiles.

☑ Extending Your Thinking

Write a paragraph to answer each question or statement.

1. How might some kinds of worms be useful to farmers?
2. Mammals have fewer young at one time than fish. Explain how this helps young mammals live and grow.

 To explore scientific methods, see Experiment Skills on pages 350–351.

Living Things Need Each Other

The hummingbird is having a meal. It is using its long, thin beak to suck sweet-tasting liquid from the flower. The bird also eats small insects that are on the flower.

Introducing the Chapter

The activity below will help you learn how to group objects. In this chapter, you will learn how scientists divide living things into groups. You also will learn how living things need other living things to stay alive.

Classifying Objects

DISCOVER!

Look at the buttons you get from your teacher. Think about how you would describe the different buttons.

Divide the buttons into two groups. You might group the buttons by their sizes, shapes, or colors. What other ways can you divide your buttons into groups? Ask a classmate to figure out how you grouped the buttons. Now think of another way to divide the buttons into groups. Ask your classmate to try to figure out how you grouped the buttons the second time.

Talk About It
1. What two ways did you group the buttons?
2. How could you divide one of your groups into two smaller groups?

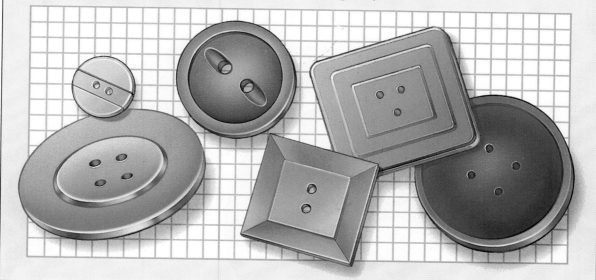

1 What Are the Five Groups of Living Things?

LESSON GOALS

You will learn
- how living things are alike.
- how scientists group living things.

organism
(ôr′gə niz′əm), a living thing.

cell (sel), the basic unit of an organism.

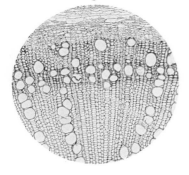

Plant cells

Look at the pictures at the bottom of these two pages. Notice that each picture looks different. All of these pictures show things that are alive.

How Living Things Are Alike

You cannot always easily tell what is alive and what is not. How can you tell if something is alive? Living things—or **organisms**—are alike in certain ways. All organisms grow. Organisms need food. They make more organisms like themselves. Organisms are made of one or more cells.

Cells are the basic units of an organism. Think about how bricks can make up a building. In much the same way, cells make up an organism. The picture on the left shows plant cells. Most cells are so tiny you need to use a microscope to see them.

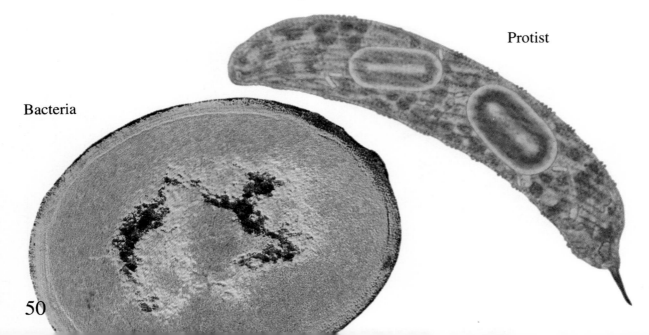

Protist

Bacteria

50

How Scientists Group Living Things

Millions of different kinds of organisms live on the earth. Scientists have divided these organisms into five groups: bacteria, protists, fungi, plants, and animals. These pictures show an organism from each group.

Bacteria are made of one cell. Some bacteria use other living things for food. Some bacteria can make their own food. Many kinds of bacteria help people. For example, certain bacteria are used to make medicines. A few bacteria cause illnesses, such as sore throats.

Protists are made of one or more cells. They live in wet places. Many protists have parts that help them move. Some protists can make their own food and some cannot. The picture shows a protist that is made of one cell. This protist moves by whipping its tail back and forth. Most seaweeds are protists. Seaweeds have many cells and make their own food.

bacteria (bak tir′ē ə), organisms made of one cell that can be seen through a microscope.

protists (prō′tists), organisms that live in wet places and have one or more cells.

Animal

Fungus

Plant

51

Kelp are large protists that live in oceans. They are used as food and in making ice cream and some medicines.

fungus (fung′gəs), an organism, such as a mold or mushroom, that gets food from dead material or by growing on foods or living things. [Plural: **fungi** fun′jī]

Mold

A **fungus** can be only one cell, but most fungi are more than one cell. Fungi cannot make their own food. Some fungi grow on foods. The mold in the picture is a fungus that grows on bread. Other fungi grow on living things and can make them sick. Mushrooms are fungi that get food from dead material in the soil.

Plants and animals are made of many cells. Plants can make food. Animals must eat food. Plants do not move from place to place on their own. Their roots keep them attached to the soil. Animals can move around. What are some ways animals move from place to place?

Lesson Review

1. How are living things alike?
2. What are the five groups of organisms?
3. **Challenge!** How are animals and fungi alike?

Study on your own, pages 320–321.

Study on your own, pages 320–321.

PHYSICAL SCIENCE

FIND OUT ON YOUR OWN

CONNECTION

Yeast is a fungus used in baking bread. Find out what gas yeast gives off that causes bread to rise.

Feeding the Jays

ACTIVITY

Purpose
Observe how the food supply affects a population in a habitat.

Gather These Materials
• 25 small paper plates • colored markers • 20 sunflower seeds

Follow This Procedure
1. Use a chart like the one shown to record your observations.
2. Write the word *Jay* on 20 paper plates.
3. Place 4 of the plates in front of you and put 5 sunflower seeds on each plate, as shown in the picture. Each Jay gets to eat 5 seeds.
4. Record the number of Jays and how many seeds each Jay gets to eat.
5. Place 1 more plate in front of you. Divide the seeds equally among all the Jays.

6. Repeat step 4.
7. Place 5 more Jay plates in front of you. Divide the seeds equally among all the Jays.
8. Repeat step 4.
9. Lay all the Jay plates out and divide the seeds equally among all the Jays.
10. Repeat step 4.
11. Make 5 more Jay plates. Divide the seeds equally.

Record Your Results

Number of Jays	Seeds each Jay had to eat
4	
5	
10	
20	
25	

State Your Conclusion
1. How did changing the number of Jays change the number of seeds that each Jay could eat?
2. How many Jays can get food in your habitat?

Use What You Learned
How might the population of Jays change when the population of sunflowers changes?

53

2 How Do Organisms Live Together?

LESSON GOALS

You will learn
- what a population is and what can cause the size of a population to change.
- how groups of different kinds of organisms live in a community.
- how each organism in a community lives in its own place.

population
(pop′yə lā′shən), organisms of the same kind that live in the same place.

Population of swans

The swans in the picture stay together most of the time. They look for food together, drink water together, and rest together. Many animals and other organisms live in groups.

Populations

A **population** is a group of organisms of the same kind that live in the same place. These swans are part of a population. What other population do you see in the picture?

The size of a population can change from time to time. Every year, some members of the population die and new members are born. Populations often grow larger when there is plenty of food. Populations often become smaller when there is not enough food. How might the amount of sunlight and water cause the size of a plant population to change?

Communities

Think of your favorite outdoor place. How many different populations live there? Most places have more than one kind of population. For example, a meadow has populations of birds, deer, and trees. An ocean has populations of fish, crabs, and seaweeds.

All the populations that live together in the same place make up a **community**. The organisms in a community depend on each other for food and shelter. The picture shows a forest community. Think about how the organisms in a forest depend on each other. This squirrel makes its nest in the tree. The rabbit eats plants. The birds feed on worms and insects that live in the forest. Insects, such as this butterfly, pollinate the plants.

INVESTIGATE!

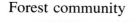

The populations in a garden need space, sun, soil, and water. Find out how pulling the weeds out of a garden affects the growth of other populations. Write a hypothesis and test it with an experiment.

community
(kə myü′nə tē), all plants, animals, and other organisms that live in the same place.

Forest community

Habitats

habitat (hab′ə tat), the place where an organism lives.

Red-necked grebe

Each organism in a community lives in its own special place—or **habitat.** An organism gets everything it needs from its habitat. It gets food, water, shelter, and space to live.

The bird in the picture lives in a pond community. The bird's habitat is its nest and the part of the pond where it swims and finds food.

Lesson Review

1. What might cause the size of a population to change?
2. What makes up a community?
3. What does an organism get from its habitat?
4. **Challenge!** How do you depend on other organisms for food and shelter?

Study on your own, pages 320–321.

LIFE SCIENCE

FIND OUT ON YOUR OWN

Choose a plant or animal that lives near you. Draw a map of the organism's habitat. Use a meter stick to measure the distances between objects. Then record the meters on a map like this.

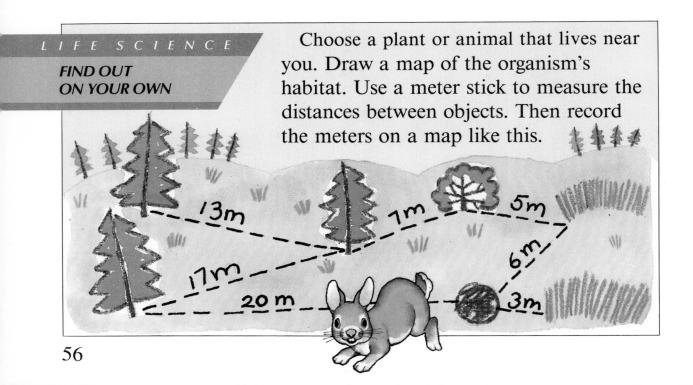

Making a Model of a Food Chain

Purpose
Make a model of a food chain and *observe* that the links of a food chain depend on each other.

Gather These Materials
•strips of paper • tape • crayons or pencil

Follow This Procedure
1. Use a chart like the one shown to record your observations.

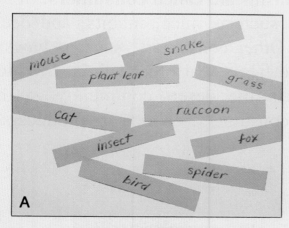

A

B

2. Picture A shows the names of plants and animals. Choose at least four of these names to make a food chain. Write the name of each of your organisms on a separate strip of paper.
3. Arrange the strips in the correct order for a food chain.
4. Tape the first paper strip so that it makes a circle.
5. Loop the second strip through the first strip and tape it to make a chain as shown in the picture.
6. Add the other links to your chain.
7. Record the names of the organisms you used.

Record Your Results

Food chain

State Your Conclusion
1. Explain how the organisms you chose make up a food chain.
2. What happens to a food chain if one of the links breaks?

Use What You Learned
Explain why two producers cannot be in the same food chain.

3 How Do Organisms Get Food?

LESSON GOALS

You will learn
- that, to get food, some organisms make food and some organisms eat food.
- how some animals catch and eat other animals.
- how organisms depend on each other for food.

producer (prə dü′sər), an organism that makes its own food.

consumer (kən sü′mər), an organism that eats food.

Think about the different kinds of food you eat every day. All living things need food. Different organisms get food in different ways.

Producers and Consumers

You learned in Chapter 1 that green plants use sunlight to make—or produce—their own food. Plants and other organisms that make their own food are called **producers.**

Most organisms cannot make their own food. They must eat—or consume—food. These organisms are called **consumers.** Some consumers, such as mice, rabbits, and deer, eat plants. Other consumers, such as hawks, wolves, and tigers, eat other animals. Which organisms in the desert community in the picture are consumers? Which are producers?

Lion hunting for food

Predators and Prey

Many consumers hunt for their food. Hawks fly over fields and look for animals to catch and eat. Some snakes quietly wait for small animals to come near. Then they catch and eat the animals. Tigers follow herds of antelope. They wait for an antelope to wander away from the herd. Then the tigers chase and catch the antelope for food.

Animals that hunt for their food are **predators.** The animals they catch and eat are their **prey.** Which animal in the picture is the predator? Which animals are the prey?

predator (pred′ə tər) organism that captures and eats other organisms.

prey (prā), organism that is captured and eaten by another organism.

Food chain

food chain, the way food passes from one organism to another organism in a community.

Food Chains

Organisms in a community depend on each other for food. A **food chain** is the way food passes from one organism to another in a community. The picture shows a food chain in a meadow. The grass makes its own food. Mice feed on the grass. Snakes eat the mice. Coyotes eat the snakes.

All communities have food chains. Food chains are found in the soil, on land, and in water.

Lesson Review

1. What is a producer? What is a consumer?
2. How are predators and prey different?
3. What is an example of a food chain in a meadow?
4. **Challenge!** Why do food chains begin with plants or some other kinds of producers?

Study on your own, pages 320–321.

LIFE SCIENCE

FIND OUT ON YOUR OWN

Look in library books to find out about marshes and the organisms that live in them. Write a few sentences explaining how these organisms depend on each other for food.

Helping Pandas Survive

The Problem   You might have trouble thinking of the animal in the picture as a picky eater. Giant pandas like this one eat a lot of mostly one food—bamboo. Wild giant pandas live in bamboo forests in the mountains of China. The problem is that populations of pandas are getting smaller. Only about 700 remain in the whole world. China is trying to protect pandas by not letting people hunt them. Even so, sometimes pandas fall into traps set for other animals. Scientists are trying to understand how pandas live to try to save them. Understanding the problem is the first step to solving it.

The Breakthrough   During the last ten years, photographs of panda habitats were taken from space satellites. These photographs show how the clearing of forests has hurt panda populations. Now scientists know that when trees are cut down, the pandas move. Sometimes they cannot find bamboo in their new home. Cleared forest areas split pandas into groups of fewer than twenty animals. If they cannot find bamboo, small groups are easily wiped out.

New Technology   Scientists have made a special kind of community

Giant panda

to help pandas live and grow. One community is in a large protected area in China. About one hundred pandas live there. Each panda in the community has its own house. A hungry panda can go to feed in a nearby bamboo thicket. When a female panda is ready to mate, she can walk around until she finds a male. Pandas do have babies, but many do not live to be adults in the wild. Scientists hope that the pandas born in their new community can be released into the wild.

What Do You Think?
1. How have people harmed pandas?
2. Why is it especially hard for a small group of pandas in the wild to produce a new generation?

Skills for Solving Problems

Using Diagrams and Pie Graphs

Problem: How does the number of producers in a marsh community compare to the number of consumers?

Part A. Using a Diagram to Collect Information

1. Look at the diagram below. All the organisms in an area make up a community. How many organisms are shown in the diagram?
2. Producers are organisms that make their own food. Plants use sunlight to make their food. How many producers are in the community?
3. Organisms that cannot make their own food are consumers. All animals are consumers. How many consumers are in the community?

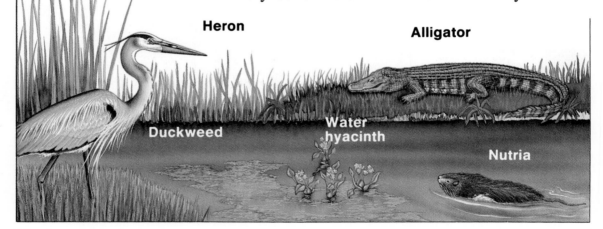

Marsh community

Part B. Using Pie Graphs to Organize and Interpret Information

4. This pie graph contains the information you collected in Part A about producers and consumers. A pie graph is a circle divided into pieces like slices. What does each slice of the graph stand for? How many organisms are shown in the pie graph?

5. In the graph, producers are pink and consumers are green. How many producers are shown? How many consumers are shown?

6. Can the number of living things in a community change? How would this affect the number of slices in the pie graph?

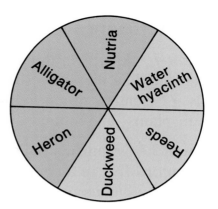

Part C. Using a Diagram and a Pie Graph to Solve a Problem

Problem: How does the number of producers in a pond community compare to the number of consumers in the community?

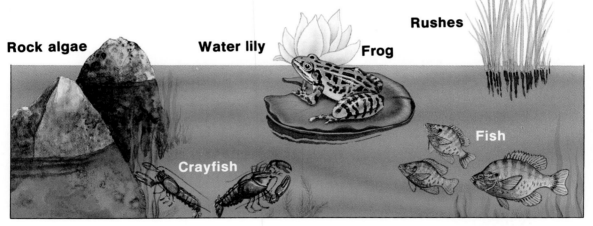

Pond community

7. Use the diagram to collect the information you need to solve the problem. Make a pie graph similar to the one shown in Part B to organize your information.

8. How many organisms are in the pond community shown here? How many of these organisms are producers? How many are consumers? How many slices does your pie graph have?

9. How is the pond community like the marsh community shown in Part A? How is it different?

Chapter 3 Review

☑ Chapter Main Ideas ━━━━━━━━━━━━━━━━━━

Lesson 1 • All living things grow, need food, make more organisms like themselves, and are made of one or more cells. • Scientists group living things into bacteria, protists, fungi, plants, and animals.

Lesson 2 • Organisms live in populations. • Different populations live in a community. • Each organism in a community has its own habitat.

Lesson 3 • Organisms can be producers or consumers. • Some animals catch and eat other animals. • Organisms depend on each other for food.

☑ Reviewing Science Words ━━━━━━━━━━━━━━

bacteria	fungi	predator
cell	habitat	prey
community	organisms	producer
consumers	population	protist
food chain		

Copy each sentence. Fill in the blank with the correct word from the list.

1. A ▨▨ is the way food passes from one organism to another in a community.
2. An animal that is captured and eaten by another animal is called ▨▨.
3. Each organism in a community lives in its own ▨▨.
4. ▨▨ are organisms that are made of one cell and sometimes cause illnesses.
5. ▨▨ are organisms that get food from dead material.
6. A ▨▨ is a group of organisms of the same kind that live in the same place.
7. The smallest living part of an organism is a ▨▨.
8. An organism that makes its own food is called a ▨▨.
9. All the organisms that live in one place make up a ▨▨.
10. Scientists have divided ▨▨ into five main groups.

11. A ▨ catches and eats another organism.
12. A ▨ is an organism that lives in a wet place and has one or more cells.
13. Living things that depend on other living things for food are ▨.

Reviewing What You Learned

Write the letter of the best answer.

1. A group of goldfish that live in a pond make up a
   (a) community.   (b) population.   food chain.   (d) habitat.
2. All organisms are made of one or more
   (a) bacteria.   (b) food chains.   (c) prey.   (d) cells.
3. A frog that catches and swallows a grasshopper is a
   (a) predator.   (b) producer.   (c) protist.   (d) prey.
4. Most seaweeds are
   (a) fungi.   (b) animals.   (c) protists.   (d) bacteria.
5. A pine tree is a
   (a) predator.   (b) producer.   (c) consumer.   (d) protist.

Interpreting What You Learned

Write a short answer for each question or statement.

1. What might happen to a plant population if the weather is unusually dry for a long period of time?
2. What are two ways plants and animals differ?
3. List these steps in a food chain in order: a bird eats a grasshopper, the grasshopper eats a plant, a fox eats the bird, the plant makes its own food.

Extending Your Thinking

Write a paragraph to answer each question.

1. What would happen to the population of mice in a field if the population of snakes grew larger? Explain.
2. Suppose all the plants in a pond died. What would happen to the food chain in the pond? Explain your answer.

 To explore scientific methods, see Experiment Skills on pages 352–353.

Chapter 4

How People Affect Plants and Animals

These raccoons find food, water, shelter, and space to live in their wooded habitat.

Introducing the Chapter

In this chapter you will learn how people affect plants and animals. You will also learn how plants and animals affect people. People make many things from plants and animals. In the activity below you will make a dye from a cabbage plant.

DISCOVER!

Making a Plant Dye

Plants have different colors. Some plants are green. Others are red, yellow, or purple. People make dyes from the colored parts of some plants. They use the dyes to color fabrics, paper, and other things.

You can use a red cabbage plant to make a dye. Then, you can use the dye to paint a picture.

Tear some cabbage into small pieces. Place the pieces into a cup. Add a few tablespoons of water to the cup. Stir the pieces of cabbage until the water becomes darkly colored. Remove the cabbage from the cup. Use the dye in the cup to paint a picture.

Talk About It
1. What part of the cabbage plant did the dye in your cup come from?
2. What are some other things people make from plants?

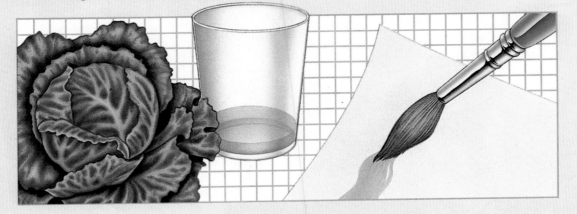

1 How Do People Change the Lives of Plants and Animals?

LESSON GOALS

You will learn
- how people change habitats.
- about endangered organisms.
- about extinct organisms.

The owl in the picture lives in a forest. Suppose people cut down the forest so they could build new houses. Then the owl would have to look for a new home.

How People Change Habitats

When people build houses, roads, or factories, they change the habitats of many organisms. An organism gets everything it needs from its habitat, such as food, water, and shelter. If the habitat changes, the organism might not be able to live there anymore.

Owl in tree

Sometimes, people change habitats by adding harmful things to them. **Pollution** is anything harmful added to the air, water, or land. Pollution can kill organisms and can destroy their habitats.

People pollute the air when they burn fuels in their homes, cars, and factories. Gasoline, coal, and oil are some kinds of fuels. When a fuel burns, it gives off harmful chemicals.

Look at the water pollution in the picture. Some factories pollute water by dumping chemical wastes into lakes and streams. The chemicals can poison fish and other organisms in the water.

When people litter, they pollute the land. Litter can change the appearance of the land. It can also change the habitats of plants and animals.

pollution (pə lü′shən), anything harmful added to the air, water, or land.

INVESTIGATE!

Find out how people can affect the plants and animals in a habitat. Write a hypothesis and test your hypothesis with an experiment. You might set up two terrariums and then observe them for a few weeks, changing one variable at a time in one of the terrariums.

Polluted river

Endangered Plants and Animals

SCIENCE IN YOUR LIFE

Scientists thought the ivory-billed woodpecker was extinct. It lived in forests in the United States. When the forests were cut down, the bird's habitat was destroyed. To their surprise, scientists found a few of the woodpeckers in Cuba in 1986.

endangered
(en dān′jərd)
organisms, kinds of organisms that are very few in number and might someday no longer be found on the earth.

Some organisms can find new homes when their habitats are changed. Other organisms cannot find new homes. Those organisms die.

When many organisms of the same kind die, that kind of organism might become endangered. **Endangered organisms** are kinds of organisms that are very few in number. Someday these organisms might no longer be found on the earth.

People have caused many kinds of organisms to become endangered by changing their habitats or by killing the organisms. Tigers are endangered animals. They used to live in many parts of Asia. Over the years, people killed many tigers for sport and for their fur. People also cut down the forests where the tigers lived. Endangered organisms live in many parts of the world. What endangered organisms do you see in the pictures?

Pitcher's thistle flower

Loggerhead turtle

Extinct Plants and Animals

Some kinds of plants and animals no longer are found on the earth. These organisms are **extinct.** The picture on the right shows a fossil of an extinct plant.

The dodo bird in the picture used to live on an island that had no people. In the 1500s, sailors landed on the island. They killed many dodo birds for food. The sailors' dogs destroyed the eggs of the dodo birds. The number of dodos became smaller and smaller. Finally, dodo birds became extinct.

extinct (ek stingkt′) **organisms,** kinds of organisms that no longer are found on the earth.

Leaves of Maidenhair tree

Dodo bird

Lesson Review

1. How do people change the habitats of plants and animals?
2. How have people caused some plants and animals to become endangered?
3. What are extinct plants and animals?
4. **Challenge!** How can people prevent tigers from becoming extinct?

Study on your own, pages 322–323.

Scientists think the weather might have caused dinosaurs to become extinct millions of years ago. Use an encyclopedia to find out how the weather might have changed the dinosaurs' habitat. Write a report about what you learned.

EARTH SCIENCE
FIND OUT ON YOUR OWN
CONNECTION

2 How Do People Protect Plants and Animals?

LESSON GOALS

You will learn
- how people protect the habitats of plants and animals.
- how people protect endangered plants and animals.

Mountain Goat in Glacier National Park

The bird in the picture is a bald eagle. At one time only 15,000 bald eagles were alive. Then, people began to protect these birds. Today, about 37,000 bald eagles live on the earth. Without the help of people, these birds might have become extinct.

Protecting Habitats of Plants and Animals

People can protect plants and animals from becoming endangered or extinct. One way of protecting organisms is by protecting their habitats. Look at the park in the picture on the left. People have made large parks such as this one to protect plants and animals. No one is allowed to disturb the habitats in these parks. People cannot build houses there. They cannot hunt animals. No one can collect plants or animals in the parks.

People have made laws that protect organisms and their habitats. Hunting laws do not allow people to hunt certain kinds of animals. Some laws limit the number of trees that can be cut down in forests. Other laws do not allow people to build houses, stores, or factories in certain places.

People can also protect habitats by trying not to pollute them. For example, some factories remove chemical wastes from water before returning the used water to lakes and streams. Factories also use certain kinds of coal that cause less air pollution when they are burned.

SCIENCE IN YOUR LIFE

Many bluebirds used to live in the eastern United States. Today, these birds are rare. Other birds took their nesting places. Now, people are trying to protect bluebirds. Some people have made boxes that are safe places for bluebirds to build nests.

Field of wildflowers

Protecting Endangered Plants and Animals

Scientists protect endangered plants by saving their seeds, growing the seeds indoors, and later putting the plants in their habitats. These people protect wildflowers.

Some endangered animals are placed in zoos. Someday the animals might be returned to their habitats.

Lesson Review

1. How do people protect the habitats of plants and animals?
2. How do people protect endangered plants and animals?
3. **Challenge!** How can you help fight pollution?

Study on your own, pages 322–323.

Study on your own, pages 322–323.

LIFE SCIENCE

FIND OUT ON YOUR OWN

The black-footed ferret is an endangered animal. Use library books to find out how many populations of black-footed ferrets remain alive, and where these animals live. Write a few sentences telling what you learned.

Making a Model of an Animal Habitat

Purpose

Identify the kind of habitat an animal lives in and *make a model* of that habitat.

Gather These Materials

- crayons or colored markers
- scissors • construction paper
- glue • shoe box

Follow This Procedure

1. Use a chart like the one shown to record your observations.
2. Choose one wild animal, such as a tiger. Draw a picture of it. Color and cut out your picture.
3. Make a model of the animal's habitat. Use construction paper for different parts of the habitat. You might cut out the outline of a tree or a rock. Glue the parts of the habitat inside the shoe box.
4. Glue the picture of the animal in the habitat.
5. List all the parts of the habitat in the chart. For each part of the habitat, write what might happen to the animal if that part was destroyed.

Record Your Results

Part of Habitat Destroyed	What Might Happen to Animal
1.	
2.	
3.	

State Your Conclusion

1. What kind of a model habitat did you make?
2. Why is the habitat you made a good place for your animal to live in?

Use What You Learned

What might happen to your animal if a road were built through the animal's habitat?

3 How Do People Use Plants and Animals?

LESSON GOALS

You will learn
• how people get foods from plants and animals.
• that some useful things are made from plants and animals.
• that some plants and animals are harmful.

Plants and animals are important to you. Many foods you eat come from plants and animals. Some of the clothes you wear also come from plants and animals. Plants and animals help keep you alive.

Food from Plants and Animals

Look at the foods in the picture. Where do these foods come from? Fruits and vegetables come from plants. Grains, such as wheat, oats, and corn, also come from plants. People use grains to make bread, macaroni, and cereal. You can see in the picture that people eat almost every kind of plant part. Grains are seeds. Lettuce is leaves. Potatoes are stems. Apples are fruits. What kind of plant part are carrots?

Meat comes from animals. A chicken leg, a hamburger, and a piece of fish are some kinds of meat. Milk and eggs also come from animals. People use milk in many ways. People drink milk. They also make cheese, butter, yogurt, and ice cream from it.

Many of the foods you eat look different from the plants or animals from which they came. Look at the foods below. What plant did the juice in the picture come from? What animal did the eggs come from?

Silk cloth comes from caterpillars called silkworms. Silkworms make long, thin threads of silk and then wrap themselves up in the silk. This silk covering is called a cocoon. People get silk by unwinding the silk threads of cocoons.

fibers (fī′bərz), strong thin threads in plants that can be used to make cloth.

Useful Things from Plants and Animals

You get more than food from plants and animals. You also get things you can use. For example, wood comes from trees. People use wood to build houses and to make furniture, paper, and toys. What are some other ways people use wood?

Look at the clothes the girl is wearing. Her blouse is made of cotton cloth. Cotton comes from cotton plants. These plants have strong, thin threads—**fibers**—that are used to make cloth. The girl's skirt is linen. Flax plants have fibers that are used to make linen cloth. The girl is also wearing leather shoes. People make leather from animal skins. The girl's sweater is woolen. Wool is made from sheep's hair.

Cotton

Wool

Flax

Leather

Black widow spider

Poison sumac

Harmful Animals and Plants

Some animals can hurt people. When the spider in the picture bites, it releases a poison that can make people very sick. What other animals are dangerous to people?

Some plants also can hurt people. If you touched the poison sumac in the picture, you might get an itchy rash. Some plants, such as buttercups, are poisonous to eat.

Lesson Review

1. What are three kinds of food people get from plants? from animals?
2. What are two useful things people get from plants? from animals?
3. How are some plants harmful to people?
4. **Challenge!** What things did you use today that came from plants or animals?

Study on your own, pages 322–323.

Use an encyclopedia to find out what chemicals are used in tanning leather to make clothes.

PHYSICAL SCIENCE

**FIND OUT
ON YOUR OWN**

CONNECTION

ACTIVITY

Looking at Fibers

Purpose
Compare the fibers in objects made from plants.

Gather These Materials
• paper • cotton cloth • linen cloth
• hand lens • paper plate • colored water

Follow This Procedure
1. Use a chart like the one shown to record your observations.
2. Tear the paper and the cloths two ways—up and down and across. Look at the edges with the hand lens. Record your observations.

3. Place a torn edge of each sample on the paper plate. Leave the opposite edge out of the plate, as shown in the picture.
4. Slowly pour some colored water into the plate until it reaches the edges of the samples. Compare how fast the samples soak up the water. Record the order of the samples from fastest to slowest.

Record Your Results

	How Fibers Looked	Order Samples Soaked Water
Paper Cotton Linen		

State Your Conclusions
1. What do plant fibers look like?
2. Which of the three samples would you use to wipe up a water spill? Why?

Use What You Learned
How do you think the fibers in wool cloth would compare with the cotton and linen fibers?

Protecting the Wilderness

More than 100 years ago, a man named John Muir decided to take a trip. He had had an accident that almost left him blind. Now he could see again. He wanted to see the beautiful world with his own eyes. On his trip, he studied plants and animals. He did see quite a lot on his trip. He walked all the way from Kentucky to Florida!

This long walk was not the only trip John Muir made. Throughout his life, he enjoyed living outdoors and traveling to new places. He visited the Yosemite Valley in California. There he saw beautiful mountains and giant trees. He could also see that cutting trees, mining, and grazing sheep might soon ruin the wilderness. This valley, like all habitats, was formed over a long period of time. If people destroyed it, they could not build it over again. Muir felt that the best idea was to save the land before it was harmed.

John Muir wrote about the valley in books and magazines. He told about trees that were thousands of years old. He told about winter snows and spring flowers and birds. He also talked to people who make laws. Many people agreed that saving the wilderness was important. Due to his hard work, the land he loved

John Muir

Waterfall in Yosemite Park

became Yosemite National Park.

Throughout his life, John Muir kept working to save wild lands and make them national parks. He wanted people like you to be able to enjoy the lands just as he did.

What Do You Think?

1. John Muir is sometimes called the father of the national parks. Why do you think people gave him that name?
2. If a forest was cut down, what do you think would happen to the plants and animals that lived there?

Skills for Solving Problems

Using Pictographs and Time Lines

Problem: How has the population of trumpeter swans changed since 1850?

Part A. Using Pictographs to Collect Information

1. The key shows that each picture in the pictograph stands for a number of swans. What do the large pictures stand for? medium-sized pictures? small pictures?
2. The pictograph shows how many swans were alive in certain years. To find out how many were alive in 1850, add the numbers the pictures for that year stand for. Many hunters shot trumpeter swans. Habitats were changed. Later, people protected the swans. How many swans were alive in 1900? in 1950? in 1980?

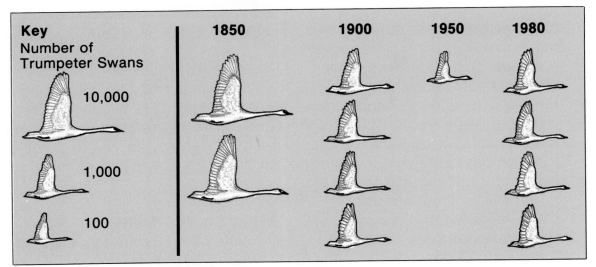

Part B. Using a Time Line to Organize and Interpret Information

3. The time line contains the information you collected. The spaces on the line stand for lengths of time. What is the length of time between the marks on the time line?

4. What happened to the swan population between the years 1850 and 1900? between 1900 and 1950? between 1950 and 1980?

5. What might have changed the population of swans between 1850 and 1980? What changes could you infer might take place by the year 2000?

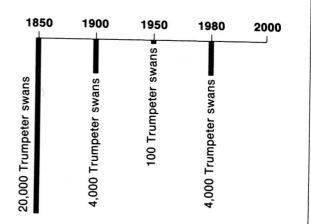

Part C. Using Pictographs and Time Lines to Solve a Problem

Problem: How has the woolly spider monkey population changed?

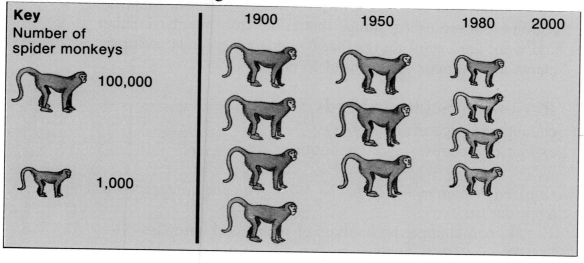

6. Use the pictograph to collect the information you need to solve the problem. Make a time line similar to the one shown in Part B to organize your information.

7. Look at your time line. The woolly spider monkey lives in the jungle forests in Brazil.

People are cutting down these forests to make farms. Compare the time line you made with the time line shown in Part A. How are they different? What might cause this difference?

8. What changes in the monkey population might take place by the year 2000?

Chapter 4 Review

✔ Chapter Main Ideas

Lesson 1 • People change the habitats of plants and animals when they build things and when they pollute. • Many kinds of organisms are endangered because people changed their habitats or killed many of them. • An extinct organism is a kind of organism that no longer is found on the earth.

Lesson 2 • People protect habitats by making large parks where habitats cannot be disturbed, by passing laws that protect habitats, and by trying not to pollute habitats. • Scientists protect endangered plants by saving their seeds and by growing the seeds indoors. Zoos protect endangered animals.

Lesson 3 • Fruits, vegetables, and grains come from plants. Meat, milk, and eggs come from animals. • Wood, linen, and cotton cloth are useful things that come from plants. Leather and wool are useful things that come from animals. • Some plants and animals are harmful to people.

✔ Reviewing Science Words

endangered organisms   fibers
extinct organisms   pollution

Copy each sentence. Fill in the blank with the correct word from the list.
1. _____ can change the habitats of plants and animals.
2. Cotton cloth is made from the _____ of a cotton plant.
3. _____ are kinds of organisms that no longer are found on the earth.
4. _____ are so few in number they might someday no longer be found on the earth.

✔ Reviewing What You Learned

Write the letter of the best answer.
1. An organism gets everything it needs from its
   (a) community.   (b) population.   (c) food.   (d) habitat.

2. When a fuel is burned, it often releases harmful
   (a) plants.   (b) chemicals.   (c) fibers.   (d) light.
3. To protect the habitats of organisms, people have
   (a) made parks.   (b) stopped making chemicals.
   (c) closed zoos.   (d) opened museums.
4. Which of the following animals are extinct?
   (a) tigers   (b) lions   (c) dodo birds   (d) goldfish
5. Scientists protect endangered plants by saving their
   (a) leaves.   (b) names.   (c) pictures.   (d) seeds.
6. Which of these animals is endangered?
   (a) tiger   (b) bee   (c) dog   (d) dodo bird
7. Grains are
   (a) roots.   (b) seeds.   (c) stems.   (d) leaves.
8. Wool is made from
   (a) cotton plants.   (b) sheep's hair.   (c) flax plants.
   (d) animal skins.
9. When a black widow spider bites, it releases
   (a) an odor.   (b) a poison.   (c) water.   (d) food.

Interpreting What You Learned

Write a short answer for each question.
1. Why might an animal not be able to live in its habitat if the habitat is changed?
2. How did tigers become endangered organisms?
3. What is the difference between endangered organisms and extinct organisms?
4. How are plants and animals important to people?

Extending Your Thinking

Write a paragraph to answer each question.
1. How might an endangered organism become an extinct organism?
2. How do people help themselves when they protect plants and animals?

 To explore scientific methods, see Experiment Skills on pages 354–355.

Careers

You can probably think of many different kinds of living things. Just imagine how many different jobs there must be for people who like living things.

Fish-culture technician

Foresters like to work with trees. They help protect forests from fire, harmful insects, and disease. They might make maps of forest areas. Foresters spend a great deal of time outside. To become a forester, you need to go to college.

Like foresters, **gardeners** work outside a great deal. They plant flower or vegetable gardens. Then they take care of the plants by watering them and pulling weeds. Gardeners usually learn their skills by working with other gardeners.

A person who likes fish might enjoy becoming a **fish-culture technician.** This person raises young fish and then lets them go into lakes or rivers. Fish-culture technicians can learn their skills on the job, or they can go to college.

Microbiologists study the tiny living things that can be seen only under a microscope. Some microbiologists study bacteria that cause disease. To become a microbiologist, you must graduate from college. Then you need to take special classes.

Some people are interested in the food we get from animals. **Meat inspectors** check meat and poultry to make sure it is safe for people to eat. They also check the place where food is handled. They make sure the place and the equipment are clean. People who want to be food inspectors must pass a special test.

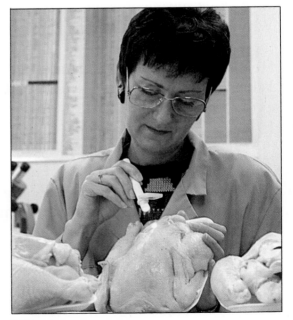
Meat inspector

An Aquarium Filter

Air, water, and gravel are three things that pet fish need to stay healthy. In a good aquarium, water always moves. It travels in a circle from the top of the tank to the bottom and back up again. At the bottom of the tank, the water passes through a gravel filter.

The filter helps keep the fish healthy. It collects leftover food and wastes from the tank. The wastes and old food could make the fish sick if they stayed in the water. Here is how an aquarium filter works.

Gravel

1 **Plastic screen**

1 A plastic screen covers the bottom of the aquarium. The plate contains many small holes. A layer of gravel rests on top of the screen.

2 An air pump pushes air into the tank. The air goes down a small tube to the bottom of the tank.

3 Then, the air goes up the large tube that is around the small tube. The flow of air up the tube pulls water along with it. Here, oxygen in the air mixes with the water. Fish take in the oxygen that is mixed with the water.

4 When water is pulled up the tube, it makes water underneath the filter move toward the tubes. This movement makes the water in the tank move down through the filter. The water carries wastes and old food along with it.

5 Wastes and food are trapped in the gravel filter. Bacteria on the gravel eat the wastes and food. The water becomes clean as it moves through the filter.

Unit 1 Review

Complete the Sentence

Fill in the blank with the correct word or words from the list.

cell   oxygen
fibers   petals
germinate pollution
gills   prey
habitat   pupa
larva   reptiles

1. ___ takes place when harmful things are added to the air, water, or land.
2. A fish uses its ___ to take in oxygen from the water.
3. The ___ of plants can be used to make cloth.
4. Plants give off the gas ___ into the air.
5. A caterpillar is the ___ of a butterfly.
6. The ___ is the basic unit of an organism.
7. A seed will ___ only when it gets enough air and water.
8. Mice, birds, and other small animals often are the ___ of snakes.
9. Snakes, turtles, and alligators are ___.
10. An organism finds everything it needs to live in its ___.
11. An insect is a ___ when it forms a hard shell around itself.
12. The ___ of a plant often are colored.

Short Answer

Write a short answer for each question or statement.

1. How are trunks of trees like stems of small plants?
2. Name two ways that pollen can be carried to the center part of a flower.
3. Why do most cold-blooded animals live in warm places?
4. Tell the order of these stages in an insect's life cycle: pupa, egg, adult, larva.
5. Name two groups of organisms that can have one cell or many cells.
6. How might a population of lions be affected by the size of their habitat?
7. Explain why all animals are consumers.
8. How do you think that eyes set toward the sides of their heads help rabbits survive?
9. What causes plants and animals to become endangered?
10. Name four ways that people use plants.

Essay

Write a paragraph for each question or statement.

1. How are reptiles and fish alike? How are they different?
2. Describe the important parts of a plant's habitat.

Unit Projects and Books

Science Projects

1. Ask permission to cut off a small piece of a house plant, such as ivy, that has trailing vines. Use scissors to cut a piece that is about 12 centimeters long. Be careful not to cut yourself with the scissors. Put the cut end of the plant in a jar of water. Observe the cut end of the plant for several weeks. Draw a picture of the plant and its new roots.

2. Obtain several mealworms from a pet store. Put the mealworms in a container with a small amount of oatmeal. Cover the container with a lid that has several tiny holes. Feed the mealworms every few days with oatmeal. Observe the mealworms for several weeks. Describe the life cycle of a mealworm. Draw pictures to illustrate the life cycle.

3. A terrarium can be thought of as a small habitat for plants. Use library books to help you make a terrarium in a clear plastic container with a lid. Watch your project for several weeks. How is your terrarium like the real world?

4. Look through magazines and cut out pictures of plants and animals. Sort these pictures into two groups. One group should be helpful organisms; the other group should be harmful organisms. Using the pictures, make a poster of helpful and harmful organisms.

Books About Science

Plants and Flowers by Brian Holley. Penworthy, 1986. Learn about plants and their flowers.

Salmon by Elma Schemenauer. Grolier, 1986. Find out about the life cycle of a salmon.

Science and Society

Protecting Habitats Some people in the community want to build a new baseball field. But other people object. The new field would be built in Henson's meadow. This meadow is the only place the Mariposa blue butterfly still lives. If the ball field is built, the butterfly might become extinct. Many members of the community do not see the problem. They wonder what difference it makes if one kind of butterfly becomes extinct. They know that playing baseball helps keep boys and girls out of trouble. They think baseball is more important than a butterfly. What are some good reasons to build the new ball field? What are some good reasons not to?

Physical Science

This picture shows some parts of a machine. Notice the jagged edges on the wheels. These edges help the wheels turn around to make the machine work.

Machines use energy to help make work easier for people. In this unit, you will learn about different kinds of energy, such as electricity. You also will discover what makes up all the objects around you.

SCIENCE IN THE NEWS During the next few weeks, look in newspapers or magazines for stories about electricity. Also look for pictures of machines that use electricity. Share the news stories and pictures with your class.

Chapter 5 Properties of Matter
Chapter 6 Work and Machines
Chapter 7 Forms of Energy
Chapter 8 Sound

Properties of Matter

Have you ever made an animal out of sand? If you look closely, you can see that many tiny parts of sand make up this dragon.

Introducing the Chapter

Many objects around you look different from each other. In some ways, all the objects are alike. In this chapter you will learn about parts that make up all the objects in the world around you. In the activity below, you can observe and describe different objects.

Observing Different Materials

DISCOVER!

Notice that each glass in the picture has a small amount of white material in it. One glass has salt. The other glass has sugar.

You can get a glass with salt and a glass with sugar from your teacher. You will not know which material is in each glass. Look at the two materials. Add a few drops of water to each glass. Touch each material. Mix a small amount of each material in water. Compare the way the materials look when they are mixed in water. Notice the smell of each material. *CAUTION: Do not taste these materials. Never taste any materials, even if you think you know what they are.*

Talk About It
1. How were the materials alike?
2. How did you find out which material was salt and which material was sugar?

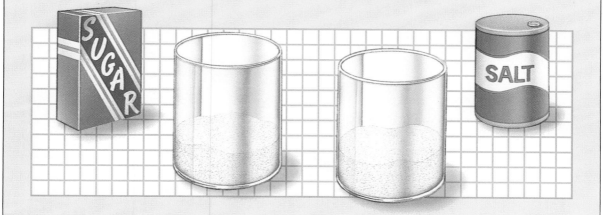

1 What Is Matter?

LESSON GOALS

You will learn
- how objects have mass and are made of matter.
- how matter can be described by its properties.
- the three forms of matter.

volume (vol′yəm), the amount of space an object takes up.

Notice how the objects in the picture look different from each other. The desk looks larger than the pencil. The notebooks have different colors. Yet all the objects are alike in some ways.

Mass and Matter

These objects are alike because they all take up space. Notice how the paper clip takes up a small amount of space. Find an object that takes up more space than the paper clip. Which object takes up the most space?

The amount of space an object fills is its **volume.** Look at objects around you. Name an object in your classroom that has a large volume. What object has a small volume?

All of these objects are made of matter.

94

All these objects are alike in another way. They all have **mass.** An object's mass is the measure of how much material makes up the object. You can use a balance to measure how much mass an object has. Find the picture of the apple on the balance. The apple has more mass than the eraser. The rock has more mass than the apple.

Everything that takes up space and has mass is called **matter.** All the objects around you are made of matter. You take up space and have mass. You are made of matter.

Imagine dreaming about your classroom. A dream does not take up space and have mass. A dream is not made of matter.

mass (mas), the measure of how much matter an object contains.

matter (mat′ər), anything that takes up space and has mass.

You can describe these objects by naming their properties.

Properties of Matter

Think about how you might describe some of the objects in the picture. The dinner plate is large. The strawberries are small and juicy. The napkin is pink and soft. How can you describe the flowers? When you describe an object, you tell about its **properties.** A property tells exactly what an object is like. You can describe matter by naming its properties.

Suppose you wanted to describe a slice of lemon. You probably would tell about its size, shape, and color. You also might describe its smell and sour taste. Size, shape, color, smell, and taste are properties of the lemon.

Matter can be solid, liquid, or gas.

States of Matter

Notice the diver in the picture. The diver is solid. The water in the picture is liquid. Find the air bubbles in the water. Air is a gas. Matter comes in three forms—solid, liquid, and gas. These forms are called the **states of matter.**

A solid keeps a certain shape and has a certain volume. Find some objects in the picture that are solid.

Suppose you poured water into a glass. The water would take the shape of the glass. A liquid takes the shape of its container. A liquid keeps its volume when it changes shape. Imagine pouring water from a glass into a bowl. The volume of water would stay the same. How would the shape change?

INVESTIGATE!

Find out if changing the shape of an object can change another property of that object. Write a hypothesis and test it with an experiment. Floating or sinking is a property of clay. You might observe how changing the shape of clay affects how it floats.

states of matter, the three forms of matter—solid, liquid, and gas.

97

Solid, liquid, and gas

Notice the different shapes of the balloons in the picture. Air is a gas that fills the balloons. A gas takes the same shape as its container. Find the broken balloon. The air from the broken balloon spread out into the whole room. The same amount of gas can spread out to fill a larger volume.

Lesson Review

1. What is matter?
2. What are properties of matter?
3. What are the three states of matter?
4. **Challenge!** Suppose you added marbles to a full glass of milk. Would the shape and volume of the milk change? Explain your answer.

Study on your own, pages 324–325.

PHYSICAL SCIENCE

**FIND OUT
ON YOUR OWN**

Find objects like those shown above to measure. Using metric measures, guess the length or height of each object. Also guess each object's mass. Then measure the objects.

Observing That Air Has Volume

Purpose
Observe that air takes up space.

Gather These Materials
• plastic glass • paper towels (or napkins) • large bowl • water

Follow This Procedure
1. Use a chart like the one shown to record your observations.
2. Loosely crumple a paper towel and put it in the bottom of the empty glass. Make sure the towel will not come out when the glass is turned upside down.
3. Run water into the large bowl. Turn the glass upside down. Push it straight down into the water as shown. Hold the glass there while you count to 30.
4. Lift the glass straight up out of the water. Pull the towel out of the glass. Record what you observe.
5. With the paper towel in the glass, turn the glass upside down and push it to the bottom of the water.
6. When the glass is at the bottom, slowly turn the glass over. Record what happens.

Record Your Results

Towel after glass is pushed straight into water	
Towel after glass is turned over under water	

State Your Conclusion
1. What kept the water from reaching the paper towel in the glass when you pushed the glass straight into the water?
2. What happened to the paper towel when you turned the glass over under water? Explain.

Use What You Learned
How could people use the results of this experiment to help them work under water?

2 What Makes Up Matter?

LESSON GOALS

You will learn
• what makes up matter.
• how particles of matter move.

SCIENCE IN YOUR LIFE

Some matter has only one kind of atom. You breathe oxygen from the air. All the atoms of oxygen are the same. Other matter has more than one kind of atom. Two different kinds of atoms join together to make water.

atom (at′əm), a small particle that makes up matter.

Small particles make up matter.

Imagine looking at a pin like the one in the first picture. The tiny pin can be hard to see. Now imagine adding more pins like those in the second picture. You can see the group of pins more easily than one pin. Each pin is like a small particle of matter. The group of pins is like matter you can see.

Particles in Matter

The particles that make up matter are called **atoms.** You cannot see atoms because they are so small. Two or more atoms can join together to form larger particles of matter. Then many of these larger particles can join together to form the matter you see.

Scientists know about many kinds of atoms. These atoms can join together in different ways to make different kinds of matter.

How Particles of Matter Move

Particles in matter are different in different states of matter. The pictures show how the particles in a solid look different from those in a liquid. Which state of matter has particles that are closer together?

The particles in solids pull toward each other. A solid keeps a certain shape because its particles stay close together. The particles in matter are always moving. Particles in solids move back and forth, but they do not exchange places.

Notice how the particles in liquids are farther apart than those in solids. The pull between particles is weaker in liquids than in solids. Liquids change shape because the particles can move around each other.

Particles in a liquid

Particles in a solid

Particles in a gas

The particles in gases do not pull together strongly. Notice how much space separates the gas particles in this drawing. Gas particles move around more than particles in liquids and solids. A gas can spread out to fill any space because its particles move around freely.

Lesson Review

1. What makes up matter?
2. How do particles move in solids, liquids, and gases?
3. **Challenge!** Can a container of gas be only partly full? Explain your answer.

Study on your own, pages 324–325.

**FIND OUT
ON YOUR OWN**

Draw a picture of a glass of water. Now imagine adding several drops of grape juice to the water. Color the picture to show how the liquid would look. Write a few sentences explaining what would cause the color to change.

Exploring the Inside of Atoms

The Problem   Our word *atom* comes from a Greek word, *atomos.* Over two thousand years ago, a Greek thinker wondered what the smallest particle of matter must be like. He called this pretend particle *atomos,* which means "not cuttable." Many years later, in 1803, an English scientist discovered the atom. He said it could not be split. However, in 1897, another English scientist found out that atoms are made of even smaller particles. Since that time, scientists have been trying to find out what the smallest particles of matter really are. You know an atom is tiny. How could scientists find out what is inside such a small particle?

The Breakthrough   In 1930, Ernest O. Lawrence made the first "atom smasher." This machine helps scientists find new kinds of particles inside the atom. Scientists first make the smaller particles inside of atoms move very fast. Then they use these fast particles to smash apart even smaller particles inside the atom. Using atom smashers, scientists found many new types of particles inside the atom.

New Technology   The picture shows part of a laboratory near

Control room at Fermilab

Chicago, Illinois, called Fermilab. This laboratory has a tunnel that contains a giant atom smasher. Small particles from atoms move around the circle, going faster and faster as they move. Using this kind of atom smasher, scientists at Fermilab and at other laboratories around the world have learned much more about matter. Soon, the United States plans to build an even larger and more powerful atom smasher. It will help scientists find out even more about the smallest particles of matter.

What Do You Think?
1. How has the meaning of the word *atom* changed?
2. How is an atom smasher like a telescope and microscope?

3 How Can Matter Change?

LESSON GOALS

You will learn
- what physical changes are and how matter can change from one state to another.
- how chemical changes can cause some kinds of matter to become new matter.

physical (fiz′ə kel) **change,** a change in the size, shape, state, or appearance of matter.

Physical changes

The pictures on these two pages show some ways you can change matter. Changes in matter happen around you every day. Some changes make matter look different. Other changes make one kind of matter become another kind of matter.

Physical Changes

Notice the different shapes of the clay. Changing the clay's shape does not change the clay into something else. The clay is still clay. **Physical changes** are changes in the way matter looks. Changes in size and shape, such as these changes in the clay, are physical changes. How is a person making a physical change in the piece of paper?

Another kind of physical change happens when matter changes from one state to another state. Matter looks different when it changes state but it stays the same kind of matter.

Notice the liquid water in the glass. What happens if you put water in the freezer? Water changes to a solid when it is cooled to a temperature of 0° Celsius (0°C). This temperature is called the freezing point of water. How do particles in ice move differently from those in liquid water?

Solids also can change to liquids. Heat speeds up the moving particles in ice. The particles move apart. Heat melts ice and changes it to liquid water.

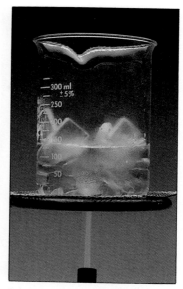

Liquid water and ice

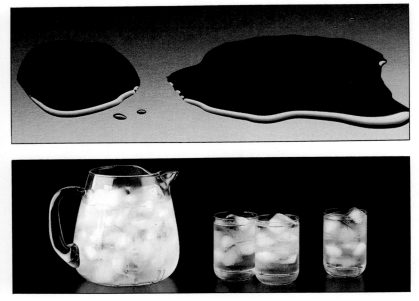

Matter can change states.

evaporate (i vap′ə rāt′), to change from a liquid state to a gas.

water vapor (wô′ter vā′pər), water in the form of a gas.

condense (kən dens′), to change from a gas to a liquid state.

You probably have seen a puddle of water that disappears after a time. The water in the puddle changes into a gas. Matter **evaporates** when it changes from a liquid to a gas. Water in the form of a gas is called **water vapor.** Compare the two puddles in the picture. Water evaporates from the top part of each puddle. Which puddle will evaporate faster?

Heat makes water particles move fast. Water quickly changes to a gas when water heats to a temperature of 100° Celsius. This temperature is the boiling point of water. Notice the bubbles in the pot of water. The gas in the bubbles is water vapor.

Cooling air causes water vapor to change to a liquid. Matter **condenses** when it changes from a gas to a liquid. This cold pitcher and the glasses cool the air around them. Then water vapor in the air condenses to small drops of water on the outsides of the containers.

106

Chemical Changes

You probably have seen different shapes carved out of wood. The wood does not change into a different material when it is carved. What kind of change happens to wood when carving changes its shape?

The wood in the picture is burning. The fire changes the wood into ashes and smoke. The wood becomes a different kind of matter. A **chemical change** takes place when matter changes to a different kind of matter.

Notice the rust on these nails. The material that makes up the nails mixes with the air to form rust. Rusting is a chemical change.

chemical (kem′ə kəl) **change,** a change that causes matter to become a new kind of matter.

Chemical changes

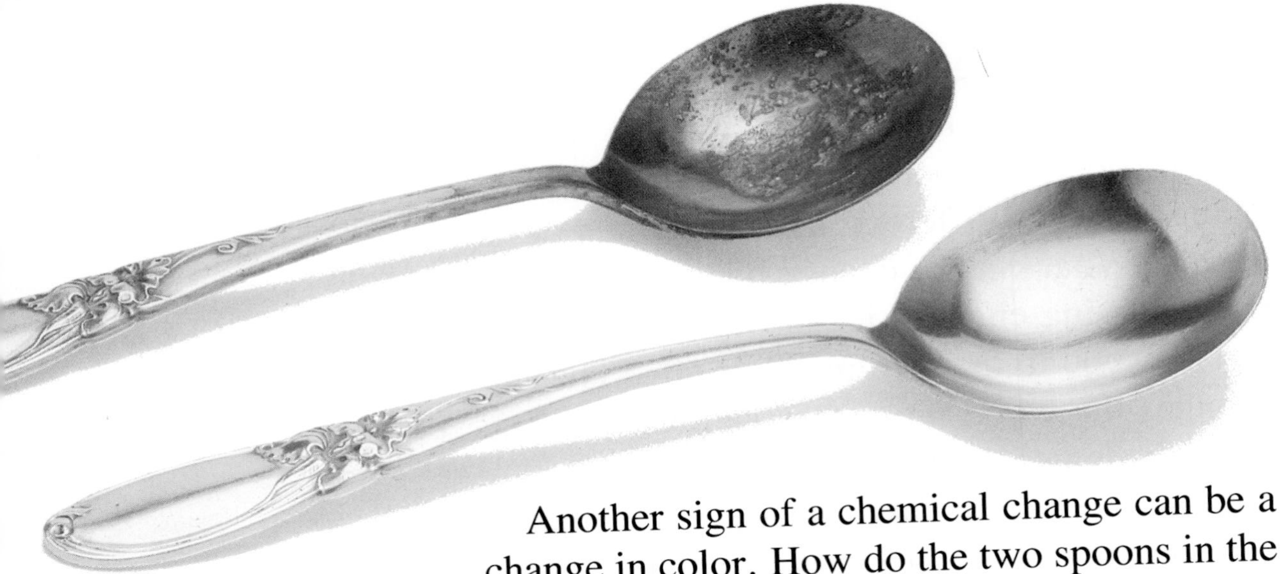

Tarnish

Another sign of a chemical change can be a change in color. How do the two spoons in the picture look different? The spoons are made of silver. A gas in the air causes a black covering called tarnish to form on silver. A chemical change takes place because tarnish has different properties from the materials that form it.

Lesson Review

1. What is a physical change?
2. What are two examples of a chemical change?
3. **Challenge!** Why can you see your breath outside on a cold day?

Study on your own, pages 324–325.

Study on your own, pages 324–325.

LIFE SCIENCE

**FIND OUT
ON YOUR OWN**

CONNECTION

Foods are often packed in dry ice to keep them safe to eat. Use library books to find out about dry ice. Write a paragraph telling how dry ice is formed. Tell whether a physical or chemical change happens when dry ice forms.

Observing Physical and Chemical Changes

ACTIVITY

Wear cover goggles for this activity.

Purpose
Observe a physical change and a chemical change.

Gather These Materials
- sugar • vinegar • baking soda
- 2 plastic cups • 2 plastic spoons
- 2 white labels

Follow This Procedure
1. Use a chart like the one shown to record your result.
2. Put one spoonful of sugar into a cup. Label the cup as shown.
3. Put 4 spoonfuls of vinegar into the cup with the sugar. Stir for one minute. Observe what happens. Record the result. *CAUTION: Do not taste.*

4. Use the other spoon to put one spoonful of baking soda into the other cup. Label the cup.
5. Put 4 spoonfuls of vinegar into the cup with the baking soda as shown in the picture. Observe what happens. Record the result. *CAUTION: Do not taste.*

Record Your Results

Sugar and vinegar	
Baking soda and vinegar	

State Your Conclusion
1. In each of these tests, did a physical change or chemical change take place?
2. What is one way you can tell that a chemical change takes place?

Use What You Learned
If you mix a spoonful of salt with 4 spoonfuls of water, the salt seems to disappear. Is this a chemical change or a physical change? Explain your answer.

Using Equal Arm Balances and Pictographs

Problem: How can the mass of solids be measured and compared?

Part A. Using balances to collect information

1. Balances measure mass. A solid is placed on the left pan of the balance. Objects of known mass are placed on the right pan. When the pans balance, the mass of the things on the right pan is the same as the mass of the solid being measured. How can you tell the pans balance?
2. Look at the first picture. What is the total mass on the right pan? What is the mass of the wood cube?
3. What is the mass of the brick cube? the sponge cube? Are all the cubes the same size?

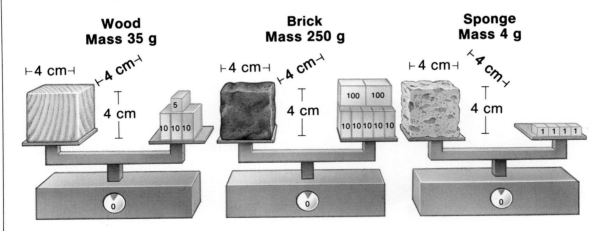

Wood
Mass 35 g

Brick
Mass 250 g

Sponge
Mass 4 g

Part B. Using a Pictograph to Organize and Interpret Information.

4. This pictograph contains the information you collected about the mass of solids in Part A. What do the large objects stand for? The medium-sized objects? The small objects?

5. Look at the pictograph on the right. The solids in the pictograph are shown in order by mass. Which object has the least amount of mass? Which object has the most mass? Are all of the objects in the pictograph the same size?

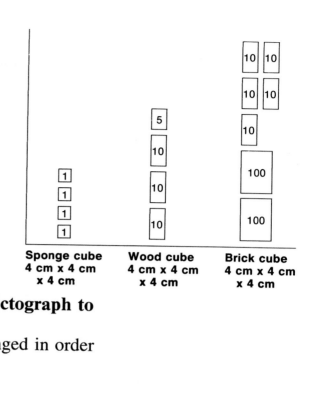

Sponge cube 4 cm x 4 cm x 4 cm	Wood cube 4 cm x 4 cm x 4 cm	Brick cube 4 cm x 4 cm x 4 cm

Part C. Using Balances and a Pictograph to Solve a Problem

Problem: How can liquids be arranged in order by mass?

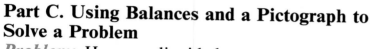

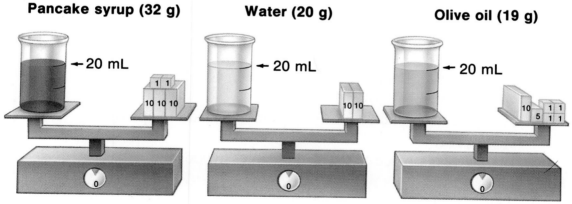

6. Use the balances to collect the information you need to solve the problem. Make a pictograph similar to the one shown in Part B to organize your information.
7. Look at your pictograph. How much liquid is in each jar?

Which jar has the liquid with the greatest mass? the least mass?
8. If you mixed the oil with the water in the same jar, which liquid would float?

Chapter 5 Review

☑ Chapter Main Ides

Lesson 1 • Everything that takes up space and has mass is matter. • Matter can be described by its properties. • The three states of matter are solid, liquid, and gas.

Lesson 2 • All matter is made of atoms. • Particles in solids are close together and move back and forth. The particles in liquids can move around each other. The particles in gases are far apart and move around freely.

Lesson 3 • Changes in the way matter looks are physical changes. A physical change takes place when matter changes from one state to another. • A chemical change takes place when matter changes to a different kind of matter.

☑ Reviewing Science Words

atom	mass	states of matter
chemical change	matter	volume
condense	physical change	water vapor
evaporates	property	

Copy each sentence. Fill in the blanks with the correct word or words from the list.

1. Color is one ▦ of matter.
2. A liquid takes the shape of its container and keeps the same ▦.
3. A ▦ takes place when fire changes wood into ashes and smoke.
4. The measure of how much matter makes up an object is called ▦ .
5. Matter ▦ when it changes from a liquid to a gas.
6. Solid, liquid, and gas are the three ▦ .
7. Cooling the air causes water vapor to ▦ .
8. A change in the shape of matter is a ▦ .
9. Water in the form of a gas is called ▦ .
10. A small particle that makes up matter is called an ▦ .
11. All the objects around you are made of ▦ .

☑ Reviewing What You Learned

Write the letter of the best answer.

1. A balance measures an object's
   (a) volume.   (b) mass.   (c) properties.   (d) atoms.
2. A chemical change can take place when matter
   (a) evaporates.   (b) condenses.   (c) burns.   (d) melts.
3. Which object has particles that move around the most?
   (a) a brick   (b) water   (c) air   (d) a pencil
4. What makes up matter?
   (a) atoms   (b) states   (c) volume   (d) properties
5. A physical change takes place when matter
   (a) rusts.   (b) tarnishes.   (c) burns.   (d) condenses.
6. When you tell about an object's length, you describe a
   (a) volume   (b) property   (c) state   (d) mass

☑ Interpreting What You Learned

Write a short answer for each question or statement.

1. How are a flower and a book alike?
2. How is the shape of a gas different from the shape of a solid?
3. How can matter be described?
4. Explain how you would put these steps in the correct order:
   a. ashes
   b. log
   c. burning log

☑ Extending Your Thinking

Write a paragraph to answer each question or statement.

1. Suppose a snowstorm covers the grass with snow. A week later, all of the snow is gone. Explain how this can happen.
2. When sugar is heated for a long time, it forms a solid black substance. What kind of change takes place? Explain your answer.

 To explore scientific methods, see Experiment Skills on pages 356–357.

113

Chapter 6

Work and Machines

People use tools to make work easier. This man is helping his grandson fix a bike. Find the tool the man is using.

114

1 What Is Work?

LESSON GOALS

You will learn
- how forces make objects move.
- how work is done.
- how work uses energy.

force (fôrs), a push or pull.

You probably have seen a shopping cart like the one in the picture. The cart cannot move by itself. A person must push or pull the cart to make it move.

Force

A push or a pull is a **force.** Which pic shows a pushing force? Which pictur a pulling force? A force changes object moves. The shopping ca same direction the person the shopping cart move You also can ch You can mak more for Yo m

Pushing and pul

115

☑ Reviewing What You Learned

Write the letter of the best answer.
1. A balance measures an object's
   (a) volume.   (b) mass.   (c) properties.   (d) atoms.
2. A chemical change can take place when matter
   (a) evaporates.   (b) condenses.   (c) burns.   (d) melts.
3. Which object has particles that move around the most?
   (a) a brick   (b) water   (c) air   (d) a pencil
4. What makes up matter?
   (a) atoms   (b) states   (c) volume   (d) properties
5. A physical change takes place when matter
   (a) rusts.   (b) tarnishes.   (c) burns.   (d) condenses.
6. When you tell about an object's length, you describe a
   (a) volume   (b) property   (c) state   (d) mass

☑ Interpreting What You Learned

Write a short answer for each question or statement.
1. How are a flower and a book alike?
2. How is the shape of a gas different from the shape of a solid?
3. How can matter be described?
4. Explain how you would put these steps in the correct order:
   a. ashes
   b. log
   c. burning log

☑ Extending Your Thinking

Write a paragraph to answer each question or statement.
1. Suppose a snowstorm covers the grass with snow. A week later, all of the snow is gone. Explain how this can happen.
2. When sugar is heated for a long time, it forms a solid black substance. What kind of change takes place? Explain your answer.

 To explore scientific methods, see Experiment Skills on pages 356–357.

6

Work and Machines

People use tools to make work easier. This man is
helping his grandson fix a bike. Find the tool the
man is using.

Introducing the Chapter

The activity below will help you learn how people move objects. The lessons in this chapter will tell you what happens when people push and pull objects. You also will learn how people can move objects quickly and easily.

Observing How People Move Objects

A person is moving this car up a ramp that was made with a book. How is the person making the car move? What are two ways a person could move the car down the ramp?

Use a book to make a ramp like the one shown. Place a crayon box at the top of the ramp. Now try to move the box down the ramp without touching the box. You can use objects to help you.

Talk About It
1. How did you move the box down the ramp?
2. What would happen if you put a Ping-Pong ball at the top of the ramp?

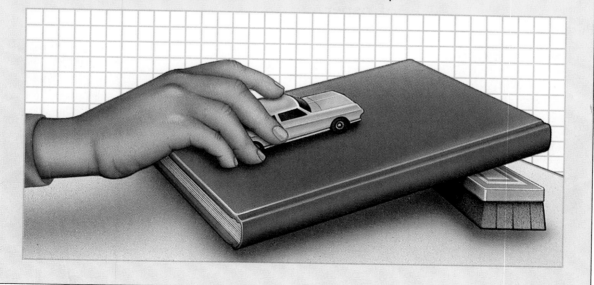

1 What Is Work?

LESSON GOALS

You will learn
- how forces make objects move.
- how work is done.
- how work uses energy.

force (fôrs), a push or pull.

You probably have seen a shopping cart like the one in the picture. The cart cannot move by itself. A person must push or pull the cart to make it move.

Force

A push or a pull is a **force.** Which picture shows a pushing force? Which picture shows a pulling force? A force changes the way an object moves. The shopping cart moves in the same direction the person pushes. Changing the direction of the force can make the shopping cart move in a different direction. You also can change the speed of an object. You can make an object move faster by using more force.

You need different amounts of force to move different objects. The heavier the object, the more force you need to move it. Would you need more force to move a book or a piece of paper?

Pushing and pulling forces

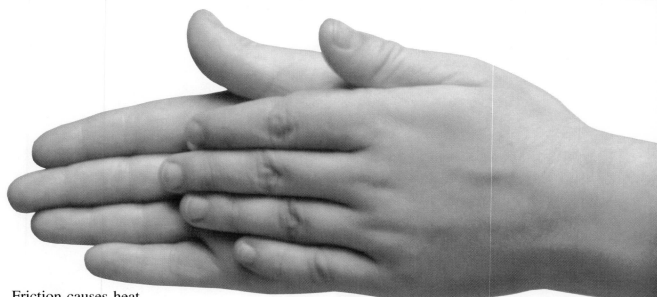

Friction causes heat.

What happens to a ball if you throw it into the air? **Gravity** will pull the ball down. The earth's gravity is a force that pulls objects toward the center of the earth.

The more mass an object has, the more gravity pulls on it. How much an object weighs tells how much gravity pulls on the object. Suppose you weigh sixty pounds. Then the pull of the earth's gravity on you is sixty pounds.

Imagine rolling a ball across a floor. Think about how the ball would stop moving. **Friction** is a force that makes moving objects slow down or stop. Two objects rubbing against each other cause friction. The friction between the ball and floor would make the ball stop moving.

Look at the hands in the picture rubbing together. Rub your own hands together. Notice how your hands feel warm. Objects always become warm when they rub together. Friction causes heat.

INVESTIGATE!

Some objects have rough surfaces. Others have smooth. Find out how the roughness or smoothness of surfaces affects the amount of friction they produce. Write a hypothesis and test it with an experiment. You might compare how an object slides across a rough surface and a smooth surface.

gravity (grav′ə tē), the force that makes objects pull toward each other.

friction (frik′shən), the force caused by two objects rubbing together that slows down or stops moving objects.

117

These students use force to lift the pumpkins.

Work

work (wėrk), something done whenever a force makes an object move through a distance.

Place a pencil on the top of your desk. Now move the pencil to the side of the desk. You need to use a force to make the pencil move. **Work** is done whenever a force makes an object move. You do work when you move the pencil across the desk.

The amount of work you do depends on how much force you use and how far the object moves. Suppose you lifted a pumpkin like one of those in the picture. You would be doing work when you used force to make the pumpkin move. Now suppose you lifted several pumpkins the same distance as you lifted the first pumpkin. You would use more force to lift several pumpkins. You do more work if you use more force to move something the same distance.

118

The children in the picture on the left are using the same amount of force to make the swings move. Look for one person in the picture who is swinging higher than the other. This boy is doing more work because he is moving his swing a greater distance. The amount of work being done depends on how far the swing moves. More work is done when the same amount of force moves an object a greater distance.

Now look at the boy in the picture on the right. This boy is not doing work because he is not making the wall move through a distance.

Which students are doing work?

Energy and Work

You can move around because you have **energy**—the ability to do work. You use energy whenever you use force to move an object through a distance. The more work you do, the more energy you need. Your body releases energy from food. You use this energy to do work. The boy in the pictures uses energy from his body to pull the dog. All objects that have energy can do work.

Lesson Review

1. What is force?
2. When do objects do work?
3. When do objects use energy?
4. **Challenge!** What makes walking on ice more difficult than walking on grass?

   Study on your own, pages 326–327.

Study on your own, pages 326–327.

PHYSICAL SCIENCE

FIND OUT ON YOUR OWN

A lubricant is a material that can lessen friction between two objects. Look in library books to find out about lubricants. Write a few sentences telling about different kinds of lubricants. Explain how using a lubricant might help a door open easily.

Observing How Friction Affects Motion

Purpose
Measure and *compare* the amount of force needed to drag a book across materials that cause different amounts of friction.

Gather These Materials
- string • large paper clip • book
- waxed paper • small towel
- metal washers

Follow This Procedure
1. Use a chart like the one shown to record your observations.
2. Tie the ends of the string together to make a loop. Put the string around the cover of the book.
3. Place the book on your desk top about 10 cm from the edge. Let the loop of the string hang over the edge of the desk.
4. Straighten a paper clip to form an *S*-shape. Hang the paper clip from the string. *CAUTION: Use the paper clip carefully.*
5. Put a metal washer on the paper clip as shown in the picture. Add metal washers one at a time, until the book begins to move. Record the number of washers needed.
6. Tape waxed paper to the desk top. Repeat steps 3–5.
7. Tape a towel to the desk top. Repeat steps 3–5.

Record Your Results

Surface	Number of washers
Desk top	
Waxed paper	
Towel	

State Your Conclusion
1. On which surface did you need the most force to move the book?
2. Compare the amounts of friction caused by each of the materials under the book.

Use What You Learned
Would it be easier to move a heavy carton across a wood floor or across a rug? Explain your answer.

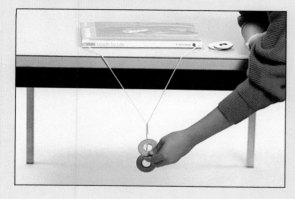

2 What Are Simple Machines?

LESSON GOALS

You will learn
- how levers and inclined planes help make work easier.
- how wedges and screws help people do work.
- how people can use a wheel and axle and a pulley to do work.

simple machine
(sim′ pəl mə shēn′), one of six kinds of tools with few or no moving parts that make work easier.

lever (lev′ər), a simple machine made of a bar that is supported underneath at some point.

fulcrum (ful′krəm), point on which a lever is supported and turns.

load (lōd), an object that is being moved.

Suppose you needed to move an object. You might use tools to help you. Machines are tools that use energy to do work. **Simple machines** are machines with a few or no moving parts. You probably have used several of the six kinds of simple machines.

Lever and Inclined Plane

Pretend you are lifting a heavy object like the one in the picture. Notice how these children use a board as a **lever.** A lever is a simple machine made of a board that is used to move objects. Find the point where the post holds up the board. The point on which a lever is held up is called the **fulcrum.** The lever moves back and forth on the fulcrum. The children push down on one end of the lever to move the object on the other end. The object being lifted is called the **load.**

Lifting a rock with a lever

A lever moves back and forth on a fulcrum.   A hammer can be used as a lever.

This seesaw is really a lever. Which person on the seesaw is the force? Which person is the load? Notice how one person can lift the other person. Which person is closer to the fulcrum? You can lift a load most easily by moving the fulcrum close to the load. Suppose the children moved the fulcrum away from the load. A person would need more force to lift the other person.

A hammer is another kind of lever. This hammer pulls a nail out of a piece of wood. Which part of the hammer is the fulcrum?

inclined (in klīnd´) **plane**, a simple machine that is a flat surface with one end higher than the other.

The man in the picture is using a ramp to move a heavy object into a truck. A ramp is an **inclined plane** that helps move objects. An inclined plane is a simple machine with a flat surface that is higher at one end. You can use an inclined plane to help move an object to a higher or lower place.

You might have seen inclined planes in other places. A slanted road is an inclined plane. The person in the picture uses an inclined plane to go into the building. A path going up a hill also is an inclined plane. Notice that this path is steeper than the ramps in the picture. You would need more force to move an object up the path than up the ramps.

Inclined planes

Find the wedges and the screws.

Wedge and Screw

Have you seen a doorstop like the one in the picture? This doorstop is a **wedge**—a simple machine used to push objects apart. Notice how two inclined planes come together to make a wedge. You might have seen other wedges. An ax is a wedge that splits wood. Find another wedge in the picture.

A **screw** is a simple machine used to hold objects together. The picture shows that a screw really is an inclined plane wrapped around a rod. Find the colored edge of the inclined plane being wrapped around the pencil. This edge is like the ridges on a screw. What are some places you have seen screws?

wedge (wej), a simple machine used to cut or split an object.

screw (skrü), a simple machine used to hold objects together.

125

Wheel and Axle and Pulley

The picture shows different kinds of wheels. Find the rod attached to each wheel. A **wheel and axle** is a simple machine made of a rod attached to the center of a wheel. A wheel and axle is a special kind of lever that moves or turns objects. The axle, or rod, turns when you put force on the wheel.

You probably have seen a wheel and axle on cars, roller skates, and wagons. A doorknob also is a wheel and axle. What other machines with a wheel and axle have you seen?

Notice the jagged edges of the wheels in the watch shown below. **Gears** are wheels with jagged edges like teeth. The teeth help the wheels turn each other. You can find gears in bicycles, cars, and many other machines.

wheel and axle (hwēl ənd ak′səl), a simple machine that has a center rod attached to a wheel.

gear (gir), a wheel with jagged edges like teeth.

Wheel and axle

126

A person pulls down on this rope to raise this paint can. The person is using a **pulley** to raise the can. A pulley is a simple machine with a wheel with a rope. The rope fits around the edge of the wheel. You can use a pulley to move a load up, down, or sideways.

A pulley can help move an object to a place that is hard to reach. For example, you might use a pulley to raise a flag to the top of a pole. A pulley also can help move a heavy load.

pulley (pul/ē), a simple machine made of a wheel and a rope.

Lesson Review

1. How can levers and inclined planes help move objects?
2. How can a wedge and a screw help make work easier?
3. How do wheels and axles and pulleys help people do work?
4. **Challenge!** What kind of simple machine is a baseball bat?

Study on your own, pages 326–327.

Find pictures of simple machines and use the pictures to make a poster. Include at least two pictures of each of the six simple machines. Label the kind of simple machine used in each tool or object.

PHYSICAL SCIENCE

**FIND OUT
ON YOUR OWN**

ACTIVITY

Observe the Force Needed to Move an Object with a Lever

Purpose
Observe that the closer the fulcrum is to the load, the less force is needed to lift an object.

Gather These Materials
• tongue depressor • pencil • 2 sugar cubes • glue • tape • metric ruler

Follow This Procedure
1. Use a chart like the one shown to record your observations.
2. Mark the tongue depressor with lines to divide it into 4 parts. Label the lines *A, B,* and *C.*
3. Glue the sugar cubes to one end of the tongue depressor.
4. Tape the pencil to your desk as a fulcrum. Place the tongue depressor on the pencil with the fulcrum at line *C* as shown.
5. Use the ruler to measure the height from the desk to the end of the tongue depressor.
6. Push on the end of the tongue depressor. Observe how much force you use to lift the sugar cubes.
7. Repeat steps 5–6 with the fulcrum at line *B* and line *A.* Compare the distances you moved the sugar cube. Compare the amount of force you needed to move the sugar cubes each time.

Record Your Results

Fulcrum	Line A	Line B	Line C
Force (easier, harder, hardest)			
Height: desk to tongue depressor end			

State Your Conclusion
1. Where was the fulcrum when you moved the sugar cubes the longest distance?
2. Compare the amount of force you used to move the sugar cubes when the fulcrum was moved from line *A,* to *B,* to *C.*

Use What You Learned
To move a heavy box with a lever, would you place the fulcrum close to the box or far away from the box? Explain.

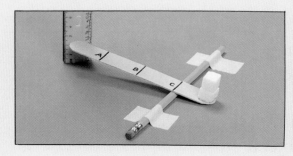

Teaching an Old Machine New Tricks

The Problem   A windmill is a machine that uses energy to produce power. People have used windmills to do work for more than a thousand years. Early windmills often had four or five blades covered with cloth sails to catch the wind. These windmills pumped water, ground corn, and sawed timber. In 1890, for the first time, a windmill pumped water to make electricity. Soon, nearly six million windmills made electricity in the United States. Then large power companies began using oil to make less costly electricity. Many people took down their windmills. In the 1970s, supplies of oil were short. The cost of oil and other types of fuel rose. People had to find a way to make electricity and run machines without using fuels.

The Breakthrough   Scientists and engineers began to work on the problem of energy needs. Windmills seemed to be part of the answer. Scientists designed new kinds of windmills, like the one in the picture. The new windmills have metal blades. The blades spin easily in wind from any direction. These windmills can work even when the wind is not blowing very hard.

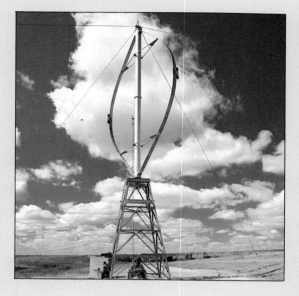

New Technology   Some of today's windmills have blades that measure 100 meters long from tip to tip. This is about the length of a football field! Some places have wind farms with several hundred large windmills. Wind farms can make as much electricity as a power plant. California has more than sixty-five wind farms that use five thousand windmills.

What Do You Think?

1. How did the low supply of oil cause people to start using windmills again?
2. Many years ago an eight-ton windmill blade tore loose from a windmill. Where should windmills be put to keep people safe?

3 What Are Compound Machines?

LESSON GOALS

You will learn
- how simple machines can be put together to make compound machines.
- that using machines carefully can help keep you safe.

compound machine
(kom′pound mə shēn′), a machine made of two or more simple machines.

Look at the different machines that make up the paddle boat in the picture. The front of the boat is a wedge that pushes through the water. Screws hold parts of the boat together. What kind of simple machine is the paddle?

Compound Machines

A **compound machine** is two or more simple machines put together. The paddle boat is a compound machine. You probably use many other compound machines. Look for the different parts of the pencil sharpener in the picture. The handle is a wheel that turns on an axle. Wedges sharpen the pencil. Find the gears that move the wedges. What kind of simple machine holds the pencil sharpener together?

Compound machines

130

Using Machines Safely

Using machines carefully is important. Asking an adult before using a machine and following safety rules can help keep you safe.

The picture shows compound machines you might use. A pair of scissors is made of two levers. The edge of each blade has the shape of a wedge. The screw that holds the two levers together is the fulcrum. You can use scissors safely by pointing them away from yourself.

What kind of simple machines make up the stapler in the picture? How can you use a stapler safely?

SCIENCE IN YOUR LIFE

A bicycle is a compound machine. Several different simple machines make up a bicycle. Handbrakes are levers. You can find a wheel and axle in the front and back wheels, as well as the pedals. The chain on the bicycle is a pulley. Screws hold parts of the bicycle together.

Lesson Review

1. What is a compound machine?
2. How can you use machines safely?
3. **Challenge!** How is a shovel a compound machine?

Study on your own, pages 326–327.

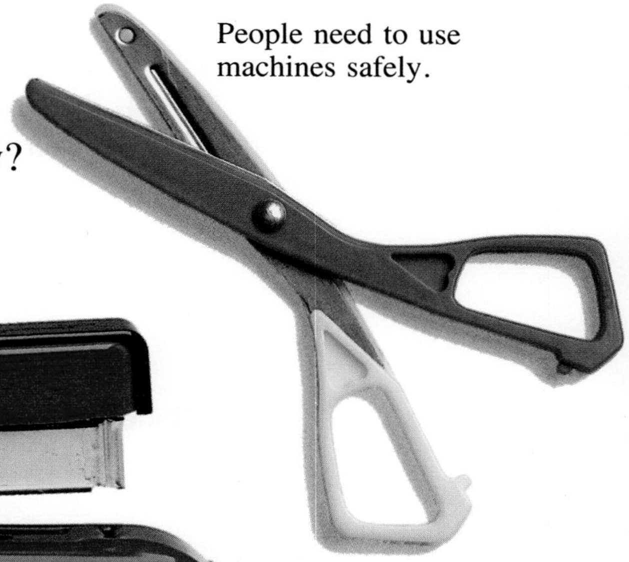

People need to use machines safely.

Invent a compound machine that people can use to exercise properly. Draw a picture of it. Label each simple machine you use in your drawing. Write a few sentences explaining what your machine would do and how it would work.

H U M A N   B O D Y
**FIND OUT
ON YOUR OWN**
C O N N E C T I O N

Using Rulers and Bar Graphs

Problem: How does the length of the longest line of an inclined plane change when the bottom changes?

Part A. Using Rulers to Collect Information
1. The diagram shows three inclined planes that have the same slant. How do they differ?
2. The sides of the planes are measured with a metric ruler. The long lines on the ruler stand for centimeters. A centimeter is divided into 10 millimeters.
3. Look at the ruler below Plane A. Count the centimeters starting from the left end of the ruler. It measures 4 cm. How long is the bottom of Plane B? Plane C?
4. Measure the upright lines at the right end of each plane. How long is each one?
5. Measure the longest line of each plane. How long is each one?

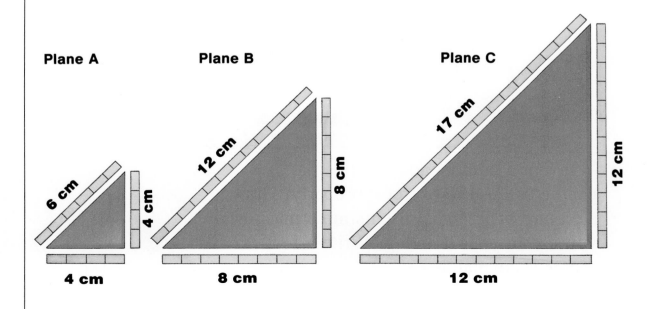

Plane A

6 cm

4 cm

4 cm

Plane B

12 cm

8 cm

8 cm

Plane C

17 cm

12 cm

12 cm

Part B. Using Bar Graphs to Organize and Interpret Information

6. This bar graph contains the information you collected about inclined planes. The bottom line and the upright line are the same length in each plane. How long is the longest line of the plane with a 4 cm bottom? an 8 cm bottom? a 12 cm bottom?

7. If a plane had a bottom line 16 cm long, how would the length of its longest line compare with the longest lines of these planes?

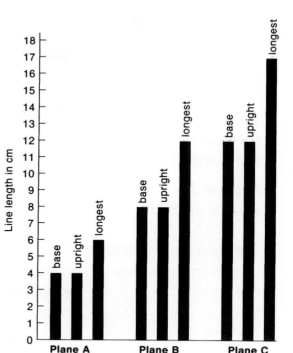

Part C. Using Rulers and Bar Graphs to Solve a Problem

Problem: How does the length of the incline change when the slant is smaller and the bottom stays the same length as in Part A?

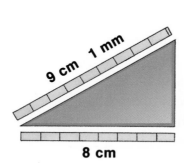

Plane A

4 cm 5 mm

4 cm

Plane B

9 cm 1 mm

8 cm

Plane C

13 cm 8 mm

12 cm

8. Use the rulers to collect the information you need to solve the problem. Make a bar graph like the one shown in Part B to organize your information.

9. Look at your bar graph.

Compare it to the bar graph you made in Part B. How does the length of the longest line change when the slant is smaller and the bottom stays the same length?

133

Chapter 6 Review

☑ Chapter Main Ideas

Lesson 1 • A force changes the way an object moves.
• Work is done whenever force makes an object move.
• Energy is used whenever work is done.

Lesson 2 • Levers and inclined planes help make work easier.
• Wedges and screws help people do work. • A person can
use a wheel and axle and a pulley to do work.

Lesson 3 • A compound machine is made of two or more
simple machines. • Using machines safely is important.

☑ Reviewing Science Words

compound machine	gravity	screw
energy	inclined plane	simple machines
force	lever	wedge
friction	load	wheel and axle
fulcrum	pulley	work
gear		

*Copy each sentence. Fill in the blank with the correct word
from the list.*

1. A _____ has jagged edges like teeth.
2. A lever turns back and forth on a _____.
3. Six different _____ can help make work easier.
4. A push or a pull is a _____.
5. A machine that turns objects is a _____.
6. A machine that pushes objects apart is a _____.
7. _____ pulls objects toward the center of the earth.
8. A pencil sharpener is an example of a _____.
9. _____ causes heat.
10. A _____ is made of a wheel and a rope.
11. A ramp is an example of an _____.
12. An object being lifted or moved is a _____.
13. _____ is done whenever a force moves an object through a
    distance.

14. A seesaw is a ___.
15. All objects that have ___ can do work.
16. A ___ is a machine used to hold objects together.

✓ Reviewing What You Learned

Write the letter of the best answer.
1. The blade of a knife is an example of a
   (a) screw.   (b) lever.   (c) wedge.   (d) force.
2. Gravity is one kind of
   (a) machine.   (b) friction.   (c) heat.   (d) force.
3. A bicycle is a
   (a) compound machine.   (b) pulley.   (c) simple machine.   (d) load.
4. A lever turns on a point called the
   (a) wedge.   (b) force.   (c) load.   (d) fulcrum.
5. How much an object weighs measures the pull of
   (a) friction.   (b) gravity.   (c) energy.   (d) work.
6. A simple machine sometimes used to raise a flag is a
   (a) wedge.   (b) pulley.   (c) gear.   (d) axle.

✓ Interpreting What You Learned

Write a short answer for each question or statement.
1. When is energy used?
2. Explain how using more force changes an object's speed.
3. Where can a fulcrum be moved to lift a load most easily?
4. Is more force needed to move an object the same distance across a level floor or up a hill?
5. What is one way a person can use scissors safely?

✓ Extending Your Thinking

Write a paragraph to answer each question or statement.
1. Explain how the wheels of roller skates can become hot.
2. How do you use energy when you throw a ball?

 To explore scientific methods, see Experiment Skills on pages 358–359.

7

Forms of Energy

Look at the many lights shining at night. Energy from electricity and light makes this city look bright.

Introducing the Chapter

In this chapter, you will read about electricity and magnets. You also will learn about heat and light. In the activity below, you will learn about the force of a magnet.

Observing Magnets

DISCOVER!

You can find out how the force of a magnet moves through different materials. Get a magnet, a paper clip, and pieces of paper, aluminum foil, and cloth.

Place the paper clip on your desk. Hold the magnet near the paper clip. Do not touch the clip with the magnet. What happens to the paper clip? Does the magnet's force move through air? Put the paper on top of the paper clip. Place the magnet against the top of the paper. Notice what happens to the paper clip. Place the aluminum foil and then the cloth between the magnet and the paper clip. Notice what happens.

Talk About It
1. How did you know the magnet had a force?
2. What happened when each of the materials was between the paper clip and magnet?

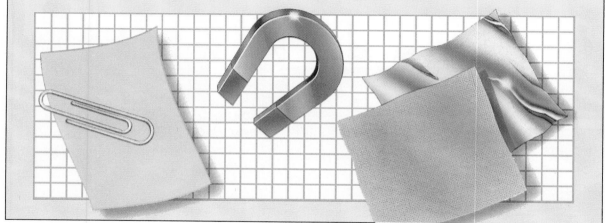

1 What Are Some Kinds of Energy?

LESSON GOALS

You will learn
- that energy comes in different forms.
- how people on earth get energy.

energy of motion
(mō′shən), energy that moving objects have.

You use energy when you move objects from one place to another. You also use energy to do other things every day.

Different Kinds of Energy

How might you make this train move? You might push it with your hand. The moving train would have **energy of motion.** Moving objects have energy of motion.

You also could turn on electricity to make this train move. Electricity carries energy that can move the train. What other objects use electric energy?

Light and sound are other kinds of energy. One kind of energy can change to another kind of energy. For example, energy from electricity changes to light energy when you turn on an electric lamp.

Electric train

How People Get Energy

A boy uses energy to kick the ball in the picture. Light from the sun brings people most of their energy on earth. How can the sun's energy help you work and play? You get energy to move your body from the food you eat. Your food comes from plants or from animals that eat plants. These plants get energy from the sun.

Lesson Review

1. What are some kinds of energy?
2. How do people on earth get energy?
3. **Challenge!** What happens to electric energy when you turn on a radio?

   Study on your own, pages 328–329.

INVESTIGATE!

Find out how wind energy affects the motion of objects. Write a hypothesis and test your hypothesis with an experiment. You might try using a toy sailboat or a kite.

Energy from the sun is called solar energy. Find out how people can use solar energy to heat buildings. For what reason might people who live in Florida use more solar energy than people who live in Alaska? Write a few sentences explaining your answer.

PHYSICAL SCIENCE

FIND OUT ON YOUR OWN

2 What Is Electricity?

LESSON GOALS

You will learn
- about electric charges and electric current.
- how magnets work.
- how electricity can be used wisely.

SCIENCE IN YOUR LIFE

Try rubbing your feet on a wool rug and then reaching for a doorknob. You might see a spark. Sometimes electric charges jump between objects with unlike charges. These jumping charges make the sparks you see.

electric charges, tiny bits of electricity in all matter.

Imagine walking into a dark room. What would you do first? You might turn on an electric light. Electric energy can help make your life easier. How have you used electricity today?

Electric Charge and Electric Current

Sometimes objects stick together. Look at the balloons in the picture. These balloons are sticking to the wall.

All matter has tiny bits of electricity called **electric charges.** Rubbing objects together can cause these electric charges to move from one object to another. These balloons were rubbed against wool cloth. The balloons picked up charges from the cloth. The balloons and the wall have unlike, or opposite, charges. Unlike charges pull on, or attract, each other. The pulling force between unlike charges makes the balloons stick to the wall.

140

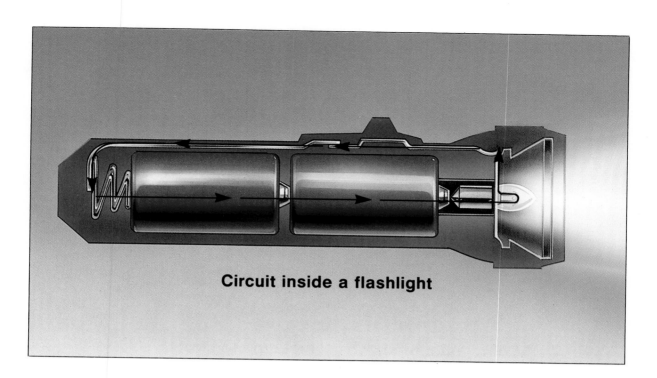

Circuit inside a flashlight

Suppose you rubbed two balloons against a piece of wool. If you held the two balloons near each other, they would push away from each other. The balloons would have charges that are alike. Like charges push away from, or repel, each other.

Think about times that you have used a flashlight. Electricity from a battery can make a flashlight work. A battery pushes electric charges from place to place. The moving of electric charges from one place to another is called **electric current.**

Follow the path of electric current shown in the picture. Notice how the current moves from one end of the battery through the wire to the bulb. Then the current moves from the bulb back to the battery. Electric current travels in a **circuit** when it travels in a path. This bulb lights because the circuit is complete.

electric current (kèr′ənt), the movement of electric charges from one place to another.

circuit (sèr′kit), the path along which electric current moves.

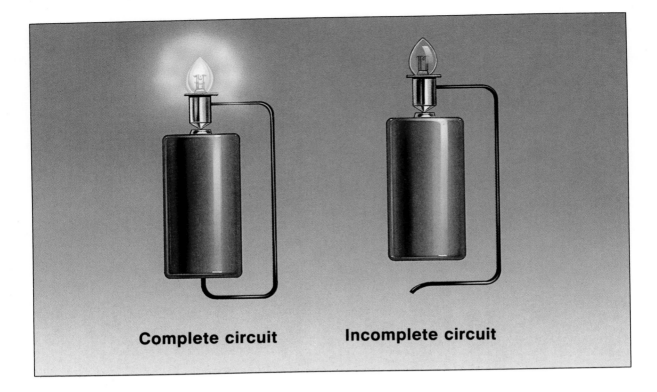

Complete circuit   **Incomplete circuit**

Compare these pictures of batteries. Follow the path of electric current shown in the picture on the left. Find the place where the path stops in the picture on the right. Notice that current cannot move from the battery through the wire back to the battery. The bulb does not light because the circuit is not complete.

Electric current can easily move through some materials, such as copper and other metals. Some other materials, such as rubber, plastic, and glass, do not carry electric current well. Look at the picture of the electric cord. Electric charges move through the copper wire inside the cord. The rubber covering keeps the charges from moving outside the cord.

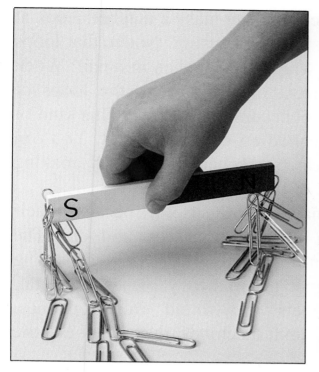

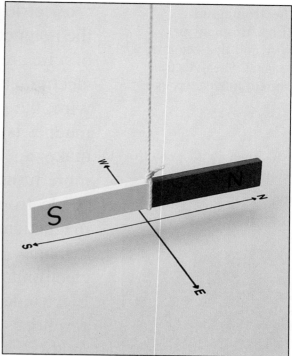

Magnetism is strongest at magnet's poles.   Poles of a magnet

Electricity and Magnets

Look at the picture of the magnet picking up paper clips. A magnet attracts objects with iron in them. Magnets have a force called **magnetism.** Does this magnet pick up more clips at its ends or at its center? The poles of a bar magnet are usually at its ends. Magnetism is strongest at a magnet's poles.

The second picture shows a magnet at the end of a string. Find the marks *N* and *S* on the poles. The magnet turns until the pole marked with an *N* points north. The pole marked *S* points in the opposite direction, or south. A north pole and a south pole are unlike poles. If you hold unlike poles of two magnets near each other, they will attract each other. Like poles of magnets repel each other.

magnetism
(mag′nə tiz′əm), the force around a magnet.

143

electromagnet
(i lek/trō mag/nit), a wire coil that becomes a magnet when electric current moves through it.

Machine with electromagnet

Using an electromagnet

Electric current can make a magnet. Look at the magnet this girl is using. Notice that loops of wire are wrapped around an iron nail. When electric current moves through the loops of wire, the nail becomes a magnet. This kind of magnet is called an **electromagnet.** You can make an electromagnet stronger by making more turns of wire in the loops.

Electromagnets are useful because their magnetism can be turned on and off. The machine in the picture uses a very strong electromagnet to lift heavy pieces of metal. Electromagnets are found in telephones, earphones, and machines that have electric motors.

Electricity can cause magnetism. Also, magnetism can cause electricity. Moving a magnet through loops of wire causes electric current to move through the wire. Power plants use magnets to make electricity. Wires carry the electricity to your home and school.

How Electricity Can Be Used Wisely

Many power plants use energy from coal or oil to make electricity. Energy from the sun long ago was stored in coal and oil. People can make supplies of coal and oil last longer by using less electricity. How can you use less electricity?

Using electricity wisely also means using it safely. Electricity can be harmful if it is not used properly. You can help keep yourself safe by following the safety rules in this chart.

Lesson Review

1. How are electric charges and electric current different?
2. How can electric current make a magnet?
3. How can electricity be used wisely?
4. **Challenge!** Many toys with batteries have switches to turn the toys on and off. What does a switch do to a circuit?

Study on your own, pages 328–329.

Safety Rules

1. Always use dry hands to touch electric appliances and switches.
2. Keep electric appliances away from water.
3. Disconnect electric appliances when not in use.
4. Keep electric cords in places where the cords will not be damaged.
5. Check electric cords to make sure they are not worn.

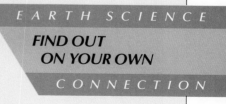

EARTH SCIENCE

FIND OUT ON YOUR OWN

CONNECTION

The earth acts like a giant magnet. Magnetism is strongest near the north and south magnetic poles of the earth. A compass is a tool that helps people use the earth's magnetism to find directions. Find out more about compasses. On a piece of paper, draw a picture of a compass. Write a few sentences explaining how you could use a compass to find directions.

Wear cover goggles for this activity.

Making an Electric Circuit

Purpose
Make an electric circuit.

Gather These Materials
- three 20 cm pieces of thin insulated wire with about 1 cm of insulation scraped from the end
- flashlight battery (size D)
- flashlight bulb • masking tape
- heavy paper

Follow This Procedure
1. Use a chart like the one shown to record your observations.
2. Tape one end of one wire to the tip of the bulb's base. Tape one end of another wire to the metal on the side of the bulb's base.
3. Tape the other end of one of the wires to the point at one end of the battery. Tape one end of the third wire to the other end of the battery.
4. Tape the wires to the paper, like the picture shows, so that the free ends of the wires are close to each other but not touching. Leave enough wire free at the ends to make them touch in the next step. Observe the bulb.
5. Touch the free ends of the wires. Observe what happens.
6. Untape the battery, and tape it in backwards. Observe what happens when you touch the free ends of the wires.

Record Your Results

	What happens to bulb
Wires not touched	
Battery first way	
Battery second way	

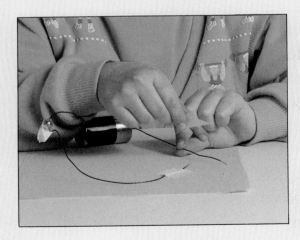

State Your Conclusion
1. Why does the bulb look different when the wires touch?
2. Explain what happens when you turn the battery backwards.

Use What You Learned
How do you think the switch on a flashlight works?

146

Finding Out About Energy

In 1938, some scientists were experimenting with a special kind of matter called uranium. They tried shooting it with tiny particles. They found that it changed to form a different type of matter! How could this happen? A scientist named Lise Meitner, along with her nephew Otto Frisch, figured out what happened to the uranium.

Dr. Lise Meitner

Dr. Meitner found that the special treatment made each atom of uranium split into two new atoms. These new atoms were different kinds of matter. Splitting up the uranium had caused the change. Dr. Meitner called this splitting nuclear fission.

Dr. Meitner knew that energy is stored in each atom of uranium. She found that uranium releases a huge amount of energy when it splits apart. Dr. Meitner figured out just how much energy was released. This energy is called nuclear energy.

Like other forms of energy, nuclear energy can be used to do work. It can be used to make electricity in the same way coal and oil are used. However, just 1 gram of uranium can make the same amount of energy as 3 million grams of coal!

Electricity made by using

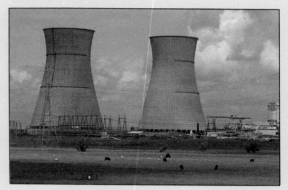

Nuclear energy plant

nuclear energy provides light and heat to many homes and factories. Also, nuclear energy can be used to run submarines and spacecraft. The energy stored in a tiny bit of matter can make big things happen.

What Do You Think?
1. Describe what happens to a uranium atom when nuclear fission occurs.
2. Which can do more work, splitting one gram of uranium or burning one gram of coal?

3 How Is Matter Heated?

LESSON GOALS

You will learn
- how heat moves through matter.
- how you can measure temperature.
- how you can control home temperature.

source (sôrs), a place from which something comes.

Energy gives off heat.

Imagine walking outside on a hot summer day. You would feel warm. The sun is an energy **source** because it gives off energy that can warm you. A source is a place from which anything comes. What are some other energy sources?

How Energy Moves Through Matter

Heat is the flow of energy from warmer places and objects to cooler ones. Pretend that you are holding an ice cube in your fist. Your hand is warmer than the ice cube. Energy from your hand moves to the ice cube. What happens to the ice cube?

Electric energy and most other forms of energy give off heat. Look at the hair dryer in the picture. When energy from electric current passes through the wires in this dryer, the wires become hot. This energy can warm air to dry the girl's hair.

148

Energy moves through matter.

You may have cooked food in a pan like this one. The burner on the stove is the energy source. Energy moves from the stove to the pan to the food. You know that the pan and the food are solids. Energy moves through one solid directly to another solid.

Materials that carry energy easily are called good **conductors.** Most metals are good conductors. Materials that do not carry energy easily are called **insulators.** Notice the wood handle on this pan. Wood is an insulator.

Energy also can move through liquids and gases. However, most liquids and gases are poor conductors.

The sun's energy can travel through empty space. When energy from the sun strikes an object, the sun's energy warms the object.

conductor
(kən duk/tər), a material that easily carries heat.

insulator (in/sə lā/tər), a material through which energy cannot easily flow.

Measuring Temperature

You might listen to a weather report to find out how hot or cold a day is. The report tells about the temperature of the air. You learned in Chapter 5 that particles in matter are always moving. Temperature is a measure of how fast particles of matter are moving. The faster the particles of matter move, the higher the temperature of the matter.

A thermometer is a tool that measures temperature. The thermometer in the picture measures temperature in degrees Celsius. What temperature does this thermometer show?

Thermometer

Thermostat

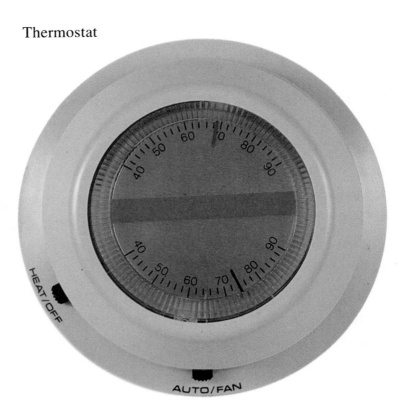

Insulating an attic

Controlling Home Temperature

A **thermostat**, like the one shown on page 150, can control the temperature in a home. When the room temperature falls below the set temperature, the thermostat turns on the furnace. A thermostat also can control cooling systems.

People can help stop heat from moving out of a building. The man in the picture lines an attic with a good insulator to help keep heat in.

thermostat
(thėr′mə stat), a tool that controls the temperature in a home or building.

Lesson Review

1. How does energy move through solids?
2. What is used to measure temperature?
3. How can home temperature be controlled?
4. **Challenge!** How does touching a cold object make your fingers feel cold?

Study on your own, pages 328–329.

Look in library books to find out how feathers keep birds warm in the winter. Write a few sentences explaining what you learned.

PHYSICAL SCIENCE
**FIND OUT
ON YOUR OWN**

4 How Does Light Travel?

You will learn
- that white light is made of colors.
- how lenses work.
- how people see.

reflect (ri flekt′), to turn back.

SCIENCE IN YOUR LIFE

Perhaps you have seen fireflies on a clear summer evening. A firefly has a tiny taillight. Part of the firefly's tail has two different materials that can give off light when they mix together.

Notice how this light travels and reflects.

Suppose you tried to draw on paper when you were in a dark room. You would not be able to see. Paper does not give off light. This boy can see his paper because he turned on a lamp. The lamp is a light source. What are some other sources of light?

The arrow shows how light travels in a straight line from the light source to the paper. Then light bounces off the paper to the boy's eyes. Light **reflects** when it bounces off an object. Light reflects best from smooth, shiny surfaces.

Light cannot go around objects. Suppose an object blocked the light from this lamp. The boy would see a shadow on his paper. A shadow forms whenever an object blocks light. Suppose your body blocks the sun's light when you are outside. What will you see?

A rainbow

Colors in White Light

Most of the light you see is white light. Have you ever seen a rainbow like this one? The rainbow shows how many different colors really make up the white light you see.

You might have seen a rainbow when the sun shines through rain. Light energy travels in waves. Raindrops in the air reflect and bend the light waves coming from the sun. Then the sunlight is separated into different colored parts. The band of colors you see in a rainbow is called the **visible spectrum.** The seven colors of the visible spectrum are red, orange, yellow, green, blue, indigo (in′də gō), and violet.

You also can use certain shapes of glass or plastic to bend white light. A **prism** is a piece of glass or plastic shaped like a triangle. A prism can separate white light into the colors of the visible spectrum.

visible spectrum (viz′ə bəl spek′trəm), the band of colors formed when a wave of white light is bent.

prism (priz′əm), a clear piece of glass or plastic that is shaped like a triangle and can be used for separating white light.

153

How Lenses Work

You might have seen a **lens** like one of those in the picture. A lens is a curved piece of glass, plastic, or other clear material. Light waves bend when they pass through a lens.

Lenses can make objects look different. What you see depends on the kind of lens you use. Notice that lenses have different shapes. Some lenses are thick in the middle and thin at the edges. This kind of lens sometimes makes objects look bigger. Other lenses are thin in the middle and thick at the edges. This kind of lens always makes objects look smaller.

Both kinds of lenses are used in eyeglasses to help people see clearly. Lenses have many uses. The lens in this magnifying glass makes objects look bigger. Cameras, telescopes, and microscopes also have lenses.

How People See

Look at these pictures of a person's eye. How are the pictures different? The black circle in the center of your eye is really an opening called the **pupil.** Light enters your eye through a clear layer that bends it. Then light passes through the pupil.

The colored part of your eye is the **iris.** Muscles in the iris control the size of the pupil. The pupil changes size to let in more or less light. The pupil opens wide when light is dim. The pupil becomes small when light is bright.

A lens is behind the pupil and iris of your eye. This lens bends light waves in much the same way as a glass lens does. The lens in your eye can change shape to help you see objects clearly. The lens becomes thicker when you look at a close object. The lens becomes thinner when you look at a faraway object.

pupil (pyü′pəl), the opening in the center of the eye that lets in light.

iris (ī′ris), the colored part of the eye.

Pupil in bright light

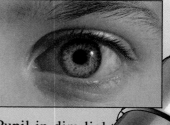

Pupil in dim light

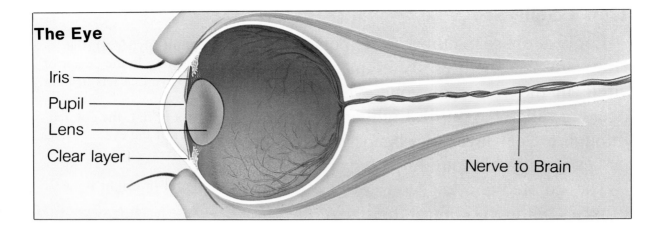

The Eye

Iris
Pupil
Lens
Clear layer

Nerve to Brain

image (im′ij), a copy or likeness.

Use this picture to help you understand what happens when light waves bounce off an object and enter your eye. With your finger, trace the path of the light waves through the pupil and the lens. An **image,** or copy, of what you see forms on the back of your eye. Cells in the back of your eye send a message through a nerve to your brain. Your brain tells you what you see.

Lesson Review

1. What makes up white light?
2. How do lenses change light waves?
3. How does light enter the eye?
4. **Challenge!** Can you see a rainbow when the sun is blocked by clouds? Explain.

Study on your own, pages 328–329.

HUMAN BODY

FIND OUT ON YOUR OWN

CONNECTION

Many people who cannot see are still able to read. Look in library books to find out about Braille. Explain how blind people use Braille to read.

Using a Prism

Purpose
Observe how a prism separates white light.

Gather These Materials
• prism • white heavy paper
• colored markers or crayons

Follow This Procedure
1. Use a chart like the one shown to record your observations.
2. Hold a prism on end in direct sunlight as shown in the picture.

3. Turn the prism until a block of colored bands appears on the wall.
4. Have your partner hold the white paper so that the colored bands can be seen on it.
5. Observe the colors you see. Notice the order in which the colors appear.
6. In the chart, draw and color what you see. List the colors.

Record Your Results

What you see	Names of colors

State Your Conclusion
1. What was the order of the colors in the visible spectrum?
2. How are the colors that you saw like a rainbow?

Use What You Learned
What do you think would happen if you passed the visible spectrum you made through a second prism?

Using Thermometers and Bar Graphs

Problem: How does temperature change when distance between a thermometer and a heat source is greater?

Part A. Using a Thermometer to Collect Information

1. Thermometers measure temperature in degrees Celsius. Spaces between the lines on a thermometer stand for 2°C. The colored liquid shows the temperature. Look at the top of the liquid in Thermometer A. What is the temperature? How far is the thermometer from the lamp?

2. What is the temperature on Thermometer B? How far is this thermometer from the lamp?

3. What is the temperature of the thermometer that is 6 cm from the lamp? 8 cm from the lamp?

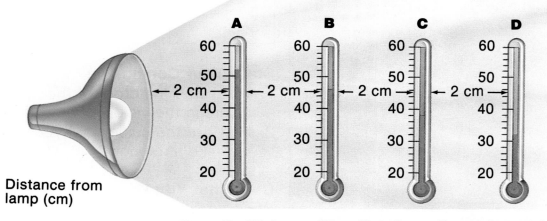

Distance from lamp (cm)

Part B. Using a Bar Graph to Organize and Interpret Information

4. The bar graph contains information you collected about how temperature changes with the distance from the heat source. The first bar shows the temperature of the thermometer that is 2 cm from the lamp. Move your finger

from the top of the
bar to the line at the left of the
graph. This point tells the
temperature on the thermometer.
What is the temperature?

5. What temperature is on the
thermometer that is 4 cm from
the lamp? 6 cm? 8 cm? How
far from the heat source is the
temperature highest? lowest?

6. What would the temperature be
on a thermometer that is 10 cm
from the lamp?

Part C. Using Thermometers and Bar Graphs to Solve New Problems

Problem: How does temperature change when the
amount of electric power, or number of
watts, of a heat source is greater?

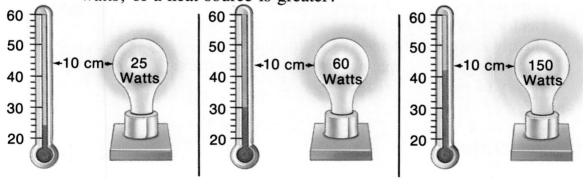

7. Use the picture to collect the
information you need to solve
the problem. Make a bar graph
similar to the one in Part B to
organize your information.

8. Look at the bar graph. How
does temperature change when
the amount of power, or

number of watts, of a heat
source increases?

9. You might want to do this
experiment and use your own
results to make a bar graph.
*CAUTION: Light bulbs can get
hot enough to cause burns. Do
not touch hot bulbs.*

159

Chapter 7 Review

☑ Chapter Main Ideas

Lesson 1 • Energy of motion, electricity, light, and sound are different kinds of energy. • People on earth get most of their energy from sunlight.

Lesson 2 • All matter has electric charges, and electric current travels in a circuit. • Electric current can make a magnet, and magnetism can cause electricity. • Electricity should be used wisely.

Lesson 3 • Heat is energy in motion. • Temperature is the measure of how fast particles of matter move. • People can control temperature in homes and buildings.

Lesson 4 • White light is made of colors. • A lens can change the way an object looks. • Light must travel through the eye for a person to see.

☑ Reviewing Science Words

circuit	image	pupil
conductor	insulator	reflects
electric charges	iris	source
electric current	lens	thermostat
electromagnet	magnetism	visible spectrum
energy of motion	prism	

Copy each sentence. Fill in the blank with the correct word from the list.

1. All matter has ▦.
2. Moving objects have ▦.
3. The ▦ is the colored part of the eye.
4. Electricity can travel in a path called a ▦.
5. Light ▦ when it bounces off an object.
6. A ▦ can control home temperature.
7. An ▦ can be made with wire and an iron nail.
8. A ▦ is a material that carries heat easily.
9. The band of colors in a rainbow is the ▦.
10. ▦ is the force around a magnet.

11. ___ is produced when charges move along a path.
12. The ___ is an opening in the eye.
13. A lamp is a ___ of light.
14. An ___ does not carry heat easily.
15. A ___ can separate white light.
16. An ___ is a copy.
17. The glass in a magnifying glass is a ___.

☑ Reviewing What You Learned

Write the letter of the best answer.
1. Which material is the best heat conductor?
   (a) wood   (b) metal   (c) water   (d) air
2. What brings people most of their energy on earth?
   (a) gasoline   (b) air   (c) wind   (d) sunlight
3. When moving particles in matter speed up, temperature
   (a) goes up.   (b) goes down.
   (c) stays the same.   (d) keeps going up and down.
4. Magnets can attract
   (a) plastic.   (b) paper.   (c) iron.   (d) glass.
5. What forms when an object blocks light?
   (a) a prism   (b) a rainbow   (c) a shadow   (d) an image

☑ Interpreting What You Learned

Write a short answer for each question.
1. What are three kinds of energy?
2. What are two ways to control home temperature?
3. What is a complete circuit?

☑ Extending Your Thinking

Write a paragraph to answer each question or statement.
1. What happens if a hot piece of metal is attached to a cold piece of metal?
2. Suppose the lens in your eye could not change shape. How would you have to move in order to see objects that were close and far away?

 To explore scientific methods, see Experiment Skills on pages 360–361.

Sound

Look at the dolphins in the picture. Dolphins make clicking sounds as they swim. They can use sounds to send messages to each other. They also listen to sounds to help them find their way.

Introducing the Chapter

In this chapter, you will learn how sounds are alike and how sounds are different. You will learn how sound travels through matter. You also will read about how people make and hear sound. The activity below will help you learn what makes sound.

Inferring What Makes Sounds

DISCOVER!

You hear many different sounds every day. You can make sound with objects in your classroom. Place a plastic ruler on your desk so that part of it hangs over the edge. Hold the ruler tightly on the desk with one hand as shown in the picture. Gently press down on the free end of the ruler with your other hand. Let go of the free end of the ruler. How does the ruler move? What do you hear? What happens when the ruler stops moving? Slide the ruler on the desk to make the part that moves longer and then shorter. Listen to the different sounds you can make.

Talk About It
1. What was happening to the ruler when sounds were made?
2. How did the sounds change when you moved the ruler?

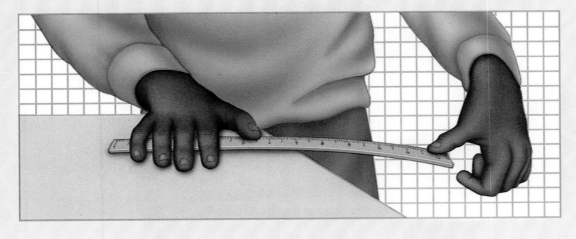

163

1 What Is Sound?

LESSON GOALS

You will learn
- how sounds are alike.
- how sounds are different.

vibrate (vī′brāt), move quickly back and forth.

You learned in Chapter 7 that you use many different kinds of energy each day. Electricity and light are some kinds of energy. Sound is another kind of energy.

How Sounds Are Alike

Suppose you took a walk outside. You might hear people, animals, or cars making sounds. All these sounds are different. Yet all sounds are alike in some ways.

Sound happens when matter **vibrates,** or moves back and forth very quickly. Look at the drum in the picture. If you hit a drum, parts of the drum will vibrate. The drum makes sound. All the sounds around you happen only when objects vibrate.

How Sounds Are Different

Suppose you lightly tapped a drum. You would hear a soft sound. Suppose you hit the drum harder. How would the sound change? The loudness or softness of a sound is called **volume.** The harder you hit the drum, the more it will vibrate. The more an object vibrates, the louder the sound will be. A loud sound has more volume than a soft sound.

Pretend you are listening to music. You probably would hear high sounds and low sounds. **Pitch** describes how high or low a sound is. Objects that vibrate slowly, such as the drum, make sounds with a low pitch. This recorder makes air particles vibrate quickly. The recorder has a high pitch. Different volumes and pitches can be combined to make pleasant music.

INVESTIGATE!

Find out if animals hear the same sounds as people. Write a hypothesis and test your hypothesis with an experiment. You might blow on a whistle with a very high pitch. See if both people and dogs can hear the sounds.

volume (vol′yəm), the loudness or softness of a sound.

pitch (pich), how high or low a sound is.

165

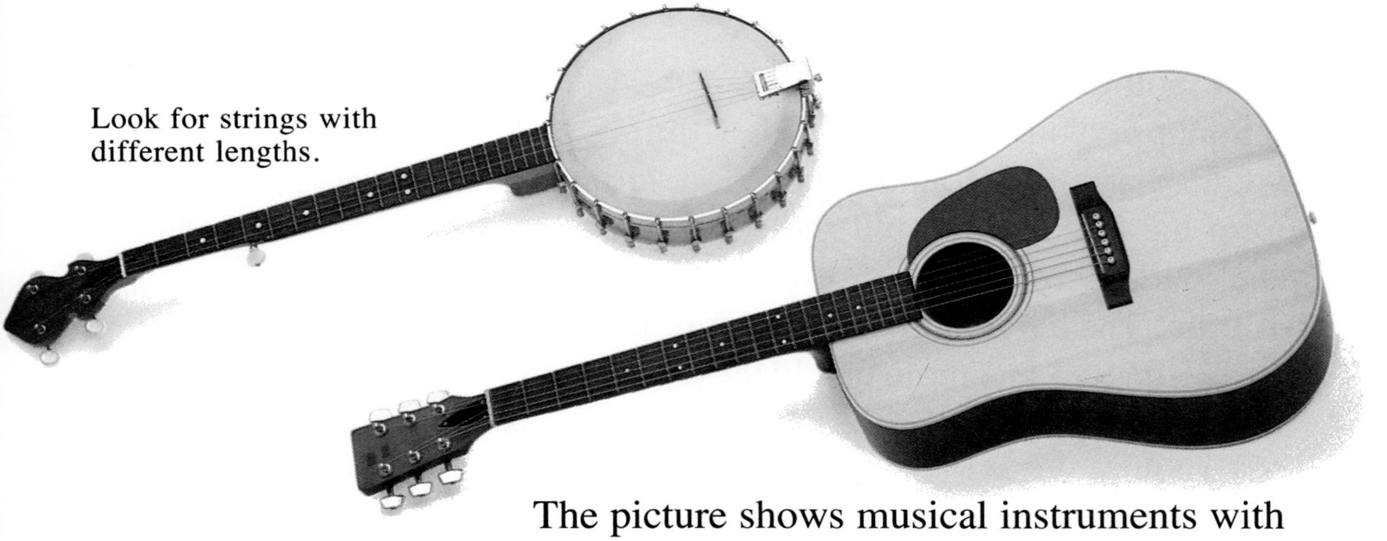

Look for strings with different lengths.

The picture shows musical instruments with strings. You can make different sounds by plucking the strings. Notice how some strings are shorter than others. As a string is shortened, it vibrates more quickly. How does making a string shorter change the pitch of the sound?

Lesson Review
1. How is sound made?
2. How are some sounds different?
3. **Challenge!** How can you change the pitch of a sound made by a vibrating rubber band?

Study on your own, pages 330–331.

Study on your own, pages 330–331.

PHYSICAL SCIENCE

FIND OUT ON YOUR OWN

Look through magazines for pictures of objects that can make sound. Use these pictures to make a poster about sound. Place the pictures in order from those that make the softest sound to those that make the loudest sound. Write the name of each object under its picture.

Predicting Sounds

Purpose
Predict how the length of a vibrating rubber band affects the sound the rubber band makes.

Gather These Materials
• large rubber band • book about 24 cm long • centimeter ruler • 2 pencils

Follow This Procedure
1. Use a chart like the one shown to record your observations.
2. Put the rubber band the long way around the book. Place the pencils under the band about 10 cm apart. *CAUTION: Handle the rubber band carefully.*
3. Ask a partner to hold a finger over the band and each pencil as shown. Gently pluck the band between the pencils. Listen to the pitch of the sound.
4. Predict how the pitch will change if you make the vibrating part of the band longer. Record your prediction.
5. Hold the rubber band and pencils 19 cm apart. Pluck the rubber band. Record the result.
6. Predict how the pitch will change if you shorten the vibrating part of the band. Record your prediction.
7. Hold the rubber band and pencils 5 cm apart. Pluck the rubber band. Record the result.

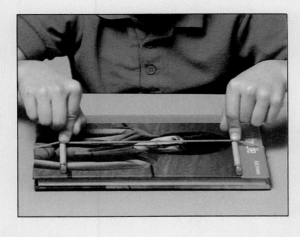

Record Your Results

	Prediction	Result
Long band		
Short band		

State Your Conclusion
1. How does the length of a vibrating object change the pitch of the sound produced?
2. At which length did the vibrating part of the rubber band vibrate the fastest?

Use What You Learned
The strings of a cello are longer than the strings of a violin. Which instrument would you use to play music with low sounds?

2 How Does Sound Travel?

LESSON GOALS

You will learn
- how sound travels through matter.
- what makes an echo.

Pretend that your friend is talking to you. Sound from your friend's voice moves through the air. You learned in Chapter 5 that particles make up matter. Sound moves from place to place by making the particles in matter vibrate.

How Sound Moves Through Matter

Sound travels in waves. The picture shows how sound waves might look if you could see them. First, the school bell vibrates when it rings. Then the air particles next to the bell begin to vibrate. The sound waves keep moving from one air particle to another. Notice how sound waves spread out in all directions.

You would hear a loud sound if you stood close to the school bell. The sound waves are strongest near the bell. These sound waves get weaker as they move away from the bell. You might hear only a soft sound from far away.

Sound waves

Suppose you placed a ticking clock in one part of a room. Now suppose you walked away from the clock. You could still hear the clock ticking. Sound waves from the clock would move through the air.

The girl in the picture is listening to a ticking clock. Notice that she places her ear on the table. Sound waves also can move through wood.

You can only hear sound when it travels through matter. Sound moves through solids, liquids, and gases. Particles of matter in solids are the closest together. For this reason, sound moves fastest and most easily through solids. Particles in liquids are farther apart. Sound moves more slowly through liquids. The particles in gases are the farthest apart. Which state of matter carries sound most slowly?

Sound waves can travel through solid matter.

Echoes

echo (ek′ō), a sound that bounces back from an object.

Pretend you see a ball like this one bouncing against a smooth wall. Use your finger to trace the path of the ball in the picture. Now imagine calling out your name in a large empty room. You might hear sound even after you stop speaking. Like the ball, sound waves can bounce off different surfaces. An **echo** is a sound bouncing back from an object. Echoes can best be heard when sound bounces from hard, smooth surfaces.

Lesson Review

1. How does sound move through different kinds of matter?
2. What is an echo?
3. **Challenge!** Could sound waves from a radio travel through a room with no air? Explain your answer.

Study on your own, pages 330–331.

LIFE SCIENCE

FIND OUT ON YOUR OWN

CONNECTION

Bats are animals that fly in the dark. Look in library books to find out what kind of sounds bats hear. Write a few sentences telling how these sounds help bats.

Listening to Sound Through Different Materials

Purpose
Test different materials to learn which substances sound travels through most easily.

Gather These Materials
- sealable bag • pencil with eraser
- water • cup • wood block

Follow This Procedure
1. Use a chart like the one shown to record your observations.
2. Fill the bag with air by blowing into the bag. Seal the bag closed.
3. Hold the bag next to your ear. Cover your other ear with your hand. Listen while your partner taps the bag lightly with the pencil eraser. Record whether the sounds are loud or quiet.
4. Use the cup to fill the bag with water. Seal the bag.
5. Repeat step 3. Record whether the sounds are louder or quieter than before.
6. Hold the block next to your ear, and cover the other ear. Ask your partner to tap lightly on the block. Record whether the sounds are louder or quieter than before.

Record Your Results

	Observation
Sounds Through Air	
Sounds Through Water	
Sounds Through Wood	

State Your Conclusion
1. Through which material did you hear the loudest sound? the quietest sound?
2. Does sound travel most easily through solids, liquids, or gases? Explain your answer.

Use What You Learned
Suppose you were trying to hear footsteps. Would you put your ear next to the ground to hear the sounds better or would you hold your head up in the air? Explain.

3 How Do People Make Sound?

LESSON GOALS

You will learn
- how people make sound.
- how people hear sound.

vocal cords (vō′kəl kôrdz), two pairs of thin, ropelike flaps at the top of the windpipe.

Think about sounds you can make with your voice. You can whisper or talk. You make sound when you laugh. You might even enjoy singing.

Making Sound

Place your fingers lightly on the front of your throat like the girl in the picture is doing. Now say your name out loud. What do you feel with your fingertips?

You probably can feel your **vocal cords** moving back and forth. Vocal cords are thin flaps at the top of your windpipe. When you talk, air comes from your lungs and passes between your vocal cords. The air makes your vocal cords vibrate. This vibrating movement makes sound.

This girl can feel her vocal cords vibrate.

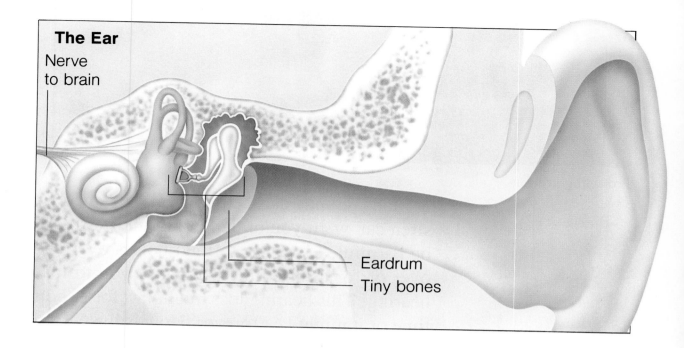

The Ear

Nerve to brain

Eardrum

Tiny bones

Hearing Sound

Imagine trying to catch a ball. You might cup your hands together. Shaping your hands this way helps you catch the ball. Now think about the shape of the outer part of your ear. This shape helps catch sound waves in the air.

Look at the picture to follow the path of the sound waves through the ear. First, the part of the ear you can see moves the sound waves to the part of the ear inside the head. Find the **eardrum**—the thin skin that covers the middle part of the ear. Sound waves make your eardrum vibrate. Then the tiny bones in the middle of your ear begin to vibrate. Find the part of the ear that is shaped like a shell. A liquid fills this part of your ear. This liquid carries sound waves to a special **nerve**—a part of the body that carries messages to the brain. Your brain tells you about the sound you hear.

eardrum, thin skin that covers the middle part of the ear and vibrates when sound waves reach it.

nerve (nėrv), a part of the body that carries messages to the brain.

173

Protecting hearing

Many sounds can help you. For example, a siren can warn you of danger. Sounds also can be harmful. Listening to loud noises over and over or for a long time can cause you to lose hearing. This hearing loss might last for a short time or it might last forever. How is the person in the picture protecting his hearing?

Lesson Review

1. How do people make sounds with their voices?
2. What path do sound waves follow through the ear?
3. **Challenge!** Do sound waves move faster through the outer part of the ear or through the tiny bones in the ear? Explain your answer.

Study on your own, pages 330–331.

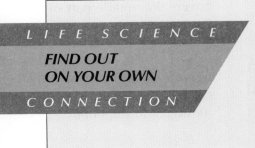

LIFE SCIENCE

FIND OUT ON YOUR OWN

CONNECTION

Many animals make sounds using different body parts. Look in library books to find out how crickets and flies make sound. Write a few sentences telling what you learned.

Sending Voices over the Telephone

The Problem   By the late 1800s, the telegraph made it possible to send messages over long distances. The telegraph changed a code into electric signals, dots, and dashes. However, only one telegraph message could be sent over the wire at one time. Also, telegraph wires could not carry human voices.

Alexander Graham Bell

The Breakthrough   Alexander Graham Bell was born into a family very interested in sound. His grandfather was an actor. His mother was a musician. His father taught deaf people to speak. Bell also became a teacher of the deaf. He became interested in electricity while working on ways to teach the deaf to imitate speech. Bell found a good partner for his experiments. Thomas A. Watson was a repair mechanic.

Bell and Watson worked together to develop the telephone. They were working with an instrument made of several metal reeds and electromagnets. A line ran from one room into the next room. In March 1876, Watson was at the end of the line in the other room. He heard Bell say, "Mr. Watson, come here. I want you!" This famous sentence was the first ever carried by a telephone. The sound waves from Bell's voice traveled as electrical signals along the line. More than one message could travel along the line at once.

New Technology   Today new technology lets us send more messages than ever before over long distances. This is possible because of fiber optics. Scientists discovered that beams of light can carry messages. Thin threads of clear glass or plastic can carry light beams for more than 30 kilometers before they fade away. These thin threads are called optical fibers.

What Do You Think?
1. In what way was teamwork an important part of the development of the telephone?
2. How does fiber optics improve the telephone?

Skills for Solving Problems

Using Rulers and Pictographs

Problem: How does the rate an object vibrates affect the pitch of a sound?

Part A. Using Rulers to Collect Information

1. Rulers measure distance in a straight line. The marks on a ruler stand for centimeters. Move your finger up a ruler in the picture. Read the number of centimeters when your finger is even with the top of the straw. How long is the longest straw?

2. Objects make sounds when they vibrate. A straw vibrates when you blow through it. The shorter the straw, the more rapidly it vibrates. Is the pitch of the longest straw high or low?

3. How long is the shortest straw? Is its pitch high or low?

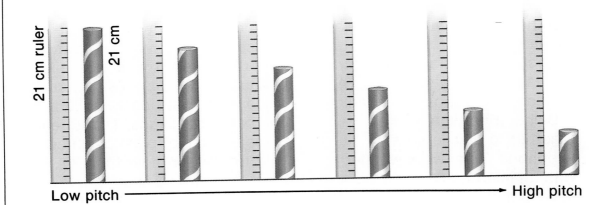

Low pitch ———————————————→ High pitch

Part B. Using a Pictograph to Organize and Interpret Information

4. The pictograph contains the information you collected about how the rate an object vibrates affects the pitch of a sound. How are the lengths of the straws different?

5. How does the rate the straws vibrate change with the differences in length? How does the pitch of the sound change?

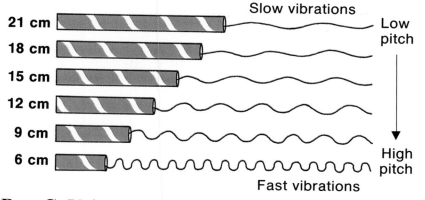

Part C. Using Rulers and Pictographs to Solve a Problem

Problem: Can the pitch change even if the length of an object that vibrates stays the same?

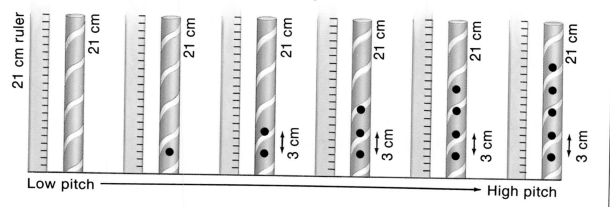

6. Use the picture to collect the information you need to solve the problem. Make a pictograph similar to the one in Part B to organize your information.

7. Look at your pictograph. Can pitch change if the length of a vibrating object stays the same?

8. Are the straws all the same length? How are the straws different from the straws in Part A? How are the straws different from each other?

9. You might want to do this experiment and use your own results to make a pictograph.

177

Chapter 8 Review

☑ Chapter Main Ideas

Lesson 1 • Sound happens when particles of matter vibrate. • How much an object vibrates controls the volume of a sound. How fast an object vibrates controls the pitch of a sound.

Lesson 2 • Sound travels in waves that spread out in all directions. Sound travels through all states of matter— solids, liquids, and gases. The speed of sound through matter is fastest through solids and slowest through gases. • An echo is sound bouncing back from an object.

Lesson 3 • People make sound when the vocal cords vibrate. • Sound waves travel through all the parts of the ear. People hear when the nerve in the ear carries messages to the brain about sound.

☑ Reviewing Science Words

eardrum   pitch   vocal cords
echo   vibrate   volume
nerve

Copy each sentence. Fill in the blank with the correct word from the list.

1. A special ____ in the ear carries messages about sound to the brain.
2. An ____ is a sound bouncing back from an object.
3. Objects that move back and forth slowly make sounds with a low ____.
4. The air particles next to a bell begin to ____ when the bell rings.
5. The more an object vibrates, the louder the ____ will be.
6. When a person talks, air comes from the lungs and passes between the ____.
7. The ____ is a skin that covers the middle part of the ear.

☑ Reviewing What You Learned

Write the letter of the best answer.

1. Sound waves travel most quickly through
   (a) solids.   (b) gases.   (c) air.   (d) liquids.
2. Which part of the ear collects sound waves?
   (a) eardrum   (b) nerve   (c) outer part   (d) bones
3. How fast an object vibrates controls
   (a) volume.   (b) pitch.   (c) echoes.   (d) hearing.
4. What makes the vocal cords vibrate?
   (a) sounds   (b) the lungs   (c) air   (d) the windpipe
5. Hitting an object harder will make the volume
   (a) softer.   (b) the same.   (c) lower.   (d) louder.
6. The liquid in the ear carries sound waves to the
   (a) bones.   (b) nerve.   (c) eardrum.   (d) brain.
7. Echoes can be heard best when sound bounces from surfaces that are
   (a) smooth.   (b) rough.   (c) soft.   (d) bumpy.
8. Objects that vibrate slowly have a pitch that is
   (a) high.   (b) loud.   (c) soft.   (d) low.

☑ Interpreting What You Learned

Write a short answer for each question or statement.

1. How are all sounds alike?
2. How can sounds be harmful?
3. How does sound move through solids more easily than it moves through air?
4. What happens when sound waves reach the eardrum? What makes the vocal cords vibrate?

☑ Extending Your Thinking

Write a paragraph to answer each question or statement.

1. How can guitar strings with different lengths make music that has different sounds?
2. Explain how covering the ears can keep a person from hearing a sound.

 To explore scientific methods, see Experiment Skills on pages 362–363.

Careers

Your books, your clothes, and even your body are made up of atoms. **Chemists** are the people who study atoms. They learn about the matter that forms when different atoms join together. Some chemists study the atoms and particles inside living things. Other chemists help make useful products, such as clothing, tape,

Chemist

and medicines. To become a chemist, you need to go to college for at least four years.

Electricians work with electric energy. Electricians put electric wires, switches, and outlets into buildings. They also repair old electric wiring. Electricians work carefully so they do not get an electric shock from the wires. To become an electrician, you need to take special classes. Then you train with an electrician for about four years.

Like electricians, **carpenters** work on buildings such as houses. To build a house, carpenters first make a wooden frame. Then they put in doors and windows. Inside the house they put up walls, cabinets, and wood trim. Carpenters use many different tools, such as saws, hammers, and drills. They must measure everything closely so that all parts of the house fit together. Carpenters can learn their skills on the job or by taking classes at a special school.

Musicians create sounds that please the ear. When a musician performs music, he or she makes sound energy. Some musicians play musical instruments. Others make music by singing, writing music, or leading groups of musicians. Many musicians start their training at a very early age. Some study music in college. Others become good musicians by practicing and performing with other musicians.

Carpenter

The Violin

A violin can make beautiful music. It can also teach a lot about sounds. A violin has 84 parts. All these parts work together to make the sound that you can hear. Together, these parts vibrate and send sound waves into the air.

The picture shows the main parts of a violin. Every part adds something to the sound the violin makes.

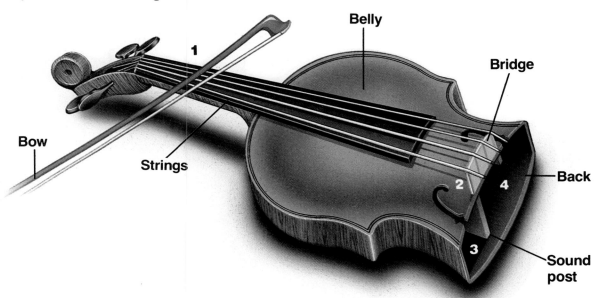

Belly

Bridge

Bow

Strings

Back

Sound post

1 The sound begins with the strings. A person draws a bow across a string. The bow makes the string vibrate. A string vibrates in many ways at once, making many different sounds. You hear all these sounds mixed together.

2 A vibrating string does not make very loud sounds. The other parts of the violin help make the sound louder. When a string vibrates, it causes the bridge to vibrate too. The bridge passes the vibrations to the belly of the violin.

3 Vibrations from the bridge also pass down the sound post to the back of the violin. The sound post and the back vibrate along with the string and the belly. Special kinds of wood are used to make the violin, because different kinds of wood make different sounds.

4 All of the vibrating parts cause the air inside the violin to vibrate too. Each vibrating part sends out sound waves and makes its own special sound. Musicians say that the violin has a rich sound. They mean that the violin has many different kinds of sounds that go together well.

Unit 2 Review

Complete the Sentence

Fill in the blank with the correct word or words from the list.

condenses   friction
conductors   nerve
echo   pitch
electromagnet   thermostat
evaporates   volume
force   work

1. The ___ controls the temperature in a home.
2. An object's ___ is the amount of space it takes up.
3. Sound is carried by a ___ from the ear to the brain.
4. An object can be made to move faster by using more ___.
5. ___ is done when an object is moved through a distance.
6. Water ___ when it changes from a liquid to a gas.
7. Energy is carried easily by materials that are good ___.
8. Objects create a sound with a high ___ when they vibrate very quickly.
9. A wire coil becomes an ___ when an electric current moves through it.
10. Water vapor ___ to a liquid on a cold glass.
11. A sound produces an ___ when it bounces back from an object.
12. Two objects rubbing together cause the force of ___.

Short Answer

Write a short answer for each question or statement.

1. Describe the change that takes place when water is boiled. Is this change a physical change or a chemical change?
2. A person removes some of the gas from a container. What happens to the volume of the gas in the container? Why?
3. Describe the forces that make a thrown ball stop moving.
4. Describe gears and tell where you might find them.
5. What kind of force do magnets have? Where is this force the strongest?
6. Why does an electric cord need to have two wires inside it?
7. How can a wood handle on a hot pot protect you from burns?
8. How does the movement of air particles change when the pitch of a flute becomes lower?
9. How are vocal cords like the strings of a violin?

Essay

Write a paragraph for each question or statement.

1. Describe a lever and explain how a lever can help lift a heavy object.
2. How can lenses make objects seem larger or smaller?

Unit Projects and Books

Science Projects

1. Compare the sizes of different objects. Use paper clips to find the perimeter of an envelope. Perimeter is the distance around the envelope. Use small squares to find the envelope's area. The number of squares needed to cover the envelope is its area. Then use the paper clips and squares to find the perimeter and area of a sheet of paper.

   Next find the perimeter and area of the envelope in metric measures. Use a ruler to find its perimeter in centimeters. Find the envelope's area by using a sheet of 1 cm graph paper. Place the envelope on top of the graph paper. Trace the outline of the envelope. Then count how many square centimeters it takes to cover the envelope. Do the same with the paper.

2. Make your own telephone. Use two paper cups. Punch a small hole through the bottom of each cup. Thread the end of a long piece of string through each hole. Fasten the string by tying large knots that will not slip through the holes. With the help of a friend, stretch the string in a straight line. Speak into one of the cups. Your friend should hold his ear close to the second cup. Can your friend hear you? Now have your friend talk to you.

Books About Science

Wheels at Work: Building and Experimenting with Models of Machines by Bernie Zubrowsky. Morrow, 1986. Learn to make a model of a pulley and a gear using readily available materials.

All About Sound by David Knight. Troll, 1983. Learn about sound, its formation, pitch, and transmission.

Science and Society

Noise Pollution More people want to fly in and out of Barnes County Airport. The airport needs to build another runway to handle more airplanes. This would bring money and jobs to the county. Neighbors of the airport object. The added noise might break their windows and damage their hearing. The airport manager agrees that there will be more noise. But she says it will only last a few hours each day. She has to think about the whole county, not just those who live near the airport. The county will buy the homes of people who want to move away. What are the arguments for a new runway? What are the arguments against the runway?

Earth Science

Over the years, the land in the picture has slowly changed. Notice the shapes of the mountains. Look at the snow on the mountain tops.

The earth is always changing. In this unit, you will discover what causes changes in land and changes in weather. You also will learn about places far away from earth.

SCIENCE IN THE NEWS During the next few weeks, look in newspapers or magazines for news about storms. Also, look for stories that tell how storms changed the land or changed the lives of people. Share the news with your class.

Rocks and Soil

Have you ever seen a rock shaped like this? Notice that you can see different colors in the rock.

Introducing the Chapter

Different kinds of rocks are made of different materials. In this chapter, you will learn about how rocks and soil are formed. You will read about ways people use rocks and soil. The activity below will help you learn about different properties of rocks.

Observing Rocks

DISCOVER!

Put the rocks your teacher gives you on your desk. Observe the rocks carefully. On a piece of paper, write some words that describe one of the rocks. Give the paper to a classmate to read. Ask your classmate to point out the rock that you described.

Talk About It
1. How are the rocks you collected alike?
2. How was the rock you described different from the others?

1 How Are Rocks Formed?

LESSON GOALS

You will learn
- that rocks are made of minerals.
- how the three kinds of rocks are formed.

Suppose you scratched the tip of a pencil with your fingernail. Part of the tip would come off. The soft, black material in a pencil tip came from a rock.

Minerals and Rocks

The tip of a pencil is made of graphite (graf′īt), a form of the mineral carbon. You learned in Chapter 1 that a mineral forms in the earth from matter that was never alive. The pictures show a few of the 2,500 known minerals. Each mineral has its own special properties. A mineral can be any color, shiny or dull, and soft or hard.

Rocks are made of one or more minerals. If you look closely at a rock, you might see different colors. Substances in the minerals cause the different colors.

Minerals

Selenite

Calcite with fluorite

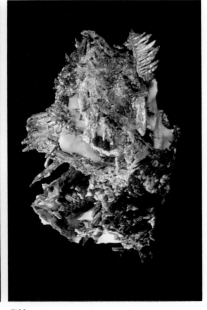

Silver

188

Kinds of Rocks

How would you group rocks in a rock collection? You might group them by their size, shape, color, or what they are made of. You also can group rocks by how they were formed.

The earth is so hot deep inside that minerals melt. Some rocks form from melted minerals inside the earth. Melted minerals sometimes move to the earth's surface. Then the minerals cool and harden into rock. **Igneous rocks** are rocks that form from melted minerals. The igneous rock in the first picture formed from melted minerals that poured out of an opening in a mountain.

Granite (gran′it) is an igneous rock that is very hard. People use granite to make buildings. What do you notice about the color of this piece of granite? Each color you see is a different mineral.

igneous (ig′nē əs) **rock,** a rock that forms from melted minerals.

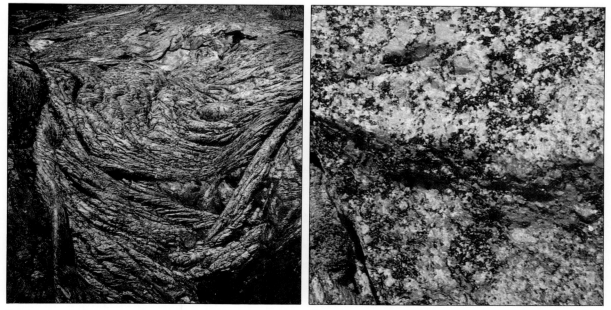

Igneous rock   Granite

189

Layers in sedimentary rock

sedimentary
(sed′ə men′tər ē) **rock,** rock that forms when layers of material are pressed together.

metamorphic
(met′ə môr′fik) **rock,** an igneous or sedimentary rock that was changed by heat or pressure.

Another kind of rock can form under water. Rivers and streams carry bits of rock, shells, and other materials into lakes and oceans. The materials sink and form layers at the bottom of the water. The top layers press down on the bottom layers. Over millions of years, the bottom layers harden into **sedimentary rock.** You can see layers of sedimentary rock in the picture.

Sometimes, igneous or sedimentary rock can be changed into a third kind of rock—**metamorphic rock.** Great heat inside the earth can change a rock's minerals into other minerals. Pressure also can change the minerals in rocks. When the minerals in a rock change, the rock becomes metamorphic rock.

190

Limestone is a sedimentary rock. When limestone is heated and squeezed inside the earth, it changes into marble—a metamorphic rock. Marble is much harder than limestone. People can use very sharp tools to carve objects out of marble.

Lesson Review

1. What are rocks made of?
2. How does each of the three kinds of rock form?
3. **Challenge!** How can an igneous rock become part of a sedimentary rock?

Study on your own, pages 332–333.

SCIENCE IN YOUR LIFE

Sometimes scientists find fossils in sedimentary rocks. Fossils are signs of past life. Some fossils are bones, teeth, footprints, or whole plants or animals that lived many years ago.

PHYSICAL SCIENCE

FIND OUT ON YOUR OWN

CONNECTION

A mineral can scratch a softer mineral. For example, the mineral graphite can scratch the mineral talc because graphite is harder than talc. However, talc cannot scratch graphite.

Read about the properties of the minerals shown here. Decide which mineral is the softest and which is the hardest. On a piece of paper, list the names of the minerals from the softest to the hardest.

Diamond can scratch quartz and gypsum.

Gypsum cannot scratch diamond or quartz.

Quartz can scratch gypsum but not diamond.

ACTIVITY

Testing Objects for Hardness

Purpose
Observe and test objects for hardness by doing a scratch test.

Gather These Materials
• pencil • chalk • penny

Follow This Procedure
1. Use a chart like the one shown to record your observations.
2. One substance is harder than another if it scratches the surface of that object. A mark that rubs off is not a scratch. Test the lead of a pencil to see if it can be scratched with your fingernail as shown in the picture. Write *yes* or *no* in the chart.
3. Test a piece of chalk and a penny to see if they can be scratched with your fingernail. Record your results.
4. Test the pencil lead and penny to see if they can be scratched by the chalk. Record your results.
5. Test the chalk and penny to see if they can be scratched by the pencil lead. Record your results.
6. Test the chalk and pencil lead to see if they can be scratched by the penny. Record your results.

Record Your Results

Object to be tested	Chalk	Pencil lead	Penny
Scratched by — Fingernail			
Chalk			
Pencil lead			
Penny			

State Your Conclusions
1. Which is harder, pencil lead or chalk?
2. List the objects you tested in order of their hardness, with the softest first.

Use What You Learned
A diamond is the hardest mineral. If you had a real diamond and a fake diamond made of glass, how could you tell which one was real?

Entering the Diamond Age

The Problem Diamonds are valuable minerals made of carbon. People dig diamonds out of the ground. Diamonds make beautiful jewelry. You might be surprised to learn that diamonds are more than beautiful. They are also the hardest substance found in nature. Their hardness makes them very useful in industry. Diamonds cut, grind, and drill holes through hard metal. Diamonds also conduct heat and electricity well. The problem is that industry needs more diamonds than are found in nature.

Diamonds

The Breakthrough In 1955, a team of American scientists made the first artificial diamonds. They used a special press to squeeze carbon under great heat and pressure. Most of the artificial diamonds were very small. They worked well in industrial uses. In 1970, American scientists also made larger artificial diamonds.

New Technology Recently, scientists learned how to coat things with thin films of diamonds. The clear films are just as hard as real diamonds. They also have other properties of diamonds. Cutting tools coated with diamond films will work better than present tools made with diamonds. New tools with diamond films will last longer and are harder all over than present diamond tools. In the future, many products may have diamond films. Windows in airplanes might be covered with a diamond film. Raindrops hitting the windows at high speed would not scratch these windows. Diamond-coated parts inside the hottest parts of cars would not melt. They could keep track of how much gas the car used. Computer parts coated with diamond film would make computers work faster. Coating computer disks with diamond film would make disks last longer.

What Do You Think?
1. Why are diamonds useful for cutting in industry?
2. How could diamond films improve eyeglasses?

2 What Is Soil Made Of?

LESSON GOALS

You will learn
- how soil is formed.
- how the three kinds of soil differ.

What do you notice about the size of this rock? Over thousands of years, the rock will slowly crumble and become part of the soil.

How Soil Is Formed

How can a large solid rock break into small pieces? If you look closely at a rock, you will see many tiny holes and cracks. When it rains or snows, water fills the holes and cracks. This water freezes and pushes against the rock. As the water continues to freeze and melt, the rock slowly breaks apart. Over many years, the water causes the rock to break into small pieces and form soil.

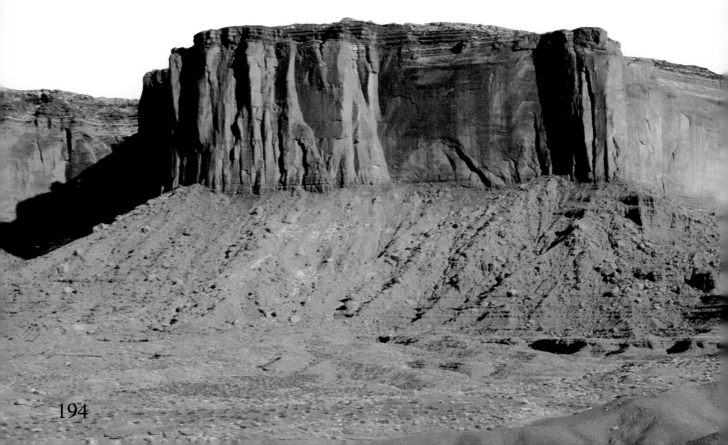

What can you notice about the rock in the picture on the right? Soil can collect in the cracks of a rock. Plants can grow in this soil. Then plant roots can break rocks apart. Over many years, the roots can help crumble a large rock.

Soil is made of more than rock. Soil also has air, water, and matter that was once alive. When plants and animals die, they **decay,** or rot. The decayed matter—**humus**—becomes part of the soil. Humus gives soil a dark color and adds **nutrients** to the soil. Nutrients are materials plants need to live and grow.

Kinds of Soil

The soil where you live might be very different from soil in other places. You might have noticed that soil can have different colors. Soil also can have pieces of different sizes. Soil can feel very soft or very hard.

SCIENCE IN YOUR LIFE

When a rock breaks apart, its minerals become part of the soil. Some minerals can give the soil a certain color. The mineral iron can give soil a red color.

decay (di kā′), to slowly break down, or rot.

humus (hyü′məs), the decayed matter in soil.

nutrient (nü′trē ənt), a material that plants and animals need to live and grow.

Plant growing in cracks in rock

Rocks help form soil.

195

Clay soil

Sandy soil

Loam

clay soil, tightly packed soil with tiny grains.

sandy soil, loose soil with large grains.

loam (lōm), good planting soil that is a mixture of clay, sand, and humus.

Compare the three kinds of soil in the pictures. Tiny grains in **clay soil** make it feel smooth. Clay soil has many nutrients and holds water well. Many plants cannot grow in clay soil because the grains are so close together.

Sandy soil is loose and easy to dig. Most plants do not grow well in sandy soil. Sand does not hold water, and it has few nutrients.

Loam is a mixture of clay, sand, and humus. Many plants grow well in this soil. Loam holds water and has many nutrients for plants.

Lesson Review

1. How is soil formed?
2. How do the three kinds of soil differ?
3. **Challenge!** What might happen to a sidewalk that has a tree growing near it?

Study on your own, pages 332–333.

Study on your own, pages 332–333.

PHYSICAL SCIENCE

FIND OUT ON YOUR OWN

CONNECTION

The part of the soil you usually see is called topsoil. Look in library books to find out about the properties of topsoil. Write a few sentences explaining why topsoil is important.

Observing Soil Samples

Purpose
Observe soil samples to see what they are made of.

Gather These Materials
- 4 soil samples in paper cups
- white construction paper
- toothpick • hand lens • plastic spoon

Follow This Procedure
1. Use a chart like the one shown to record your observations.
2. Put two spoonfuls of soil from each sample on the white paper.
3. Use the toothpick to separate one soil sample into different materials. Look for light pieces, dark pieces, and soft material. Pile like pieces together.
4. Label each pile with a letter. Carefully look at each pile with a hand lens, as shown in the picture. Look at the color, hardness or softness, size, and shape of the bits in each pile. Record your observations.
5. Repeat steps 3 and 4 with the other three soil samples.

Record Your Results

Sample part	a	b	c	d
Color				
Hard or soft				
Size (large, medium, or small)				
Shape				

State Your Conclusions
1. How many different kinds of bits did you find in the first soil sample?
2. Did one of your piles have humus? How do you know?

Use What You Learned
Which kinds of soil were in your samples? Would plants be able to grow well in your soil samples?

3 How Do People Use Rocks and Soil?

ore (ôr), rock that is rich in useful minerals.

Objects that came from rocks and soil

This glass is made of minerals that came from rocks. The juice and the salad came from plants that grew in soil. Every day, people use objects that came from rocks and soil.

How Rocks and Soil Are Important

People eat plants that grow in soil. People get meat from animals that eat plants. Some materials in clothing, such as cotton, also come from plants. The paper in this book was made from trees that grew in soil. What other ways do you use objects that came from soil?

Rocks are important to people too. Some rocks—called **ores**—have large amounts of useful minerals. People can separate the minerals from the rocks. The ore in the picture has the mineral copper. People use copper to make coins, electric wires, and pots and pans.

Copper

Open-pit mine

Some ores have more than one kind of useful mineral. For example, an ore might have the minerals lead and silver. Lead is used to make batteries and some kinds of pipes. People use silver to make film, jewelry, and mirrors.

Sometimes ores are found deep under the ground. Miners must dig deep tunnels to get the ores out. Other times ores are found near the earth's surface. Miners remove the soil and top layers of rock to reach the ores. As you can see in the picture, this kind of mining leaves a large pit in the ground. Miners must fill in the pit after the ores are mined. Then, people can use the land again.

natural resource
(nach′ər əl ri sôrs′),
something people use
that comes from the
earth.

recycle (rē si′kəl), to
change something so it
can be used again.

Using Natural Resources Wisely

A **natural resource** is something people use that comes from the earth. Minerals and soil are two kinds of natural resources. The earth has a limited amount of natural resources. People must be careful not to waste them.

Some materials can be used over and over again—or **recycled.** People use the machines in these pictures to recycle aluminum (ə lü′mə nəm) cans. Aluminum is a metal found in some minerals. The machine chops the used cans into small pieces. Then, the pieces are melted and rolled into sheets. People use the aluminum sheets to make new cans.

People can recycle some materials

Field of peas

People can grow plants in ways that use soil wisely. Some plants, such as these peas, add nutrients to the soil. Different plants use up different nutrients in the soil. People can change the kinds of plants they grow each year. Then the lost nutrients have time to build up again in the soil.

Lesson Review
1. How are rocks and soil important?
2. Why should people not waste natural resources?
3. **Challenge!** Paper is made from trees. How do people use natural resources wisely when they take newspapers to be recycled?

Study on your own, pages 332–333.

INVESTIGATE!

Fertilizers have nutrients that plants need. Find out how fertilizers affect the growth of plants. Write a hypothesis and test your hypothesis with an experiment. You might try growing one plant with fertilizer and another one without fertilizer.

Think of one way you can avoid wasting minerals or soil. Write your idea on a piece of paper. Then, make a poster that shows your idea for using minerals or soil wisely.

EARTH SCIENCE
FIND OUT ON YOUR OWN

Using Graduated Cylinders and Bar Graphs

Problem: How much water will pass through different kinds of soil?

Part A. Using Graduated Cylinders to Collect Information

1. Graduated cylinders measure volume. Each line on these cylinders stands for 10 mL.
2. Each funnel has 100 cc of soil in it. When 100 mL of water is poured into a funnel, the water soaks the soil. Extra water goes through the soil into the cylinder. Look at the line on the cylinder that measures the level of the water. How many mL of water passed through the sandy soil? the clay soil? the loam soil?

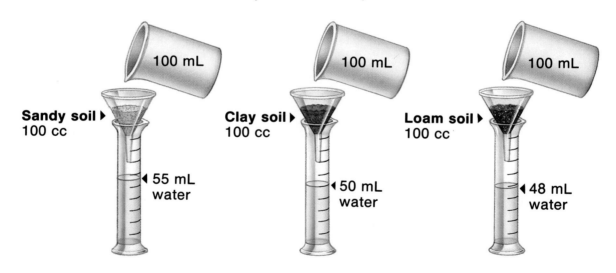

Part B. Using a Bar Graph to Organize and Interpret Information

3. This bar graph contains the information you collected about how much water will pass through soil. Each bar shows how much water passed through one kind of soil. What does each line on the scale on the left stand for?

4. The first bar shows how much water passed through the sandy soil. Trace with your finger from the top of the bar across to the scale on the left. The bar shows that 55 mL of water ran into the cylinder. How much water ran into the second cylinder? the third?

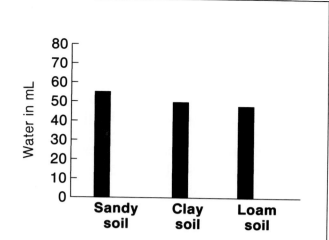

Part C. Using Graduated Cylinders and a Bar Graph to Solve a Problem

Problem: Does changing the amount of soil in the funnel affect how much water passes through it?

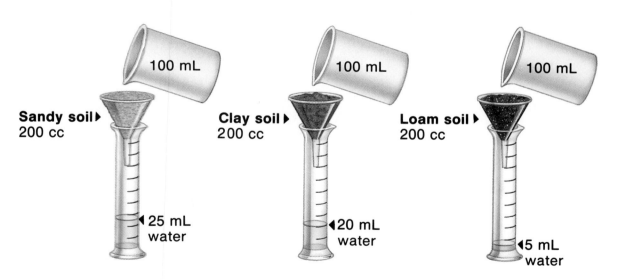

Sandy soil ▶
200 cc

◀ 25 mL water

Clay soil ▶
200 cc

◀ 20 mL water

Loam soil ▶
200 cc

◀ 5 mL water

5. Use the graduated cylinders to collect the information you need to solve the problem. Make a bar graph similar to the one shown in Part B to organize your information.
6. Look at your bar graph. Does changing the amount of soil in the funnel affect how much water passes through it?
7. You might want to do this experiment and use your own results to make a bar graph.

Chapter 9 Review

☑ Chapter Main Ideas

Lesson 1 • Rocks are made of one or more minerals.
• Igneous rocks, sedimentary rocks, and metamorphic rocks
are three kinds of rocks that formed in different ways.

Lesson 2 • Rock can break apart into small pieces and form
part of the soil. Soil also has air, water, and decayed matter.
• Three kinds of soil are clay soil, sandy soil, and loam.

Lesson 3 • Many objects people use come from rocks and
soil. • People should use natural resources wisely.

☑ Reviewing Science Words

clay soil   loam   ore
decays   metamorphic rock   recycle
humus   natural resources   sandy soil
igneous rock   nutrient   sedimentary rock

*Copy each sentence. Fill in the blank with the correct word
from the list.*

1. A rock becomes a ▨▨ when heat or pressure changes the
   minerals in an igneous or sedimentary rock.
2. ▨▨ is loose soil with large grains.
3. A plant ▨▨ when it slowly breaks down, or rots.
4. ▨▨ is a mixture of clay, sand, and humus.
5. A ▨▨ is a material in the soil that a plant needs to
   grow.
6. People can ▨▨ some kinds of minerals so that they can be
   used again.
7. A rock that is formed from melted minerals is an ▨▨.
8. Smooth soil with tiny grains is ▨▨.
9. ▨▨ is formed when layers of material are pressed
   together.
10. Minerals and soil are two kinds of ▨▨.
11. ▨▨ is decayed matter in soil.
12. A rock that has a large amount of useful minerals is an
    ▨▨.

✓ Reviewing What You Learned

Write the letter of the best answer.

1. Most plants grow well in
   (a) sandy soil.   (b) clay soil.   (c) ores.   (d) loam.
2. The soft black material in a pencil tip comes from
   (a) a plant.   (b) a rock.   (c) sandy soil.   (d) humus.
3. The grains in clay soil are
   (a) close together.   (b) far apart.   (c) very large.
   (d) loose and easy to dig.
4. Miners remove soil and top layers of rock to reach
   (a) igneous rocks.   (b) loam.   (c) ores.   (d) clay.
5. What kind of rocks can form in layers under water?
   (a) igneous   (b) sedimentary   (c) humus   (d) loam
6. Which plant parts often break rocks apart?
   (a) roots   (b) stems   (c) flowers   (d) leaves
7. Which kind of rock is marble?
   (a) sedimentary   (b) ore   (c) igneous
   (d) metamorphic
8. Which kind of soil has few nutrients?
   (a) loam   (b) clay soil   (c) humus   (d) sandy soil

✓ Interpreting What You Learned

Write a short answer for each question or statement.

1. How does humus help plants grow?
2. Explain how water can break a large rock apart.
3. Describe the steps in recycling an aluminum can.
4. How can a farmer grow plants to use soil wisely?
5. How does clay soil differ from sandy soil?

✓ Extending Your Thinking

Write a paragraph to answer each question or statement.

1. Which would dry faster after a rainstorm, a sandy beach or
   a field with many different plants? Explain your answer.
2. Most minerals are mined only in places where they are
   found in large amounts. Give one possible reason for this.

 To explore scientific methods, see Experiment Skills on pages 364–365.

Changes in the Earth

Notice how the water flows over these rocks. Over the years, the water has worn away some of the rock.

Introducing the Chapter

In this chapter, you will read about the inside and outside of the earth. You will learn how the earth can change. In the activity below, you will learn how a drop of water can change the land.

Observing Drops of Water

DISCOVER!

Suppose you dug a small hole in a field. This would not change the land much. Suppose you and your classmates spent a week digging holes in the field. Then the field would look very different.

Place a small mound of sand on a piece of waxed paper. Use a medicine dropper to let a drop of water fall on the sand, as shown in the picture. Notice what happens to the sand. Now hold the dropper higher above the sand. Squirt all the water in one place on the sand. Refill the dropper several times. Squirt all the water in the same place.

Talk About It
1. What did one drop of water do to the mound of sand?
2. What happened when you let a lot of water fall quickly on the sand in the same place?

1 What Is the Inside of the Earth Like?

LESSON GOALS

You will learn
- that the earth has three layers.
- how scientists study the inside of the earth.

People used to think the earth was flat. They believed that if you sailed a boat far out into the ocean, the boat would fall off the earth. Today people know this is not true. The earth is not flat. It is shaped like a ball. The earth only seems flat because it is so large. When you look around you, you are seeing only a small part of the earth.

Layers of the Earth

Compare the picture of the peach with the picture of the earth. You can see that they both have three layers.

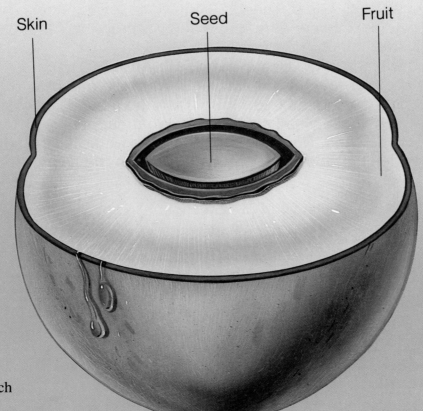

Skin   Seed   Fruit

Parts of a peach

208

Find the outer layer of the earth. This layer is like the skin of the peach. The outer layer, or **crust,** of the earth is made up of rocks and soil. The land you walk on and the land under the oceans are part of the crust.

What part of the earth is like the middle part of the peach? The middle layer of the earth is the **mantle.** It is mostly made of rock. Some of the rock in the mantle is partly melted.

Notice that the center part of the earth is like the peach seed. The center of the earth—the **core**—is mostly iron. The outside part of the core has liquid iron. The inside part has solid iron. The core is the hottest part of the earth. The temperature of the core is almost as hot as the surface of the sun!

Some parts of the top of the earth's crust are stronger than others. When workers build a very tall building, they first test the ground. The workers need to find out if the crust is strong enough to hold up the building.

---

crust (krust), the outer layer of the earth.

mantle (man′tl), the middle layer of the earth.

core (kôr), the center part of the earth.

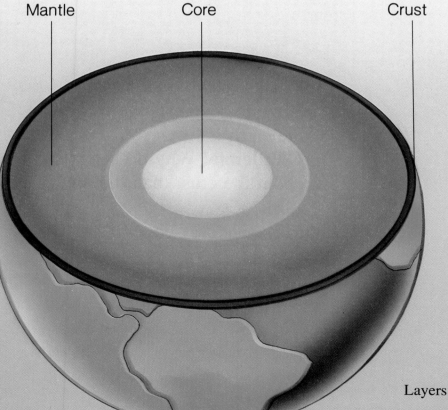

Mantle   Core   Crust

Layers of the earth

Studying the inside of the earth

How Scientists Study the Inside of the Earth

The earth's mantle and core are too far down to reach. Scientists study the inside of the earth from the outside. Movements of the earth's crust give scientists information about the inside of the earth. Scientists also use instruments to find out about the inside of the earth.

Lesson Review

1. What makes up each layer of the earth?
2. How do scientists know what the inside of the earth is like?
3. **Challenge!** Why do scientists know more about the crust than the other layers of the earth?

Study on your own, pages 334–335.

PHYSICAL SCIENCE

FIND OUT ON YOUR OWN

CONNECTION

A seismograph is one machine that scientists can use to learn about the earth's crust. Look in library books to find out how a seismograph works. Write a few sentences telling what you have learned.

Inferring Shapes From Sounds

Purpose
Describe the sounds hidden objects make when they move in a box and *infer* the shapes and types of the objects.

Gather These Materials
• covered box containing several objects • tape

Follow This Procedure
1. Use a chart like the one shown to record your observations.
2. Tilt, turn, and shake the box. Listen to the sounds the objects make. Do they sound like they are sliding or rolling? What do they sound like when they hit the sides of the box? How many objects do you think are in the box?
3. Record your observations. Write the names of the objects you think are in the box.
4. Open the box. Write the names of the objects in the chart.
5. Make up another mystery box like the one in the picture. Use objects that you get from your teacher. Seal the box with tape. Trade boxes with a partner.
6. Repeat steps 2, 3, and 4.

Record Your Results

Sounds Made	Objects you think are in box	Objects in box

State Your Conclusion
1. How did the sounds help you to tell what was in the box?
2. How did you tell how many objects were in the box?

Use What You Learned
What are some things you could not learn about the hidden objects by shaking the box? Explain your answer.

2 How Do Water and Wind Change the Earth's Crust?

LESSON GOALS

You will learn
- how rocks weather.
- how water and wind cause erosion.

weather (weᴛʜ′ər), to wear down or break apart rocks.

Notice how smooth the rocks in the picture look. These rocks used to have very sharp edges. Over many years, these sharp edges have worn away.

Weathering

You learned in Chapter 9 that rocks crumble and wear away. When rocks break down, they **weather.** Most rocks weather slowly, over many years. Rocks can weather in several different ways.

Freezing water weathers rocks. You know that water can fill the holes and cracks in a rock. What happens to the rock as the water continues to freeze and melt?

Moving water can wear away rocks.

Plants also help weather rocks. You learned that plant roots can grow in soil that collects in the cracks of rocks. The roots can break rocks apart as they grow. The roots of a large plant, such as a tree, can break a boulder apart.

Sometimes, rainwater and gases in the air can weather rocks. You learned in Chapter 1 that carbon dioxide is a gas in the air. Carbon dioxide can mix with water, such as rain, to form a new material. This material can turn hard minerals in rocks to soft clay. Then the rocks slowly break apart. Sometimes, materials in the water eat away the minerals in rocks and leave hollow spaces. Some of these hollow spaces are beautiful underground caverns, like the one in the picture.

INVESTIGATE!

Find out how moving water affects the beaches along lakes and oceans. Write a hypothesis and test it with an experiment. You might make a model to show wave action using a pan, water, and sand.

Weathered rocks can form underground caverns.

Erosion

erosion (i rô′zhən), the movement of soil or rocks by wind or water.

Every year, wind and water move tons of soil and rocks. **Erosion** is the moving of soil and rocks by wind or water. Erosion changes the earth's crust. Most of the time these changes happen very slowly, over many years.

Look at the paths on the hill. The paths were made by erosion. As rainwater rolled down the hill, it picked up some of the soil. The water carved out the paths as it moved the soil down the hill. The soil has collected at the bottom of the hill.

Soil erosion

214

Wind erosion

Wind erosion formed the large piles of sand in the picture. Strong desert winds blew the sand over long distances. When the winds calmed down, the sand stopped moving. Over time, the large piles of sand were formed.

Lesson Review
1. How do rocks weather?
2. What is erosion?
3. **Challenge!** How can erosion be both harmful and helpful?

Study on your own, pages 334–335.

Plants help keep soil from being eroded by protecting the soil from wind and water. The plants' roots help to hold down the soil. Use an encyclopedia to find out how farmers use plants to stop erosion on their land. On a sheet of paper, describe two ways that farmers fight erosion.

LIFE SCIENCE
FIND OUT ON YOUR OWN
CONNECTION

ACTIVITY

Making A Model of Erosion

Purpose
Observe how rocks erode in moving water.

Gather These Materials
• 30 small, rough stones • 2 coffee cans, half filled with water, with lids • 2 large, clear plastic cups • 3 sheets of paper towel • masking tape • marking pen

Follow This Procedure
1. Use a chart like the one shown to record your observations.
2. Divide the stones into three equal piles. Use the tape and the pen to label the piles A, B, and C.
3. Put pile A into one coffee can and pile B into the other can. Label the cans A and B.
4. Hold can A with both hands as shown in the picture. Shake the can 100 times. Ask another person in the group to shake the can 100 times.
5. Pour the water from can A into a cup. Look at the water.
6. Put the stones from can A on the paper towel. Look at the stones. Record what you see.
7. Repeat steps 4, 5, and 6 with can B. Have ten people shake the can 100 times. Compare the three piles of stones.

Record Your Results

	Water	Stones
Can A		
Can B		
Pile C		

State Your Conclusion
1. Compare the way the water in can A looks with the way the water in can B looks.
2. How are the stones in piles A, B, and C different from each other after the shaking?

Use What You Learned
How are the stones moving in the cans like the rocks moving in a stream of water?

Science and Technology

Predicting Earthquakes

The Problem   One of the clearest signs that the earth is always changing is an earthquake. Over a hundred years ago, an earthquake shook the city of Los Angeles. In 1906, an earthquake caused a lot of damage in San Francisco. In 1987, a big earthquake hit Los Angeles. Scientists have been studying the causes of earthquakes. They know that large pieces of crust called plates cover the earth. Plates move only a few millimeters each year. Earthquakes occur when two plates hit each other or move apart. If scientists could tell when the earthquakes might happen, they might help save lives.

The Breakthrough   Scientists looked for ways to keep track of small movements of the earth's surface. Several discoveries in the 1960s gave them the tools they needed. Scientists learned how to send satellites into space. They also learned how to make a special kind of light, called a laser. Laser light travels long distances in a very straight line. Lasers can make measurements over long distances.

New Technology   Today, scientists shoot laser light at satellites from ground stations.

These stations are on each edge of a plate in the earth's surface. Scientists time how long the laser light takes to reflect back from the satellite. Computers record the time and the position of the satellite. If the light travels back faster or slower, the station must have moved. If the station moved, then the crust must have moved. This helps people measure shifts in the earth's crust. Then they can predict that an earthquake is likely to occur. However, no one can tell exactly where or when an earthquake will hit.

What Do You Think?
1. What steps would you take if you lived where earthquakes were likely to occur?
2. Why is being prepared for earthquakes just as important as knowing when they might happen?

3 How Do Earthquakes and Volcanoes Change the Earth's Crust?

LESSON GOALS

You will learn
- how earthquakes change the earth's crust.
- how volcanoes change the earth's crust.

earthquake
(ėrth′kwāk′), a shaking or sliding of the earth's crust.

Earthquakes change the earth's crust.

Weathering and erosion usually change the earth's crust very slowly. Sometimes, however, the crust changes very quickly. The picture shows where a large crack occurs in the earth's crust. Land on either side of this crack can suddenly move a couple meters in a minute.

Earthquakes

An **earthquake** is a shaking or sliding of the earth's crust. Earthquakes happen when rocks inside the earth move. As the rocks move, they may form new cracks in the crust. Sometimes, the movement of the rocks makes the land move up, down, or sideways. The picture shows land after an earthquake. How did the earthquake change the land?

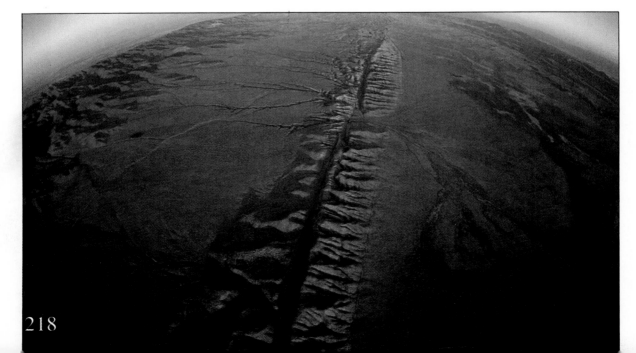

Most earthquakes are too weak for people to notice. However, some earthquakes are strong enough to shake buildings. The walls of buildings might fall down during a strong earthquake. The picture shows the kind of damage an earthquake can do. The movement of the ground twisted these railroad tracks as if they were a rubber band. Earthquakes can injure or kill people. Many people are hurt by falling objects.

Scientists try to predict earthquakes. Knowing when an earthquake will happen can save lives. People would have time to go to a safe place.

If you are indoors during an earthquake, stay away from windows and furniture that could slide or fall over. If outdoors, stay away from high buildings and other objects that could fall.

Earthquake damage

Lava

Magma

A volcano

Kilauea Volcano in Hawaii

Volcanoes

Hot, melted rock is shooting out from the volcano in the picture. A **volcano** is a mountain with an opening at the top. When a volcano erupts, melted rock, ashes, and other materials burst out from its opening.

What causes a volcano to **erupt**? The picture shows that hot, melted rock—or **magma**—lies deep inside the earth. The magma is squeezed up through the crust. Sometimes, the magma is forced up through the volcano, and the volcano erupts.

volcano (vol kā′nō), a mountain with an opening through which lava, ashes, rocks, and other materials come out.

erupt (i rupt′), to burst out.

magma (mag′maə), hot, melted rock deep inside the earth.

220

Magma that comes out of a volcano is called **lava.** When the lava cools, it hardens into solid rock. The rock forms new crust. Like earthquakes, volcanoes can change the earth's crust very quickly.

When a volcano erupts, it can hurt people and damage property. Hot lava that flows down a volcano can burn homes.

Scientists look for warning signals to predict when a volcano will erupt. Small earthquakes near a volcano might mean that magma is rising inside. A bulge on a volcano also might mean that the volcano is about to erupt.

Lesson Review

1. How can earthquakes change the earth's crust?
2. What causes a volcano to erupt?
3. **Challenge!** Why do earthquakes occur when magma rises in a volcano?

Study on your own, pages 334–335.

SCIENCE IN YOUR LIFE

A volcano can form new land. The Hawaiian Islands were formed by underwater volcanoes. The islands are the tops of volcanoes in the Pacific Ocean.

lava (lä′və), hot, melted rock that flows from a volcano.

Look in an encyclopedia to find out where earthquakes occur most often on the earth. Then, write the answers to the following questions.

EARTH SCIENCE

FIND OUT ON YOUR OWN

1. What part of North America has the most earthquakes?
2. What parts of the earth have the fewest earthquakes?
3. Do more earthquakes occur under water or on land?

4 How Do Living Things Change the Earth's Crust?

LESSON GOALS

You will learn
• how people change the earth's crust.
• how plants and animals change the earth's crust.

Whenever you dig a hole in the ground or split a rock in half, you are changing the earth's crust. People, plants, and animals change the earth's crust every day.

How Animals and Plants Change the Earth's Crust

Some animals, such as earthworms, live in the earth's crust. These animals change the earth's crust as they dig through the soil. Other animals look for food in the soil. How is the animal in the picture changing the land?

Plants also help change the earth's crust. Plants can protect the land from erosion by holding the soil down. How can plants help change rocks into soil?

A prairie dog

How People Change the Earth's Crust

When people build things, they change the land. People dig rocks and soil out of the ground to build roads and buildings. People cut down plants. Then wind and water can easily erode the soil. You learned in Chapter 9 that people dig mines to reach ores. Digging mines changes the earth's crust. Look at the picture. How are these workers changing the land?

Lesson Review

1. How can plants and animals change the earth's crust?
2. How do people change the land when they build things?
3. **Challenge!** Why do plants grow better in soil in which animals live or dig?

Study on your own, pages 334–335.

Study on your own, pages 334–335.

SCIENCE IN YOUR LIFE

You might have seen cracked sidewalks near trees. As the trees' roots grew, they pushed up on the sidewalks. The pushing caused the sidewalks to break apart.

Building a road

Long ago, there were no living things on the earth. Try to imagine what the earth might have looked like then. How was the earth's surface different from the surface today? Write a short paragraph that describes what you think the earth's crust used to be like. Then, use library books to find out what scientists think the earth was like at that time in history.

E A R T H S C I E N C E

FIND OUT ON YOUR OWN

Skills for Solving Problems

Using Balances and Line Graphs

Problem: What effect do plants have on soil erosion?

Part A. Using a Balance to Collect Information

1. The pictures below show three trays of soil. Tray A is fully covered with grass plants. Tray B has only half the number of plants as Tray A. How many plants does Tray C have?

2. Each tray had the same amount of water sprinkled over it. The soil that washed away from each tray was collected and put on a balance. Each balance shows the mass of soil that was eroded from each tray. Tray A had 4 grams of soil eroded from it. How much soil was eroded from Tray B? Tray C?

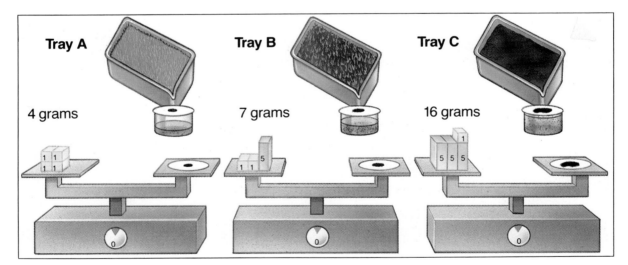

Part B. Using a Line Graph to Organize and Interpret Information

3. The line graph contains the information you collected in Part A. The dots on the graph show how many grams of soil were eroded from each tray. The line connecting the dots shows that erosion in each tray increased. If the line between two dots is not steep, the

increase in the amount of erosion was small. If the line is steep, the increase in the amount of erosion was great. Where is the line the steepest on the graph? Between which two trays did erosion increase the most? Between which two trays did erosion increase the least?

4. What effect do plants have on soil erosion?

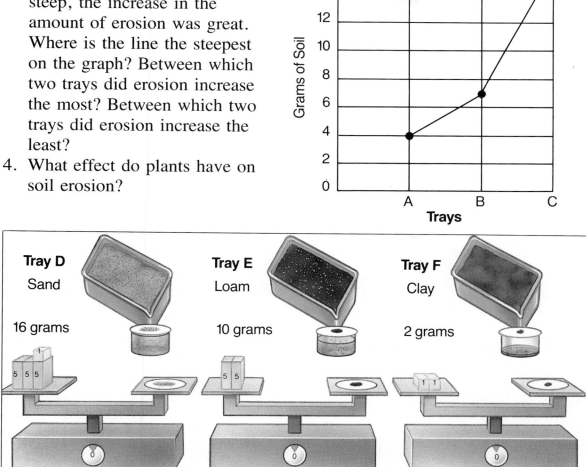

Part C. Using a Balance and Line Graph to Solve a Problem

Problem: How are different types of soil affected by erosion?

5. Use the pictures above to collect the information you need to solve the problem. Make a line graph similar to the one shown in Part B to organize your information.

6. Look at your line graph. Which kind of soil eroded the most? The least?

225

Chapter 10 Review

☑ Chapter Main Ideas

Lesson 1 • The earth has three layers—the crust, the mantle, and the core. • Scientists learn about the inside of the earth by studying movements of the earth's crust and by using instruments.

Lesson 2 • Water, plants, and air help weather rocks. • Water and wind help cause erosion of the soil.

Lesson 3 • Earthquakes cause fast changes in the earth's crust. • Volcanoes cause the earth's crust to change very quickly.

Lesson 4 • Plants change the earth's crust by breaking rocks apart; animals change the earth's crust by digging in the soil. • People change the earth's crust by building roads and buildings, cutting down trees, and mining.

☑ Reviewing Science Words

crust	erupts	mantle
core	lava	volcano
earthquake	magma	weather
erosion		

Copy each sentence. Fill in the blank with the correct word from the list.

1. ___ is hot, melted rock deep inside the earth.
2. The movement of soil or rocks by wind or water is ___.
3. The ___ is the middle layer of the earth.
4. A ___ is a mountain with an opening through which lava, ashes, rocks, and other materials come out.
5. Rocks ___ when they wear down or break apart over a long time.
6. The outer layer of the earth is the ___.
7. A volcano ___ when melted rock, ashes, and other materials burst out from its opening.
8. A shaking or sliding of the earth's crust is an ___.
9. The ___ is the inner layer of the earth.
10. ___ is hot, melted rock that flows from a volcano.

☑ Reviewing What You Learned

Write the letter of the best answer.

1. The mantle is mostly made of
    (a) water.   (b) rock.   (c) metal.   (d) soil.
2. Which of the following makes slow changes in the earth's crust?
    (a) volcano   (b) earthquake   (c) erosion   (d) lava
3. Plants help change rocks into
    (a) soil.   (b) magma.   (c) volcanoes.   (d) lava.
4. Plants can help change the earth's
    (a) core.   (b) mantle.   (c) magma.   (d) crust.
5. The earth's core is mostly
    (a) cold.   (b) water   (c) iron.   (d) soil.
6. What mixes with carbon dioxide to turn hard minerals into clay?
    (a) air   (b) water   (c) lava   (d) rock
7. When large blocks of rock in the earth's crust move, they form
    (a) an earthquake.   (b) erosion.   (c) lava.   (d) weathering.
8. When lava cools, it forms
    (a) humus.   (b) sandy soil.   (c) clay.   (d) rock.

☑ Interpreting What You Learned

Write a short answer for each question or statement.

1. What are three ways people can change the earth's crust?
2. How do scientists study the inside of the earth?
3. How does the way an earthquake changes the land differ from the way erosion changes the land?
4. Explain how water can cause rocks to weather.
5. How can people protect themselves during an earthquake?
6. What is one warning signal that a volcano is about to erupt?

☑ Extending Your Thinking

Write a paragraph to answer each question or statement.

1. How could you get an idea of how deep a hole is without really looking into it?
2. In which place would you find more erosion, a thick forest or a bare hill?

 To explore scientific methods, see Experiment Skills on pages 366–367.

Clouds and Storms

Think about the last time you saw a storm. You might have seen large clouds like these in the sky. You also might have seen lightning.

Introducing the Chapter

In this chapter, you will find out how clouds form. You also will learn what causes rainy and stormy weather. The air always has some water in it—even on a clear day. This activity will help you learn about water in the air.

DISCOVER!

Observing How Water Changes

Wear cover goggles for this activity.

Wet a paper towel and squeeze out the extra water. Use the paper towel to make a wet mark on a chalkboard. Look at the chalkboard as it dries.

Place one end of a straw inside a small plastic bag. Hold the edges of the bag tightly around the sides of the straw. Now blow through the straw. How does the plastic bag look? Open the plastic bag. Run your finger along the inside of the bag. How does the inside of the bag feel?

Talk About It
1. Where did the water go as the chalkboard dried?
2. How did the inside of the plastic bag become wet?

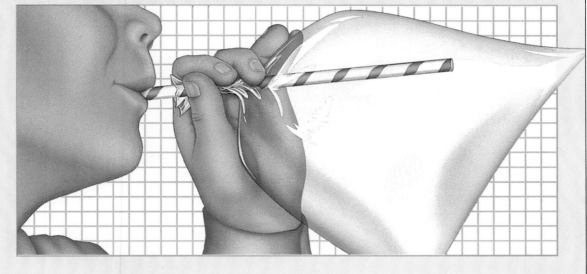

1 How Do Clouds Form?

LESSON GOALS

You will learn
- how water evaporates and condenses.
- how clouds form.
- how three kinds of clouds differ.

dew (dü), water vapor that condenses on cool surfaces, usually during the night.

Imagine climbing out of a swimming pool like the girl in the picture will do. Your skin would feel wet. Suppose you sat in the sun for a few minutes. How would your skin feel?

How Water Changes Forms

You learned in Chapter 5 that water can change from one state to another. Water on your skin evaporates and becomes water vapor. Heat from the sun helps water evaporate. Wind also helps water evaporate.

Sometimes you might notice water on the grass in the morning. When air cools during the night, water vapor in the air condenses into small drops of water. These drops of water —called **dew**—settle on the grass. What other places might you see dew?

Water evaporates from your skin.

230

How Clouds Form

You probably have seen your breath in the air on a cold day. Water vapor is in your warm breath. This water vapor condenses when it meets the cold air. What happens if you breathe out onto a cold window?

Water vapor in the air condenses in much the same way as water in your breath does. As warm air rises, it cools. As air cools, the water vapor in the air condenses into tiny droplets of water. The picture shows that many of these droplets come together to form clouds.

Sometimes the air just above the ground cools quickly. Then the water vapor in the air condenses to form **fog**—a cloud near the ground. You might notice that the air around you feels wet when fog forms.

INVESTIGATE!

Find out how a low temperature affects water vapor. Write a hypothesis and test it with an experiment. You might place a metal pan in a freezer for several hours. Take it out and observe what happens.

fog, a cloud that forms just above the surface of the earth.

Forming Clouds

Clouds form

Air cools

Warm air rises

231

Cirrus clouds

Cumulus clouds

Stratus clouds

cirrus (sir′əs) **clouds,** high, feathery white clouds made of tiny pieces of ice.

cumulus (kyü′myə ləs) **clouds,** fluffy clouds that look like puffs of cotton.

stratus (strā′təs) **clouds,** clouds that form in sheets or layers and spread out over the sky.

Kinds of Clouds

The pictures show three kinds of clouds. **Cirrus clouds** are made of tiny pieces of ice. These feathery clouds float high in the air. You often see cirrus clouds in good weather.

Cumulus clouds look like cotton. You usually see these clouds in good weather. Weather can become stormy when cumulus clouds become large.

Stratus clouds form in layers. These clouds usually spread across the sky. You often see stratus clouds during a rain.

Lesson Review

1. How can water change forms?
2. How do clouds form?
3. How do three kinds of clouds differ?
4. **Challenge!** How can you make water in a glass evaporate faster?

Study on your own, pages 336–337.

EARTH SCIENCE

FIND OUT ON YOUR OWN

Keep a cloud diary for a week. On a piece of paper, write down the kinds of clouds you see every day. Next to the name of each kind of cloud, write a sentence describing the weather.

Measuring Temperature at Which Dew Forms

Purpose
Measure the temperature at which dew forms.

Gather These Materials
• shiny can • water • ice cubes or crushed ice • stirring stick
• thermometer

Follow This Procedure
1. Use a chart like the one shown to record your observations.
2. Use the thermometer to measure the temperature in your room.

CAUTION: Handle thermometers carefully.
3. Half fill the can with water. Place the thermometer into the can of water as shown in the picture. Record the temperature of the water.
4. Add ice, a little at a time, to the water. Slowly stir the ice and water with the stirring stick.
5. Carefully watch the can. Read the thermometer when water forms on the outside of the can. Record the temperature.

Record Your Results

Air temperature	
Water temperature	
Temperature at which water forms on can	

State Your Conclusion
1. How did the temperature at which water formed on the can compare with room temperature?
2. What caused water to form on the outside of the can?

Use What You Learned
What **can** happen to water vapor in the air when it rises and cools?

2 What Happens to Water in the Clouds?

LESSON GOALS

You will learn
- how rain and snow form.
- how all the water on earth keeps moving through the water cycle.

precipitation
(pri sip′ə tā′shən), moisture that falls to the ground.

The Water Cycle

Think about water vapor condensed on a mirror. What happens if you push the tiny drops of water together? The drops become large. They get heavy and run down the mirror. Rain drops form in much the same way.

Forming Rain and Snow

The tiny drops of water in clouds are light enough to float in the air. The drops can bump into each other and form larger drops. The large drops are too heavy to float in the air. These drops fall as rain. The rain that falls from clouds is called **precipitation.** Snow is another kind of precipitation. Snowflakes are feathery bits of ice formed in clouds where air is freezing.

The Water Cycle

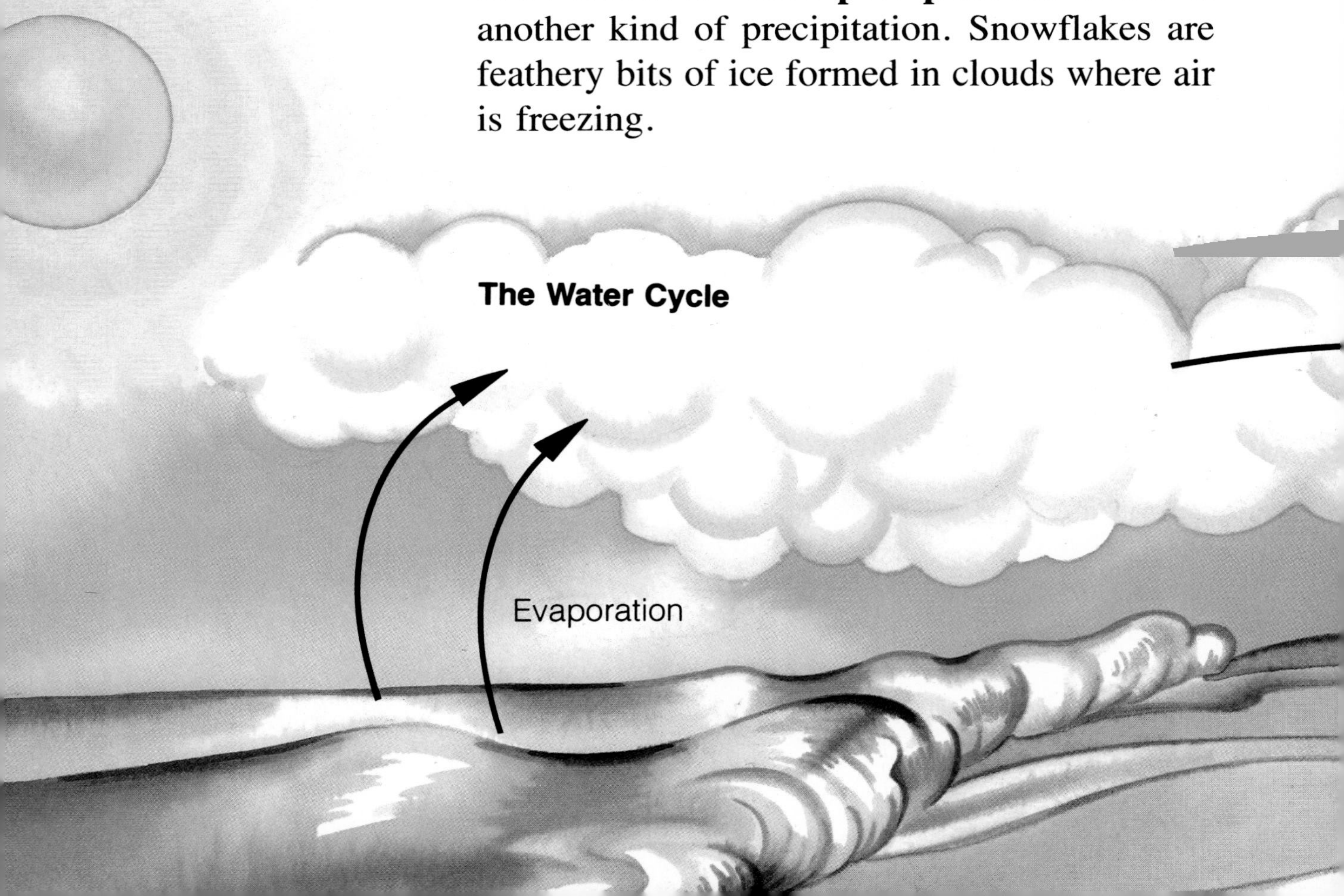

Evaporation

The Water Cycle

All the water on earth keeps moving and changing forms. The movement of water on the earth by evaporation, condensation, and precipitation is called the **water cycle.**

Use your finger to trace the raindrop's path through the water cycle in the picture. Suppose a raindrop falls on a hillside. Imagine the drop of water running down the hillside into a stream. Where does the water in the stream flow? Energy from the sun makes some of the water evaporate. Then the drop of water changes to water vapor. Some of the water vapor might condense into a tiny drop and form part of a cloud. Rain or snow might fall. Then the whole water cycle repeats itself.

SCIENCE IN YOUR LIFE

Hail is a kind of precipitation made up of lumps of ice. These icy lumps are formed inside storm clouds. Most hailstones are about the size of a pea. Some hailstones can get as big as a baseball.

water cycle (sī′kəl), the movement of water from the ground to the air and back to the ground by evaporation, condensation, and precipitation.

Condensation

Precipitation

235

All the water on earth is part of the water cycle.

Some water evaporates from land and small bodies of water like the one in the picture. Much of the water from rivers and streams reaches lakes and oceans. Most of the earth's water is in oceans, so most water evaporates from oceans. Water evaporates, condenses, and falls as precipitation over and over again.

Lesson Review

1. How do rain and snow form?
2. What are the parts of the water cycle?
3. **Challenge!** Explain how water from your faucet might once have been in the ocean.

Study on your own, pages 336–337.

Look in library books to find out about shapes and patterns of snowflakes. Use white paper to cut out different kinds of snowflakes. Write a few sentences explaining how snowflakes are different and how they are alike.

Observing Part of the Water Cycle

Wear cover goggles for this activity.

Purpose
Observe how water moves in the water cycle.

Gather These Materials
• large jar • hot tap water • ice cubes • plastic wrap • rubber band

Follow This Procedure
1. Use a chart like the one shown to record your observations.
2. Half fill the jar with hot water.
3. Place the plastic wrap over the opening of the jar. Let the plastic wrap droop to make a bowl shape.
4. Put a rubber band around the top of the jar to hold the plastic wrap in place.
5. Place 2 or 3 ice cubes on the plastic wrap, as shown in the picture. Wait 5 minutes.
6. Remove the ice cubes. Observe the plastic wrap. Record what you observe.
7. Replace the ice cubes on the plastic wrap. Wait 5 more minutes. Remove the plastic wrap from the jar. Observe the bottom of the plastic wrap. Record what you observe.

Record Your Results

After 5 minutes	
After 10 minutes	

State Your Conclusions
1. What happened to some of the hot water in the jar?
2. What did putting ice on the plastic wrap do to the warm air in the jar?

Use What You Learned
What part or parts of the water cycle were shown in this activity?

237

3 What Causes Storms?

LESSON GOALS

You will learn
- how a thunderstorm forms.
- how hurricanes and tornadoes form.
- how people can keep safe during storms.

How Storms Form

Imagine walking outside on a sunny day. Suddenly, the sky gets dark. The wind blows and rain begins to fall. Lightning flashes in the sky. A thunderstorm is beginning.

Thunderstorms

The picture shows what happens when a thunderstorm forms. Warm, moist air quickly moves up in the sky. As cool air replaces the rising air, winds begin to blow. Large cumulus clouds form. Water droplets in the clouds become large and heavy. The rain begins to fall.

You learned in Chapter 7 that electric charges can jump between objects. You see lightning when electric charges jump between clouds or from a cloud to the ground. You often can hear thunder after lightning flashes. How can you describe the sound of thunder?

How Storms Form

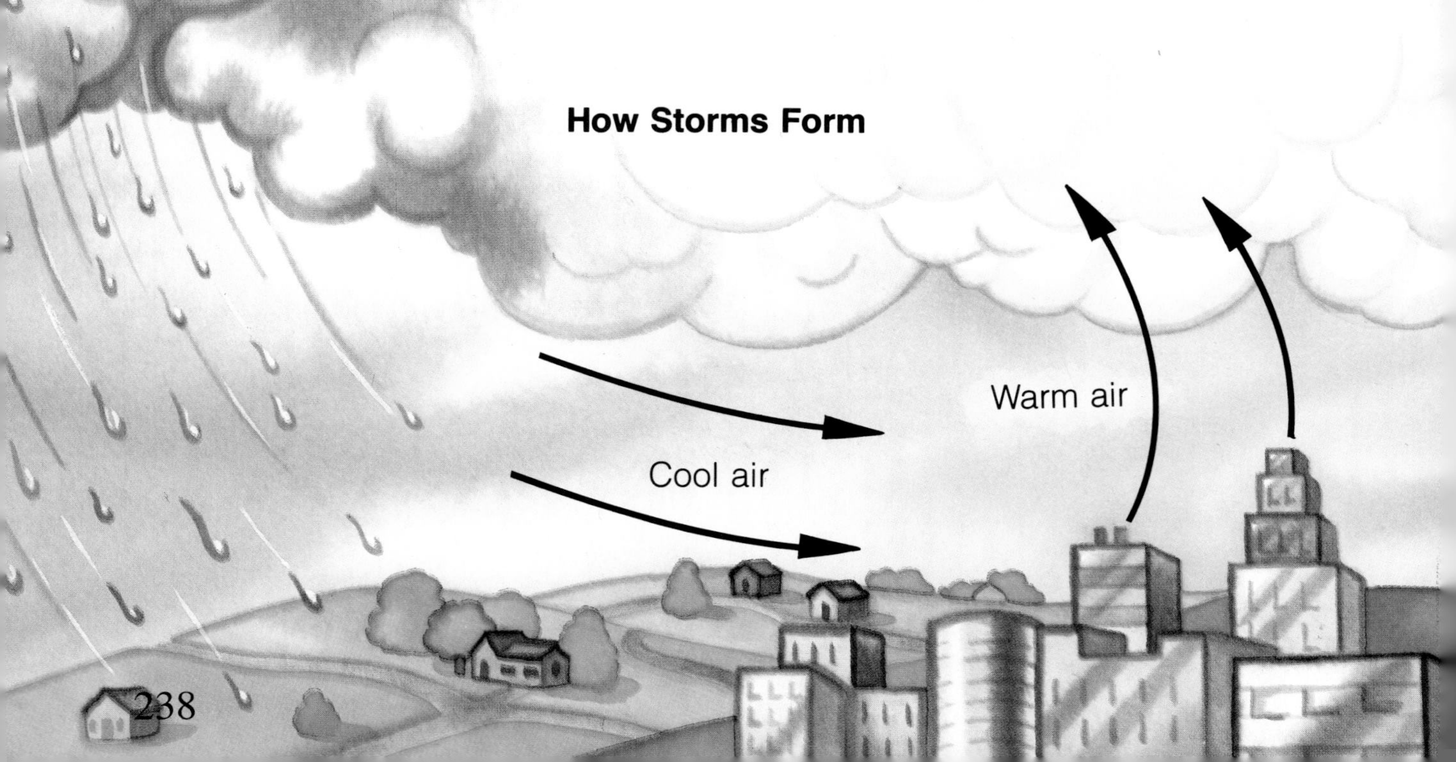

Warm air

Cool air

238

A tornado

Hurricanes and Tornadoes

A **hurricane** is a huge storm that forms when warm, moist air begins to rise very quickly from a warm ocean. The water vapor condenses to form clouds. Cool air moves in to replace the warm air that rises. The air and the clouds begin to spin around and around. As more water vapor rises from the ocean, more air begins to spin and the storm grows stronger. A hurricane has powerful winds that can destroy buildings and heavy rains that can cause floods. When a hurricane moves over land, it dies out.

Look at the **tornado** in the picture. A tornado can form during a thunderstorm when air rises very quickly. The air twists into a funnel-shaped cloud that moves along a narrow path. A tornado has the fastest winds on earth. Usually, tornadoes stay in the air. A tornado that touches the ground can destroy objects in its path.

hurricane (hėr′ə kān), a huge storm that forms over a warm ocean and has strong winds and heavy rains.

tornado (tôr nā′dō), a funnel cloud that has very strong winds and moves along a narrow path.

239

A tornado drill

A lightning rod is a metal rod placed on top of a building. The rod is connected to the ground. If lightning strikes a lightning rod, the electric charges move through the rod and into the ground. Then, the electric charges do not harm the building.

Keeping Safe During Storms

You can help keep yourself safe during a thunderstorm. Going inside a building or a car with a hard top can help protect you. If you cannot go indoors, lie down in a low place. Stay away from trees and water.

Learn about the emergency plans in your community for hurricanes and tornadoes. These children are having a tornado drill at school. They stay indoors away from windows.

Lesson Review

1. How does a thunderstorm form?
2. How do hurricanes and tornadoes form?
3. How can people keep safe during thunderstorms?
4. **Challenge!** Why does a hurricane die out when it moves over land? Explain.

Study on your own, pages 336–337.

A barometer measures air pressure. Look in library books to learn more about barometers. Write a few sentences explaining how a barometer works. Tell how a barometer can be useful for learning about weather.

Mapping Tornadoes

"The United States has the biggest and the best," says Dr. Ted Fujita. "That's why I came here from Japan." Dr. Fujita is not talking about mountains or baseball games. He is talking about tornadoes. He has been interested in these storms his whole life. Now as a scientist, he knows more about tornadoes than almost anyone in the world.

Dr. Fujita knows that in the middle of the United States tornadoes form easily. Cold winds from Canada blow south and east. Warm, moist winds from the Gulf of Mexico blow north. When these winds meet, they can twist together to make a tornado.

No one can tell just when a tornado will strike. However, Dr. Fujita found a way to help people make a good guess. He put together a map to show where tornadoes occurred from 1930 to 1978. In that time, about 23,000 tornadoes occurred. By using this map, Dr. Fujita and other scientists can tell where tornadoes are most likely to happen.

Most tornadoes last a short time—less than one hour. They usually travel just a short distance. However, tornadoes are so powerful that they can toss railroad cars and flatten houses.

Dr. Ted Fujita

Dr. Fujita thinks that the more people learn about tornadoes, the more lives can be saved.

What Do You Think?
1. Why do you think a tornado is sometimes called a twister?
2. Why do you think tornadoes are not common in Oregon?

Skills for Solving Problems

Using Rain Gauges and Charts

Problem: How can rainfall be measured?

Part A. Using Rain Gauges to Collect Information

1. Rain gauges are containers that are used to collect and measure rainfall. Look at the rain gauges below. Each line on these rain gauges is 1 centimeter. What is the abbreviation for centimeter?

2. The rain gauge in example A collected 1 centimeter of rain. How much rain was collected in examples B, C, and D?

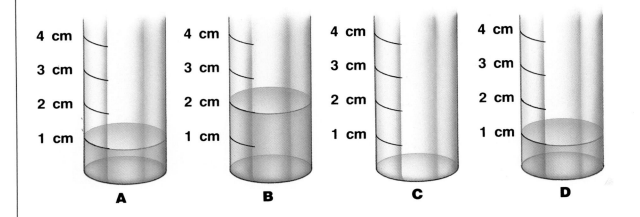

Part B. Using a Chart to Organize and Interpret Information

3. This chart contains the information you collected from the four rain gauges. Which rain gauge collected the most rainfall? Which rain gauge collected no rainfall?

Rain Gauge	Rainfall collected
A	1 cm
B	2 cm
C	0 cm
D	1 cm
Total rainfall	4 cm

4. Look again at the rain gauges. Which rain gauges collected the same amount of rainfall?

5. What is the total amount of rainfall that was collected by all of the rain gauges?

Part C. Using Rain Gauges and Charts to Solve a Problem

Problem: What was the total rainfall for one week?

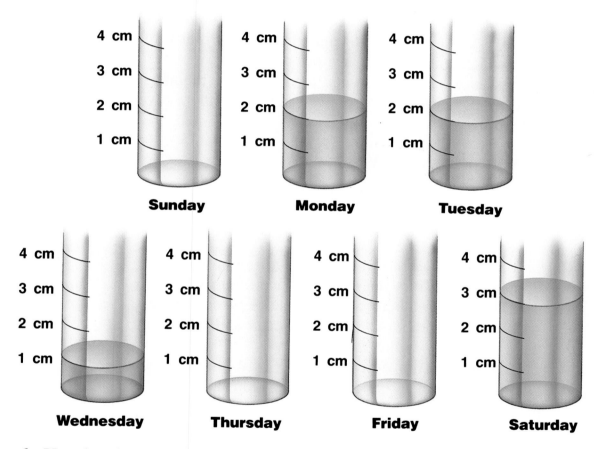

6. Use the picture to collect the information you need to solve the problem. Make a chart similar to the one in Part B to organize your information.

7. Look at your chart. How many days of the week did it rain?

8. What was the total rainfall for the week?

Chapter 11 Review

☑ Chapter Main Ideas

Lesson 1 • Water changes forms when it evaporates and condenses. • Water vapor in the air condenses to form clouds. • Cirrus clouds, cumulus clouds, and stratus clouds are three kinds of clouds.

Lesson 2 • Rain and snow are forms of precipitation. • Water on earth evaporates, condenses, and falls as precipitation over and over again as it goes through the water cycle.

Lesson 3 • A thunderstorm forms when warm, moist air rises. • A hurricane forms when warm ocean water evaporates and rises very quickly; a tornado can form during a thunderstorm when air rises quickly. • People can help keep themselves safe during storms.

☑ Reviewing Science Words

cirrus clouds	fog	stratus clouds
cumulus clouds	hurricane	tornado
dew	precipitation	water cycle

Write a short answer for each question or statement.
1. Rain that falls from the clouds is one kind of _____.
2. _____ are high, feathery clouds made of pieces of ice.
3. A storm that forms over a warm ocean and has strong winds and heavy rains is a _____.
4. The _____ is the movement of water between the ground and the air by evaporation, condensation, and precipitation.
5. Clouds that look like puffs of cotton are _____.
6. A cloud that forms just above the surface of the earth is called _____.
7. _____ is water vapor that condenses on cool surfaces, usually during the night.
8. _____ are clouds that form in layers and spread out over the sky.
9. A funnel cloud that has strong winds and moves along a path is called a _____.

Reviewing What You Learned

Write the letter of the best answer.

1. The fastest winds on earth are in a
   (a) hurricane.　(b) tornado.　(c) rainstorm.　(d) stratus cloud.
2. How does wind change the speed at which water evaporates?
   (a) makes it faster　(b) makes no change
   (c) makes it slower　(d) stops water from evaporating
3. One kind of precipitation is
   (a) fog.　(b) snow.　(c) dew.　(d) water vapor.
4. Clouds form when water vapor
   (a) warms up.　(b) freezes.　(c) evaporates.　(d) condenses.
5. A hurricane forms over a warm
   (a) desert.　(b) river.　(c) ocean.　(d) lake.
6. Which kind of clouds can usually be seen during a thunderstorm?
   (a) cumulus　(b) icy　(c) stratus　(d) cirrus
7. Most of the earth's water is in
   (a) rivers.　(b) lakes.　(c) oceans.　(d) soil.
8. What forms when air just above the ground cools quickly?
   (a) a storm　(b) dew　(c) rain　(d) fog

Interpreting What You Learned

Write a short answer for each question.

1. What should you do if you are outdoors during a thunderstorm?
2. What causes lightning and thunder?
3. Suppose a raindrop falls. What steps in the water cycle would the raindrop then follow?
4. How is a cloud like condensed water vapor on a mirror?

Extending Your Thinking

Write a paragraph to answer each question.

1. How could you explain to someone that you take in water every time you breathe?
2. Which place would be safer during a tornado, the top floor of a building with many windows or a basement with no windows? Explain your answer.

 To explore scientific methods, see Experiment Skills on pages 368–369.

12

The Sun, Moon, and Planets

For hundreds of years people wondered what caused parts of the moon to look light or dark. Scientists now know that mountains and plains make the shades you see on the moon.

Introducing the Chapter

Think about the moon shining on a clear night. Light from the sun causes the moonlight you see. The activity below will help you learn what causes the earth's moon to shine. In this chapter, you will learn about the sun and the planets and their moons. You also will read about space travel.

Observing Light

DISCOVER!

Hold a flashlight in one hand and a dark-colored ball in the other hand. This picture shows you how to shine the flashlight directly on the ball. Pretend that the light from the flashlight is light from the sun and the ball is the earth's moon.

Move the ball slowly to the right. Notice the change in the light on the ball. Now continue to move the ball until it is completely out of the light.

Talk About It
1. Describe how the ball looked when the flashlight was shining on it.
2. How did the light on the ball change when you moved the ball away from the light?

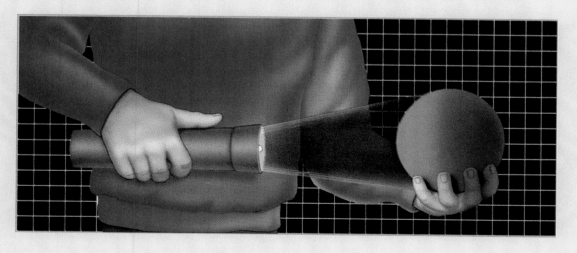

1 How Do the Earth and Moon Move?

LESSON GOALS

You will learn
- how the earth moves during 24 hours and 1 year.
- what the moon looks like and how the moon moves.
- about phases of the moon.

axis (ak′sis), an imaginary straight line through the center of the earth around which the earth rotates.

rotation (rō tā′shən), the act of spinning on an axis.

Have you ever seen a top spinning around and around? The earth spins around in much the same way as a top does.

How the Earth Moves

The earth spins around an imaginary line that runs through its center. This line is called the **axis.** Every twenty-four hours, the earth makes one complete spin, or a **rotation.**

Follow what happens to point A as the earth rotates. How does the time change? The rotation of the earth causes day and night. The part of the earth toward the sun has daylight. The part away from the sun has night.

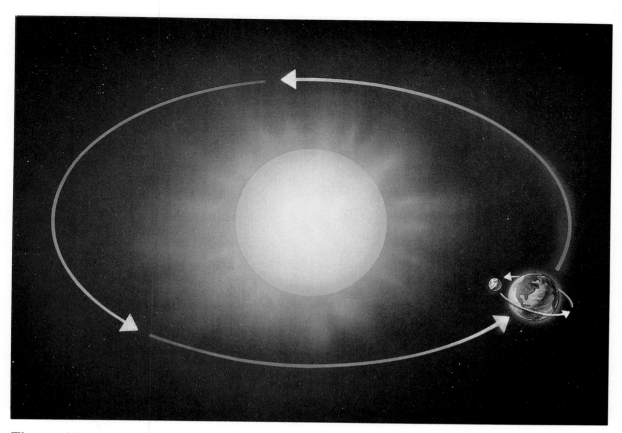

The earth's orbit around the sun

This morning you might have seen the sun in one part of the sky. Will you see the sun in the same part of the sky in the late afternoon? The sun really is not moving across the sky. The way the earth rotates makes the sun appear to move.

The earth also moves in a path around the sun. This path is called an **orbit.** Notice in the picture that the path is shaped almost like a circle. Use your finger to trace the orbit of the earth around the sun. The force of gravity from the sun pulls on the earth and keeps the earth in its orbit. Each complete orbit around the sun is called one **revolution.** The earth takes about 365 days, or one year, to make one revolution.

orbit (ôr′bit), a closed, curved path that an object follows as the object moves around another object.

revolution (rev′ə lü′shən), movement of an object in an orbit around another object.

249

The moon's orbit around the earth

INVESTIGATE!

Find out if the earth rotates in an east-to-west or a west-to-east direction. Write a hypothesis and test it with an experiment. You might observe the directions in which the sun rises and sets. Then compare this to a model of the earth and the sun using two balls.

satellite (sat′l it), object that revolves around another object.

How the Moon Moves

Find the earth's moon in the picture. What is its shape? Like the earth, the moon has rocks and soil. The moon also rotates on its axis. Yet the earth's moon is different from the earth. This moon has no water or air.

The moon is called a **satellite** of the earth because it revolves around the earth. Use your finger to trace the moon's orbit. The moon takes about one month to make one revolution around the earth.

The moon does not give off its own light. The light you see comes from the sun's light reflecting off the moon. As it rotates, the part of the moon facing the sun reflects sunlight. The other part of the moon is dark. From the earth, you only see the lighted part of the moon that faces you. As the moon revolves, you see different amounts of its lighted part.

250

Half moon   Full moon

Phases of the Moon

You probably have seen different shapes of the moon. These shapes are the **phases** of the moon. You can see all the moon's phases as the moon makes one revolution around the earth.

During the new moon phase, the lighted part of the moon faces away from the earth and you cannot see it. As the moon revolves, you can see more and more of its lighted part. About one week after the new moon, the moon looks like a half circle. It is sometimes called a half moon. Find the half moon in the picture.

As the moon continues to revolve, you can see more and more of its lighted part. About a week after the half moon, you can see a complete circle. This phase is called a full moon, shown in the picture. After the full moon, you can see less and less of the moon each night. About two weeks after the full moon, the new moon phase comes again.

phase (fāz), the shape of the lighted part of the moon as it is seen from the earth.

Sometimes you might see the moon during the daytime. You can see a full moon only at night. All the other phases of the moon can be seen during the day as well as at night.

Lesson Review

1. How does the earth move every twenty-four hours? every year?
2. How does the moon move?
3. What are the phases of the moon?
4. **Challenge!** Suppose the earth made a rotation around its axis every ten hours. How many hours would pass from the start of one day to the start of another day?

Study on your own, pages 338–339.

Study on your own, pages 338–339.

EARTH SCIENCE

**FIND OUT
ON YOUR OWN**

This picture was taken during a solar eclipse. Look in a book about space to find out about a solar eclipse. Draw a picture of the sun, earth, and moon during a solar eclipse. Write a paragraph that explains your picture.

Comparing the Sun And Moon

Purpose
Infer how the sun and moon can look the same size.

Gather These Materials
• large ball • small ball • meter stick • chalk

Follow This Procedure
1. Use a chart like the one shown to record your observations.
2. Ask a classmate to hold up a large ball. Pretend that the large ball is the sun.
3. Ask another classmate to hold up a small ball in front of the sun. Pretend that the small ball is the moon.
4. Stand in front of the classmate holding the moon, as shown.

The distance between you and the sun should be about 5 meters.
5. Ask the classmate holding the moon to move back and forth between you and the sun. When the moon and the sun appear to be the same size, tell the classmate to stop moving.
6. Use chalk to mark an X where you are standing. Measure the distance between the X and the moon. Record the distance.
7. Measure the distance between the X and the sun. Record the distance.

Record Your Results

Distance to Moon	
Distance to Sun	

State Your Conclusion
1. Was the moon closer to you or closer to the sun when it looked the same size as the sun?
2. In what way does distance affect how large an object looks?

Use What You Learned
Why do the sun and moon in the sky appear to be the same size?

2 What Are the Sun and the Planets Like?

LESSON GOALS

You will learn
• what the sun is like and how the sun produces energy.
• that the sun and the planets and their moons make up most of the solar system.

Scientists have learned many things about the sun. They know the sun is much larger than the earth. They also know that the sun is the most important source of energy for the earth.

The Sun

Have you ever watched twinkling stars at night? Each star is made of hot, glowing gases. The sun is a star. The sun looks much larger than other stars because it is closer to the earth. Objects that are closer to you often seem to be larger. You cannot see other stars during the day because the sun is so bright.

This picture shows that the sun is shaped like a ball. Notice how the sun glows. The temperature at the sun's surface is about twelve times hotter than the hottest temperature you need to cook food. The temperature in the center of the sun is even hotter. Changes in matter take place in the center of the sun. Energy comes from these changes. This energy produces the sun's heat and light.

Even though the sun is the closest star to earth, it is still very far away. The light from the sun you see now really left the sun eight and one-half minutes ago.

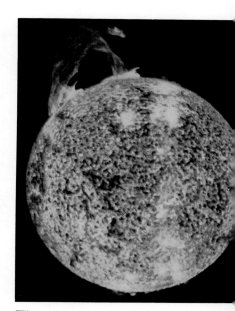

The sun

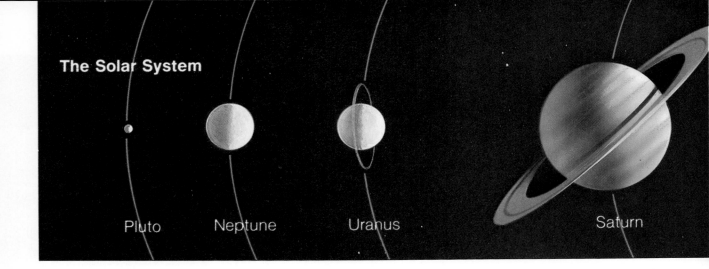

The Solar System

Pluto   Neptune   Uranus   Saturn

The Planets and Their Moons

planet (plan′it), a large body of matter revolving around the sun.

solar system (sō′lər sis′təm), the sun, the planets and their moons, and other objects that revolve around the sun.

You know that the earth revolves around the sun. Earth is a **planet**—a large body of matter that revolves around the sun. The other planets also revolve around the sun. The nine planets are Mercury, Venus, Earth, Mars, Jupiter, Saturn, Uranus, Neptune, and Pluto. The sun and the planets and their moons make up most of the **solar system.**

Look at the picture of the solar system. Notice that Mercury, Venus, Earth, and Mars are the closest planets to the sun. All of these planets are rocky. Mercury and Venus are very hot. The temperatures on Mars are a little cooler than those on Earth.

Different planets have different numbers of moons. Scientists know about two moons that revolve around Mars. They know about sixteen moons that revolve around Jupiter. How many moons revolve around Earth?

Compare the sizes of the planets. Jupiter is the largest planet. More than one thousand planets the size of Earth could fit into Jupiter. What is the smallest planet?

256

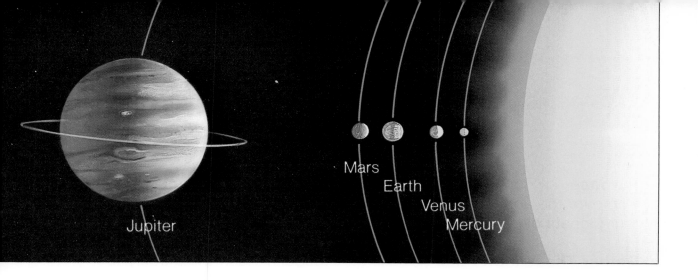

Jupiter

Mars

Earth

Venus

Mercury

Jupiter, Saturn, Uranus, and Neptune are made mostly of gases. These planets are cold because they are far away from the sun. Notice the rings around Saturn. Scientists have learned that these rings are made of millions of pieces of ice. Scientists are still learning about the planets and their moons.

Lesson Review

1. What is the sun made of?
2. What makes up the solar system?
3. **Challenge!** What is one reason why Mercury is hotter than Earth?

Study on your own, pages 338–339.

Study on your own, pages 338–339.

SCIENCE IN YOUR LIFE

The time a planet takes to revolve around the sun is called a year. Mercury makes one revolution around the sun every 88 days. Therefore, a year on Mercury is only 88 days long. Jupiter takes twelve of Earth's years to revolve around the sun. A year on Jupiter is twelve Earth years long.

Look in recent books about space to find out more about Mars. Draw a picture of Mars. Next to your picture, tell what minerals give Mars its color.

PHYSICAL SCIENCE

FIND OUT ON YOUR OWN

CONNECTION

ACTIVITY

Making Models of Planets

Purpose
Compare the appearances of the four planets closest to the sun.

Gather These Materials
• cardboard • compass • ruler
• string • scissors • crayons or markers • coat hanger

Follow This Procedure
1. Use a chart like the one shown to record your observations.
2. Cut out 2 circles for each planet you make. The table shows how wide to make the circles for each planet.
3. Use the ruler to draw a line from the center of each circle to the edge. Cut each line.
4. Use crayons or markers to color your circles.

5. Using the two circles for each planet, push the circle together at the slits as shown.
6. Tape string to each planet model. Attach the models to the coat hanger, as shown. Attach the models in the correct order as shown in the table.
7. In the chart, draw a picture of each planet model you made. Write the name of the planet under the picture.

Planet	Width of Circle
Mercury	3 cm
Venus	7 cm
Earth	8 cm
Mars	4 cm

Record Your Results

Picture of Planet			
Name of Planet			

State Your Conclusion
1. How do Mercury, Venus, Earth, and Mars compare in size?
2. What is the order of the first four planets from the sun?

Use What You Learned
Which of these planets takes the longest to orbit the sun? Explain.

Doing Experiments in Space

Sally Ride saw an advertisement in the newspaper. It said that the space program needed new astronauts, and they wanted scientists. Dr. Ride was a scientist who was interested in stars and planets. She decided to try to get the job. More than 8,000 other people also wanted to become astronauts, but only thirty-five were chosen. When Dr. Ride found out she was one of them, she was so excited she wanted to go up in space the next day! However, she and the other new astronauts needed to spend several years training before they were ready to fly. The picture shows Dr. Ride training for her flight.

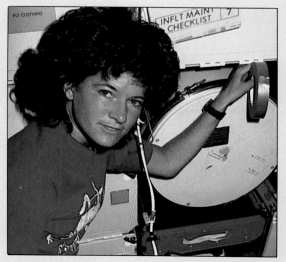

Dr. Sally Ride

Finally, Dr. Ride got her chance. She became the first American woman to fly in space in 1983. On her flight, the spacecraft made one orbit around the earth every 90 minutes. In her six days in space, she went around the earth ninety-eight times!

One of Dr. Ride's main jobs on the flight was to use a robot arm to reach out from the spacecraft. Dr. Ride and another astronaut used the arm to practice releasing and picking up satellites in space. One of the satellites was a space lab. This type of satellite could be left in space to do experiments and take pictures. Later, another spacecraft could pick it up and bring it back to Earth.

Dr. Ride also did experiments to see how plants grow when they do not feel the pull of gravity. What she learned could help scientists plan for future farms in space.

The work that Sally Ride did helps everyone understand more about space. Dr. Ride and the other astronauts know that a great deal is still left to discover.

What Do You Think?
1. Why do you think some experiments are done on a space lab satellite and not by astronauts in flight?
2. How would farms in space be useful?

3 What Do Scientists Learn From Space Travel?

LESSON GOALS

You will learn
- how space travel helped scientists learn about the moon.
- how spacecraft helped scientists learn about Mars, Venus, and other planets.

People have always wondered about objects in the sky. For many years, people thought everything in the sky revolved around the earth. Almost four hundred years ago, a man named Galileo first used a telescope to study distant objects in the sky. Galileo found mountains and valleys on the moon. He found that Venus has phases like the moon. Galileo also saw four moons revolving around Jupiter. The telescope helped scientists prove that the earth was not the center of the solar system.

Today, people use large telescopes like this one to study objects in space. Scientists also use spacecraft that carry special cameras and other tools that help us find out about the solar system.

Using a telescope

Astronaut James Irwin

Rocket on a launch pad

Learning About the Moon

Rockets, like the one in the picture, have carried people to the moon. **Astronauts** are people who travel in space. Astronauts Neil Armstrong and Buzz Aldrin were the first people to land on the moon and return to the earth. They traveled in the spacecraft named Apollo 11.

The picture shows another astronaut on the moon. American astronauts landed on the moon six times. They visited different parts of the moon. They saw large **craters** on the moon. A crater is a hole in the ground that is shaped like a bowl. Most scientists think that rocks from space crashed into the moon and caused these craters. Scientists on earth study rocks that astronauts collected to learn about the moon.

astronaut (as′trə nôt), a person who travels in space.

crater (krā′tər), a large hole in the ground that is shaped like a bowl.

261

Scientists learn about planets.

Learning About the Planets

Scientists use spacecraft to study planets. The Viking spacecraft landed on the planet Mars. No astronauts traveled on this spacecraft. Cameras on the Viking took many pictures of Mars. Scientists learned that Mars has many hills and valleys. The pictures also showed large volcanoes.

Scientists sent spacecraft into orbit around Venus. Spacecraft also have landed on Venus. Clouds always cover Venus. Spacecraft also have taken pictures of rocks under the clouds.

The scientists in the picture are studying photographs of Venus to learn more about this planet.

Spacecraft also have taken pictures of Jupiter, Saturn, and Uranus. Scientists will keep learning about the planets as they send more spacecraft into space.

Lesson Review

1. How has space travel helped scientists learn about the moon?
2. How have spacecraft helped scientists learn about the planets?
3. **Challenge!** Suppose you stood on the surface of Venus. Would you be able to see the earth and the stars? Explain your answer.

Study on your own, pages 338–339.

The pictures show satellites made by people. Scientists have sent such satellites into orbit around the earth. Look in library books to find out how some of these satellites help scientists learn about weather on earth. Write a few sentences explaining what you learned.

EARTH SCIENCE

**FIND OUT
ON YOUR OWN**

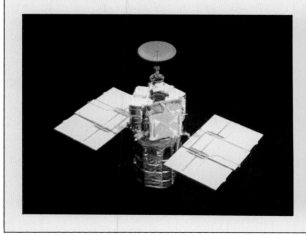

Skills for Solving Problems

Using Calendars and Charts

Problem: How many days pass between full moons?

Part A. Using Calendars to Collect Information

1. A calendar divides time into years, months, and days. Calendars tell about time. How many months does this calendar show?

2. A full moon is when you see all of the lighted side of the moon. Between each full moon, the moon revolves once around the earth. The dates of the full moons are circled below. When was the full moon in January? in February? How many days passed between the two dates?

3. How many days passed between full moons in February and in March? in March and in April? in April and in May? in May and in June?

		January				
S	M	T	W	T	F	S
					1	2
3	4	5	6	⑦	8	9
10	11	12	13	14	15	16
17	18	19	20	21	22	23
24	25	26	27	28	29	30
31						

		February				
S	M	T	W	T	F	S
	1	2	3	4	⑤	6
7	8	9	10	11	12	13
14	15	16	17	18	19	20
21	22	23	24	25	26	27
28	29					

		March				
S	M	T	W	T	F	S
		1	2	3	4	5
⑥	7	8	9	10	11	12
13	14	15	16	17	18	19
20	21	22	23	24	25	26
27	28	29	30	31		

		April				
S	M	T	W	T	F	S
					1	2
3	4	⑤	6	7	8	9
10	11	12	13	14	15	16
17	18	19	20	21	22	23
24	25	26	27	28	29	30

		May				
S	M	T	W	T	F	S
1	2	3	④	5	6	7
8	9	10	11	12	13	14
15	16	17	18	19	20	21
22	23	24	25	26	27	28
29	30	31				

		June				
S	M	T	W	T	F	S
			1	2	③	4
5	6	7	8	9	10	11
12	13	14	15	16	17	18
19	20	21	22	23	24	25
26	27	28	29	30		

Part B. Using Charts to Organize and Interpret Information

4. The chart contains the information you collected about the number of days between the full moons. What do the numbers in the column on

the right stand for? What periods of time are shown in the left column?

5. What might be the reason that the number of days between full moons is not always exactly the same?

Times	Number of days
January to February	29 days
February to March	30 days
March to April	30 days
April to May	29 days
May to June	30 days

Part C. Using Calendars and Charts to Solve a Problem

Problem: How many days pass between new moons?

		January							February							March			
S	M	T	W	T	F	S	S	M	T	W	T	F	S	S	M	T	W	T	F	S
					1	2		1	2	3	4	5	6			1	2	3	4	5
3	4	5	6	7	8	9	7	8	9	10	11	12	13	6	7	8	9	10	11	12
10	11	12	13	14	15	16	14	15	16	17	18	(19)	20	13	14	15	16	17	18	19
17	18	19	20	(21)	22	23	21	22	23	24	25	26	27	(20)	21	22	23	24	25	26
24	25	26	27	28	29	30	28	29						27	28	29	30	31		
31																				

		April							May							June			
S	M	T	W	T	F	S	S	M	T	W	T	F	S	S	M	T	W	T	F	S
					1	2	1	2	3	4	5	6	7				1	2	3	4
3	4	5	6	7	8	9	8	9	10	11	12	13	14	5	6	7	8	9	10	11
10	11	12	13	14	15	16	15	16	(17)	18	19	20	21	12	13	14	15	(16)	17	18
17	(18)	19	20	21	22	23	22	23	24	25	26	27	28	19	20	21	22	23	24	25
24	25	26	27	28	29	30	29	30	31					26	27	28	29	30		

6. Use the calendar to collect the information you need to solve the problem. Make a chart similar to the one in Part B to organize your information.

7. Look at your chart. How many days pass between new moons?

8. Compare your chart with the chart in Part B. How are the numbers of days between full moons and the numbers between new moons alike or different?

Chapter 12 Review

☑ Chapter Main Ideas

Lesson 1 • The earth rotates on its axis and revolves in an orbit around the sun. • The moon rotates on its axis and revolves around the earth. • All the phases of the moon can be seen as the moon makes one revolution.

Lesson 2 • The sun is a ball of hot, glowing gases and is the most important source of energy for the earth. • The sun and the planets and their moons make up most of the solar system.

Lesson 3 • Space travel has helped scientists learn about the moon. • Spacecraft have helped scientists learn about Mars, Venus, and other planets.

☑ Reviewing Science Words

astronaut	phase	rotation
axis	planet	satellite
crater	revolution	solar system
orbit		

Copy each sentence. Fill in the blank with the correct word from the list.

1. The earth rotates around an imaginary straight line called its ____.
2. A ____ is a hole in the ground that is shaped like a bowl.
3. The full moon is one ____ of the moon.
4. The earth makes one ____ when it makes one complete spin around its axis.
5. The moon is called a ____ of the earth because it revolves around the earth.
6. Each complete orbit the earth makes around the sun is called a ____.
7. An ____ is a person who travels in space.
8. A large body of matter that revolves around the sun is called a ____.
9. The sun and the planets and their moons make up the ____.
10. An ____ is a path an object follows as it moves around another object.

✓ Reviewing What You Learned

Write the letter of the best answer.

1. The earth rotates once every
   (a) 15 hours.　　(b) 18 hours.　　(c) 20 hours.　　(d) 24 hours.
2. The earth revolves around the sun once every
   (a) month.　　(b) 365 days.　　(c) day.　　(d) 29 days.
3. Which phase of the moon looks like a bright circle?
   (a) new moon　　(b) complete moon
   (c) full moon　　(d) half moon
4. The spacecraft Apollo 11 landed on
   (a) the moon.　　(b) Mars.　　(c) Pluto.　　(d) Venus.
5. What is the most important source of energy on earth?
   (a) moon　　(b) solar system　　(c) sun　　(d) planets
6. The planet closest to the sun is
   (a) Pluto.　　(b) Earth.　　(c) Neptune.　　(d) Mercury.
7. Which is the largest planet?
   (a) Neptune　　(b) Jupiter　　(c) Earth　　(d) Mars
8. The Viking landed on
   (a) Mars.　　(b) Uranus.　　(c) Saturn.　　(d) Venus.

✓ Interpreting What You Learned

Write a short answer for each question or statement.

1. Name two planets that are colder than Earth.
2. Name three ways Mars and Earth are alike.
3. What makes the moon shine?

✓ Extending Your Thinking

Write a paragraph to answer each question or statement.

1. Neptune takes longer to revolve around the sun than Mercury does. What can explain this difference?
2. Suppose the moon revolved completely around the earth in one week. How long would it take to see all the phases of the moon?

 To explore scientific methods, see Experiment Skills on pages 370–371.

Careers

Can you imagine trying to measure the height of a mountain? How would you measure the distance around a very large lake? If you were a **surveyor,** you would know how to solve these problems. Surveyors measure different distances on the earth. They might figure out the boundary lines between houses. They might measure the length and width of rivers. People who make maps use their measurements. Surveyors spend a great deal of time outdoors. Sometimes they must walk long distances carrying heavy equipment. Surveyors learn their skills by taking special classes after high school. They also learn by working with other surveyors.

Aerial photographers also help map makers. These photographers use special cameras to take pictures from above the earth. They might take pictures while riding in an airplane or a helicopter. A map maker might use these pictures to check the exact location of a lake. Then he or she can place the lake correctly on a map. Aerial photographers take courses in photography. They improve their skills by practicing on the job.

Many other careers involve earth science. **Volcanologists** study volcanoes. They collect lava samples from volcanoes. One of their most important jobs is to try to predict when volcanoes will erupt. You need to go to college for at least four years to become a volcanologist.

Other careers involve watching for severe storms. Hurricanes are dangerous storms with strong winds, rain, and thunder and lightning. They are like tornadoes at sea. When hurricanes come near land, they can cause great damage to communities. **Hurricane hunters** search for these storms. They try to find hurricanes in time to warn people in the path of a hurricane. Many other careers involve the world beyond earth. For example, **aerospacecraft assemblers** build spacecraft. The space shuttles are built by teams of assemblers. Aerospacecraft assemblers must be very careful to put parts together in exactly the right way. They learn their skills during two years of college.

Aerospace assemblers

Space Suits

This astronaut is ready to travel in space outside her spacecraft. Living in outer space will be very different from living on earth. For one thing, she will find no oxygen in space. She must have oxygen to breathe and stay alive. Also, space will be very cold. She will feel no gravity in space. Gravity is the force that holds you to the earth. Without gravity, a person just floats around.

Also, space contains many kinds of harmful rays like the ones that cause sunburn. In space, these powerful rays can kill a person easily. This diagram shows parts of the astronaut's space suit that protect her.

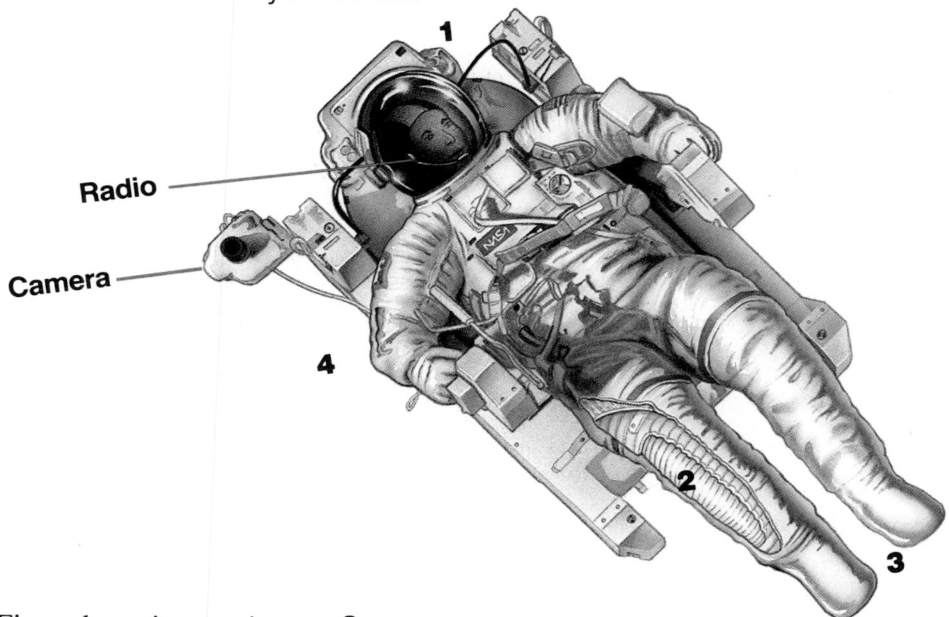

Radio

Camera

1 First, the suit contains a tank filled with oxygen. The tank is carried in her backpack. It has enough oxygen for her to work in space for many hours.

2 The suit is made of special materials that keep heat inside. These materials are like the ones in a winter coat, but they are much better at holding in heat.

3 The astronaut's shoes are special too. Sometimes they have a sticky material on the bottom. The material helps the astronaut stick to the spacecraft. Sometimes the shoes contain heavy weights. The weights would help the astronaut walk on the moon, where gravity is low.

4 The outside coating on the suit contains a thin layer of metal. The metal reflects harmful rays and keeps them out of the suit.

5 The suit also contains other special items. Inside the helmet is a radio set. The radio lets the astronaut talk and listen to other astronauts and to people on the earth.

Unit 3 Review

Complete the Sentence

Fill in the blank with the correct word or words from the list.

axis ores
core precipitation
craters phase
decay sedimentary rock
dew tornado
magma weather

1. Plants and animals ___ when they die.
2. Objects from space create ___ when they crash into the moon.
3. Snow and rain are two kinds of ___.
4. The earth rotates around its ___.
5. Useful minerals are found in some rocks called ___.
6. A volcano erupts when ___ comes up through the crust.
7. A ___ has the most powerful winds on earth.
8. The layers in ___ are formed when material is pressed together.
9. The ___ is the center part of the earth and is its hottest layer.
10. A complete circle can be seen during the ___ called the full moon.
11. Water and gases in the air ___ rocks slowly.
12. During the night, ___ often forms on cold surfaces.

Short Answer

Write a short answer for each question or statement.

1. How can you tell that a rock has many different minerals by looking at it?
2. What are two kinds of natural resources?
3. How are weathering and erosion alike?
4. Why does erosion happen faster on hilly land than on flat land?
5. How do you know magma and lava are made of the same minerals?
6. What is the main difference between fog and a cloud?
7. Why are places far away from oceans safe from hurricanes?
8. How many times does the earth orbit the sun in one year?
9. The moon has no water and almost no wind. Would you see erosion on the moon? Explain your answer.

Essay

Write a paragraph for each question or statement.

1. Describe the steps in the water cycle.
2. Tell how the earth and other planets are alike and how they are different.

Unit Projects and Books

Science Projects

1. When animals of long ago died, some fell into soft mud or clay. This made a hole. The animals rotted, and the hole, or mold, was filled in with sand, mud, and other materials. The materials hardened and formed a cast. Molds and casts are two kinds of fossils. You can make a mold and a cast. Obtain some clay. Press it out into a rectangle. Place the clay in a shallow box. Press objects, such as a shell and a twig into the clay. Remove the objects from the clay. Now mix some plaster of Paris with water so that it looks like thick soup. Pour the plaster into the molds. Allow the plaster to dry. Remove the plaster cast from the clay mold.

2. Use a clear plastic container with straight sides as a simple rain gauge. Set your rain gauge outside. After rain has fallen, place a centimeter ruler up against the outside of the container. How many centimeters of rain did you collect?

Books About Science

Natural Wonders of North America by Catherine O'Neill. National Geographic Society, 1984. Discover the natural wonders of North America created by the powers of nature.

To Space and Back by Sally Ride, with Susan Okie. Lothrop, 1986. Learn about the space shuttle flight with Sally Ride, the first woman astronaut.

Science and Society

Land Use About fifty people live in the forests and meadows of Bayonne Ridge. The town is close to a large city. Some people want a new housing development. Here is what some people of Bayonne Ridge are saying about this development: "We need better schools and new stores." "We like the Ridge just the way it is. We love the trees, the animals, and space." "But if we build new houses, city people would move here and create new businesses. So what if we have to tear down a few trees?" "Maybe, but clearing the land might cause erosion and water pollution." What are some good reasons to build a new development on Bayonne Ridge? What are some good reasons not to build the development?

Human Body

These children know that active play can help them get exercise. Getting enough exercise helps keep your bones and muscles strong. It also helps you feel your best.

Following good health habits can help keep all the parts of the body healthy. In this unit, you will discover how your bones and muscles work. You also will learn about ways you can reduce your chances of getting some illnesses.

SCIENCE IN THE NEWS During the next few weeks, look in newspapers or magazines for stories about bones and muscles. Also, look for news about eating habits that can help people stay healthy. Share the news with your class.

Chapter 13 The Body's Support

Chapter 14 Your Body's Health Needs

Chapter

The Body's Support

How is this person using her body? Notice how she twists and turns her body in different ways. She is using many different parts of her body.

Introducing the Chapter

In this chapter you will learn about what makes up your body. You will also learn how bones and muscles are important to your body. The activity below will help you learn how one part of your body works.

Observing Body Parts

DISCOVER!

Bend your right elbow. Have your partner put a hand on your upper arm as shown. Squeeze your right hand into a fist and then let go. Notice how your upper arm changes. Repeat several times. Ask your partner to feel different parts of your arm moving. Exchange places with your partner and repeat the activity.

Talk About It
1. How did your upper arm change when you made a fist?
2. What parts of your arm would move if you lifted a book?

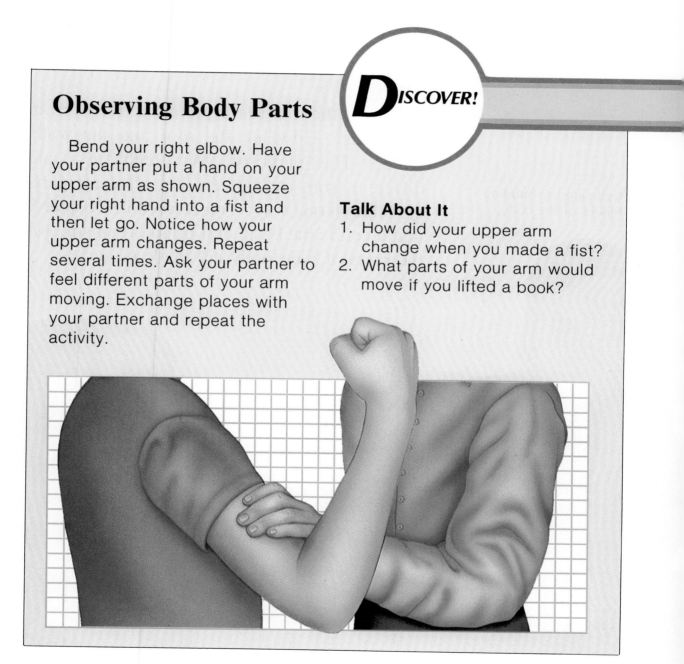

1 What Makes Up Your Body?

LESSON GOALS

You will learn
- that different kinds of cells are found in the body.
- how cells form tissues, organs, and systems in the body.

Notice how the students in the picture use small blocks to make a house with different parts. The house has windows, walls, and a roof. Your body has many different parts too. You have bones and muscles. You also have a brain, a stomach, and a heart. You need all these parts for your body to work properly.

Cells

Cells are the building blocks of the body.

How is the roof in the picture different from the walls? How are the roof and the walls alike? The parts of your body also are different from each other. Yet all these parts are alike in one way. You learned in Chapter 3 that a cell is the basic unit of an organism. All the parts of your body are made of cells.

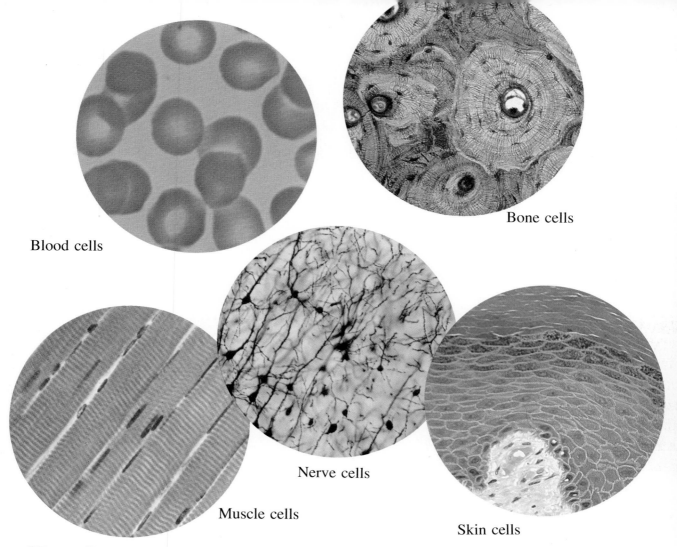

Blood cells

Bone cells

Muscle cells

Nerve cells

Skin cells

How Cells Make Up the Body

Billions of cells make up your body. Notice how the cells in the picture look different from each other. Each kind of cell does a different job in the body. For example, skin cells cover and protect your body. Notice how the nerve cells look different from the muscle cells. Find the blood cells in the picture.

Groups of cells form the parts of your body. A group of the same kind of cells forms a **tissue.** A group of bone cells forms bone tissue. A group of muscle cells forms muscle tissue. What does a group of nerve cells form?

SCIENCE IN YOUR LIFE

Scientists use microscopes to study cells. Most body cells are colorless. Cells can be stained with special dyes. Then the cells can be seen under a microscope.

tissue (tish′ü), a group of cells that look alike and do the same job.

277

organ (ôr′gən), a group of tissues that work together to do a job in the body.

system (sis′təm), a group of organs that work together to do a job in the body.

System that moves blood through the body

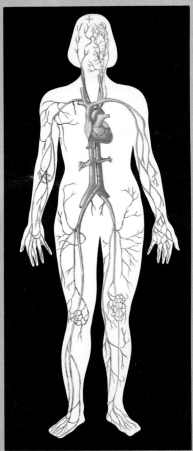

A group of different tissues forms an **organ.** The tissues in an organ work together to keep you alive. Your heart, stomach, eyes, and brain are some of your body organs.

Different organs in your body work together. The picture shows your heart and other organs that move blood through your body. Different organs working together are called a **system.** Your body has many systems. Each body system works to keep you healthy.

Lesson Review

1. What makes up all of the parts of the body?
2. What makes up a body system?
3. **Challenge!** Look at your hand. Feel the different parts. What different kinds of tissues do you have in your hand?

Study on your own, pages 340–341.

Study on your own, pages 340–341.

HUMAN BODY

FIND OUT ON YOUR OWN

Look in library books to find out about a body system. Draw a picture that shows the different parts of the system. Write a few sentences explaining how this system helps keep the body alive and healthy.

Using Computers to Make Joints

The Problem   More than 31 million people in this country have arthritis—a disease of the joints. People with arthritis feel pain, stiffness, or swelling in their joints. Arthritis cripples many people. Often, a joint of an elderly person will simply wear out. This form of joint disease cannot be cured. Doctors can only try to relieve the pain.

Designing a joint with a computer

The Breakthrough   For many years, doctors have tried to replace badly damaged joints. In 1890, a German doctor made the first artificial hip. He replaced the natural joint of the hip with a joint made of ivory. Soon, doctors in America and Europe began using other materials to repair joints. It was not easy to make a new joint. First, a designer looked at the patient's X ray. Then a model of the new joint was drawn. A technician would try to shape a block of metal to fit the patient. The doctor sometimes would have to cut away bone and tissue to make the new joint fit.

New Technology   Today, with the help of computers, people make artificial joints that fit the patient better. These new joints take less time to make and are cheaper. The computer gets some information about the patient from the X rays. Then the doctor tells the computer how much the patient weighs and how active the patient is. The computer uses this and other information to choose a design. The design appears on the screen, as you can see in the picture. The doctor checks the design to make sure it will fit. The doctor tells the computer when everything looks fine. The computer then sends instructions to the computer-run equipment. The equipment cuts out the new joint. During surgery, the doctor replaces the patient's joint with the new one.

What Do You Think?
1. Why are computers better at making new joints than people?
2. How can computers be used to design and make cars?

2 How Are Bones Important?

LESSON GOALS

You will learn
- that bones protect certain body parts and give the body shape and support.
- that joints allow bones to move in different ways.

What can make this puppet move? What might happen if a person let go of the puppet? The hand inside the puppet holds up the puppet. The hand also makes the puppet move.

Bones

Think about how your body is like the puppet. Your body needs help to stay up and to move. The bones of your body make up your skeleton. Your skeleton helps hold you up. Your bones also work with your muscles to help you move.

Your bones help protect organs in your body. Look at this picture of the skeleton. Find the ribs. These bones protect your heart and lungs. The bones of the head protect your brain.

Look at the many different kinds of bones in this skeleton. Notice how the long, narrow parts of your body have long, narrow bones. All the different kinds of bones help give your body shape.

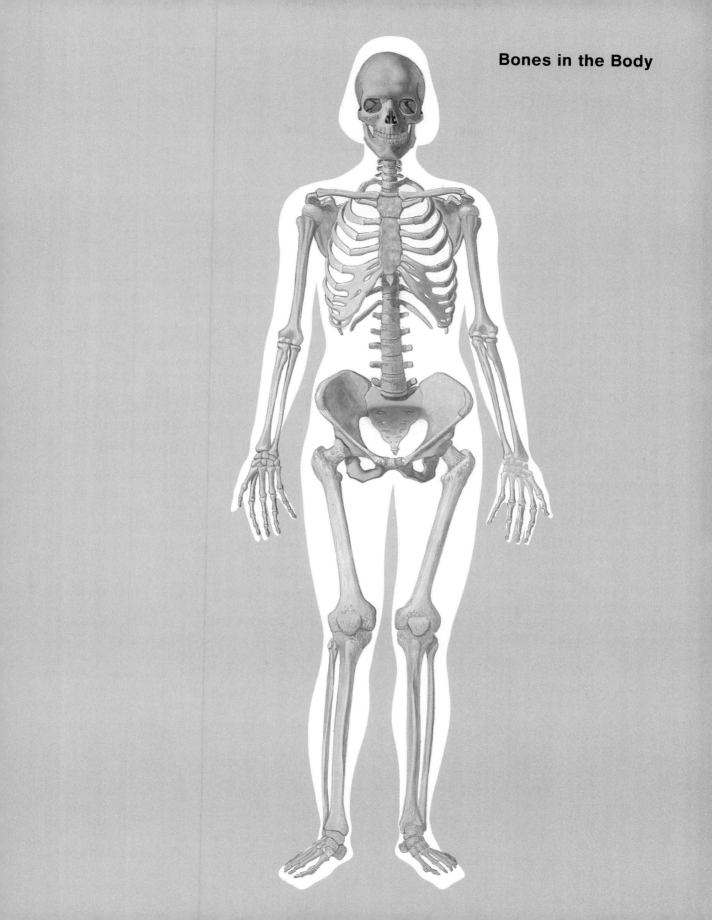

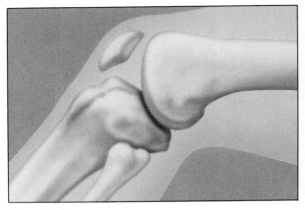

Knee joint   Shoulder joint

Joints

The pictures show places in the body where two bones come together. These places are called **joints.** Move your arm at your shoulder joint. Now move your arm at your elbow joint. Move your fingers. Notice how you can move different parts of your body. Different kinds of joints allow bones to move in different ways.

Lesson Review

1. What are three ways bones help the body?
2. How do joints help the body?
3. **Challenge!** Hinges on a door allow the door to move back and forth. Where is one joint that allows parts of your body to move back and forth?

Study on your own, pages 340–341.

INVESTIGATE!

Animals with backbones have joints. Find out how the different joints help them move in different ways. Write a hypothesis and test it with an experiment. You might compare the joints in a chicken's skeleton to those in your body.

joint, a place where bones join together; different joints allow different movement.

PHYSICAL SCIENCE

*FIND OUT
ON YOUR OWN*

CONNECTION

Some parts of your body are simple machines. What parts of your arms and legs act like levers? How do the levers move?

Observing Cells

Purpose
Observe the cells in an onion skin.

Gather These Materials
• microscope slide • hand lens
• onion skin • paper clip • cover
slip • black construction paper

Follow This Procedure
1. Use a chart like the one shown to record your observations.
2. Wet the microscope slide.
3. Get a very thin slice of onion skin from your teacher. Lay the onion skin flat on the wet slide.
4. Use the paper clip to flatten out the onion skin.
5. Place the cover slip on the slide over the onion skin.
CAUTION: Be careful handling the glass slide and the cover slip.
6. Stand near a bright light or window. Hold your hand lens and your slide above a black piece of paper.
7. Look at the onion skin through the hand lens as shown in the picture. Does it look like the onion skin is made of little boxes?

Record Your Results

How the onion skin looks

State Your Conclusion
1. Can you see the pieces that make up an onion skin without a hand lens?
2. Do you see the tiny pieces that make up the onion skin more clearly in the light or dark places of the onion skin?

Use What You Learned
If the onion skin is made of thousands of pieces, what can you infer about the whole onion?

3 How Are Muscles Important?

These children are playing soccer. They use their muscles to run and kick the ball. Your muscles help you move your body.

Kinds of Muscles

Muscles also help you in another way. Feel the back of your leg and the top of your arm. Muscles give your body its shape.

Look at the picture of the muscles on the next page. You can control many of these muscles. Muscles you can control are called **voluntary muscles.** You use voluntary muscles to turn your head and move your arms.

Other muscles in your body work without you thinking about them. Muscles that work without your control are called **involuntary muscles.** Some kinds of involuntary muscles help you breathe and keep your heart working.

LESSON GOALS

You will learn
- that the body has different kinds of muscles.
- how muscles help the body move.

voluntary (vol′ən ter′ē) **muscle,** the kind of muscle a person can control.

involuntary (in vol′ən ter′ē) **muscle,** the kind of muscle that works without a person's control.

Muscles help people move.

284

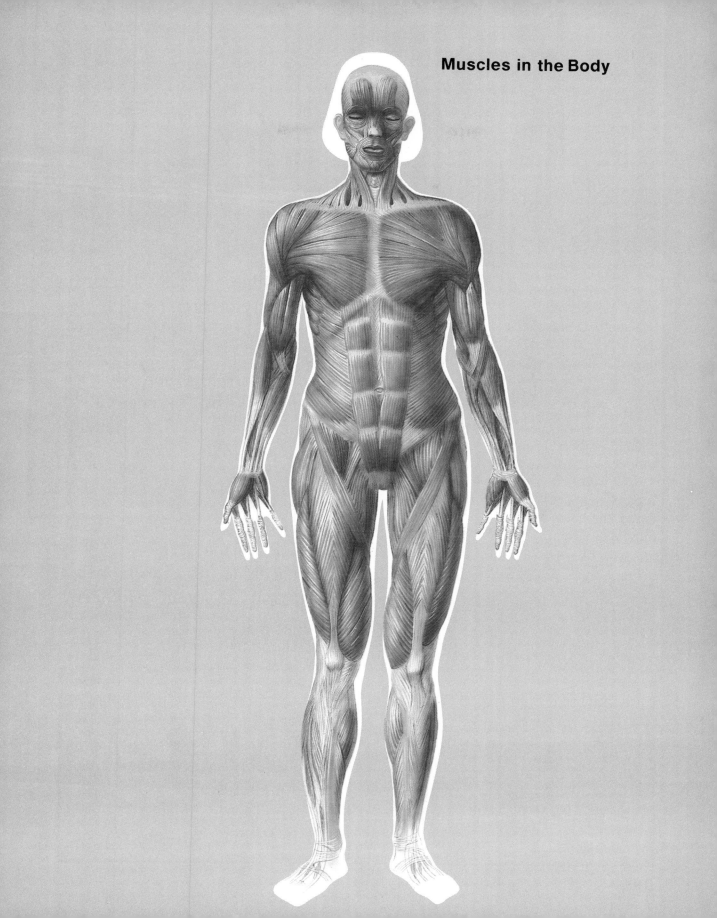

Muscles in the Body

Muscles change shape.

How Muscles Work

Muscles change shape when you move. The picture shows how one muscle becomes shorter and thicker, or **contracts,** to lift the hand. How does this muscle look when the hand is down?

Bones and muscles work together. Muscles are connected to bones by tissues called **tendons.** When a muscle contracts, the tendon causes a bone to move.

Lesson Review

1. What do muscles do?
2. What are two kinds of muscles?
3. **Challenge!** What kind of muscle helps move food around in your stomach? Explain your answer.

Study on your own, pages 340–341.

H U M A N   B O D Y

**FIND OUT
ON YOUR OWN**

Proper stretching helps keep muscles healthy. Find a book about exercise for children. Learn a stretching exercise. Write the directions for the exercise on a piece of paper. You might want to teach this exercise to others in your classroom.

Making a Model of Arm Muscles

Purpose
Observe how muscles work in pairs by *making a model* of upper arm muscles.

Gather These Materials
• cardboard • scissors • paper punch • paper fastener • string • tape

Follow This Procedure
1. Use a chart like the one shown to record your observations.
2. Ask a partner to trace your lower arm and hand on a piece of cardboard. Draw a rectangle about the same size as your upper arm on another piece of cardboard. The rectangle will be used for the upper arm shape. Cut out the shapes.
3. The picture shows how the pieces of cardboard should be joined. Punch holes in the upper and lower arm shapes. Join the two elbow holes with the paper fastener.
4. Thread the strings through the holes. Tie the lower end of each string in a loop. Place a piece of tape over each string.
5. Hold the back edge of the upper arm. Pull up on the string on the inside of the elbow, as shown in the picture.
6. Hold the front edge of the upper arm. Pull on the string on the back side of the elbow.

Record Your Results

String pulled	How arm model looks
Back edge	
Front edge	

State Your Conclusion
1. What happens when you raise each of the two strings?
2. Compare your arm muscles to the model and explain how muscles work in pairs.

Use What You Learned
How do your arm muscles change in length when you raise and lower your lower arm?

Skills for Solving Problems

Using Metric Scales and Line Graphs

Problem: How does the amount of air boys can breathe out change with age?

Part A. Using Metric Scales to Collect Information

1. An involuntary muscle below your lungs helps you breathe. You can meaure how many cc of air you can let out. What does cc stand for?
2. Look at the picture. People breathed into the tubes that go to the upside down jars. Air rises up into the top part of the jar. The metric scale on each jar shows how many cc of air entered the jar. Look at the level of air in the first jar. The scale reads 1100 cc. How much air did the 7-year-old boy breathe out? the 8-year-old?
3. How is the amount of air a 6-year-old breathed out different from that of a 9-year-old?

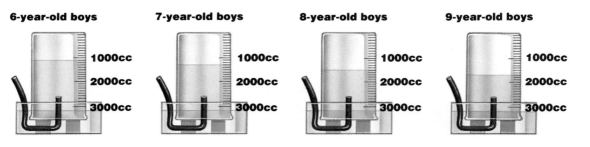

| 6-year-old boys | 7-year-old boys | 8-year-old boys | 9-year-old boys |

Part B. Using a Line Graph to Organize and Interpret Information

4. The line graph contains the information you collected about how much air boys of different ages can breathe out. What does the scale on the left stand for? the scale at the bottom?
5. Look at the first dot on the graph. Move your finger down until you reach the scale at the

bottom of the graph. What does the dot show? Move your finger to the scale at the left. What else does the dot show?

6. Look at the next dot. How much air can 7-year-olds breathe out? 8-year-olds? 9-year-olds?

7. Does the amount of air a boy can breathe out change as he gets older? How much air do you think a 10-year-old boy could breathe out?

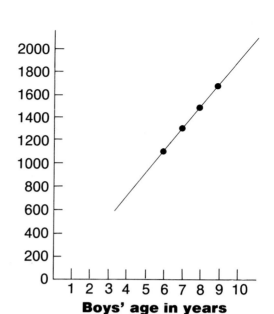

Boys' age in years

Part C. Using Metric Scales and Line Graphs to Solve a Problem

Problem: How does the amount of air girls can breathe out change as they get older?

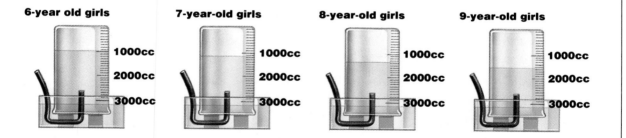

6-year old girls   7-year-old girls   8-year-old girls   9-year-old girls

8. Use the picture to collect the information you need to solve the problem. Make a line graph similar to the one shown in Part B to organize your information.

9. Look at your line graph. Does the amount of air girls can breathe out change as they get older? How is the amount of air 6-, 7-, 8-, and 9-year-old girls can breathe out different?

10. Compare your graph with the line graph in Part B. Is the amount of air girls can breathe out different from the amount boys can breathe out? How?

11. You might want to do this experiment and use your own results to make a line graph.

Chapter 13 Review

☑ Chapter Main Ideas

Lesson 1 • The body is made up of billions of cells. Many different kinds of cells make up the body. • Groups of cells work together, forming tissues, organs, and systems.

Lesson 2 • Bones support the body and help a person move. Some bones protect organs in the body. • The body has different kinds of bones that come together at places called joints. Different kinds of joints allow the body to move in different ways.

Lesson 3 • The body has muscles that work with bones to help a person move. • A person can control the use of voluntary muscles. Involuntary muscles work without a person's control.

☑ Reviewing Science Words

contracts	organ	tissue
involuntary muscles	system	voluntary muscles
joints	tendon	

Copy each sentence. Fill in the blank with the correct word or words from the list.
1. Muscles that a person cannot control are ▨▨▨.
2. ▨▨▨ allow the bones in the knee and the shoulder to move in different ways.
3. A group of tissues that work together form an ▨▨▨.
4. A group of the same kind of cells form a ▨▨▨.
5. The stomach works with other organs to form a ▨▨▨.
6. Muscles a person can control are called ▨▨▨.
7. A muscle becomes shorter and thicker when it ▨▨▨.
8. A ▨▨▨ is a tissue that connects a muscle to a bone.

☑ Reviewing What You Learned

Write the letter of the best answer.
1. The building blocks of the body are
   (a) tissues.   (b) systems.   (c) organs.   (d) cells.

2. A group of bone cells form bone
   (a) tissue.   (b) organ.   (c) organisms.   (d) system.
3. A heart is an example of
   (a) a cell.   (b) a tissue.
   (c) an organ.   (d) a system.
4. Different organs that work together are called a
   (a) tissue.   (b) system.   (c) cell.   (d) brain.
5. Bones help a person
   (a) think.   (b) see.   (c) move.   (d) feel.
6. An elbow is a
   (a) nerve.   (b) muscle.   (c) joint.   (d) bone.
7. The muscles of the upper arm are
   (a) voluntary muscles.   (b) involuntary muscles.
   (c) systems.   (d) tendons.
8. When a muscle contracts it becomes
   (a) longer.   (b) thinner.   (c) softer.   (d) shorter.

☑ Interpreting What You Learned

Write a short answer for each question or statement.
1. Put the following groups in the correct order: tissue, systems, cells, organs.
2. What is one way bones protect inside parts of the body?
3. What are two joints in your body?
4. How do voluntary muscles and involuntary muscles differ?
5. Tell what happens to the muscle on the top of the upper arm when a person bends the elbow.

☑ Extending Your Thinking

Write a paragraph to answer each question or statement.
1. What do different sized and shaped bones do to help the body? Give examples.
2. How could a bone injury change the way a person uses his or her muscles?

 To explore scientific methods, see Experiment Skills on pages 372–373.

Your Body's Health Needs

All of the members of this family enjoy good health.
They know that good health helps them work and
play better.

Introducing the Chapter

Exercise is a good health habit that can help all the parts of your body. The activity below will help you learn about exercising. In this chapter, you will learn how you can help protect yourself from certain diseases. Following good health habits and saying *no* to drugs also can help keep you healthy.

DISCOVER!

Observing How Exercise Changes Breathing

Find out what happens to your breathing when you exercise. First, sit quietly in a chair. Use a clock or watch with a second hand to count how many times you breathe in one minute. Write this number on a sheet of paper.

Now run in place about twenty-five times. When you stop running, count how many times you breathe in one minute. Write this number on the sheet of paper. Compare the two numbers on your paper.

Talk About It
1. Did you breathe faster before or after you exercised?
2. What other way did your breathing change when you exercised?

1 How Can You Stay Healthy?

LESSON GOALS

You will learn
- that eating properly can help you stay healthy.
- that exercising can help keep your body healthy.
- that getting enough sleep is important for your health.

Eating, exercising, and getting enough sleep are good health habits. Following these habits can help keep your body working well.

Eating Properly

How can you plan healthy meals? You can follow the four food group plan shown in the picture. You need to eat foods from each of these food groups. This plan tells you how much of each kind of food to eat each day.

You learned in Chapter 9 that plants and animals need nutrients. Foods contain nutrients that your body uses to grow and stay healthy. Eating the right amounts of foods from each food group helps you get all the nutrients you need.

Vegetable-fruit group
Four servings

Bread-cereal group
Four servings

Exercising Properly

What kind of activities do you enjoy? Exercising can help build **physical fitness.** Physical fitness helps you work and play without getting tired or hurt easily. Playing sports and active games can help build physical fitness. Walking, dancing, or riding a bicycle also can help you keep fit.

Your heart is a muscle. Your heart beats faster during exercise. When you exercise properly, you help your heart get stronger. When your heart is strong, you can work and play for a long time without getting tired.

Exercise helps all the parts of your body work well. Exercise also helps you sleep well. Getting enough exercise helps you look and feel your best. How can playing every day give you the exercise you need?

INVESTIGATE!

Find out if different kinds of exercises affect how fast your heart beats. Write a hypothesis and test it with an experiment. You might count your heartbeats for one minute after walking. Then run in place and count your heartbeats again for a minute.

physical (fiz′ə kəl) **fitness,** the ability to work, play, and exercise without getting tired or injured easily.

Meat-poultry-fish-bean group
Two servings

Milk-cheese group
Three servings

This girl works better when she gets enough sleep.

Getting Enough Sleep

Your body needs time to rest after a busy day. You need sleep to grow properly. Your body makes and repairs cells while you sleep. Sleep also helps give you energy for the next day. This girl knows she can work, play, and learn better when she gets enough sleep.

Lesson Review

1. How can you plan healthy meals for a day?
2. How does exercise help a person stay healthy?
3. How does sleep help the body?
4. **Challenge!** What are some ways to make exercise fun?

Study on your own, pages 342–343.

HUMAN BODY

FIND OUT ON YOUR OWN

Cut out pictures from magazines to make a poster about healthy meals. Show healthy meals and snacks for a day. The pictures of the four food groups will give you some ideas for foods to choose. Write a few sentences telling about your poster.

Testing Foods for Sugar

Purpose
Classify different types of foods according to the presence or absence of sugar.

Gather These Materials
• sugar test paper • several kinds of food

Follow This Procedure
1. Use a chart like the one shown to record your observations.
2. Touch the sugar test paper against each of your foods as shown in the picture. The paper will change color when it touches foods that have sugar. Record what you see.

Record Your Results

Food	Sugar (yes/no)
1.	
2.	
3.	

State Your Conclusion
1. Which of your foods have sugar? How do you know?
2. Which of your foods do not contain sugar?

Use What You Learned
If you want to eat only snacks that do not have sugar, what foods can you eat?

2 What Causes Disease?

LESSON GOALS

You will learn
- how some diseases can spread from person to person.
- about diseases that do not spread from person to person.

disease (də zēz′), an illness.

Cover your nose and mouth when you sneeze.

Think about a time when you felt sick. Most people become sick from time to time. In many cases, you can help keep yourself well by following good health habits.

Diseases That Spread

The girl in the picture has a cold. Her nose is runny and her eyes are watery. A cold is a **disease,** or illness, that can spread from person to person.

Germs cause colds and can cause other diseases that spread. Germs are too small for you to see. They are found everywhere. They are in air and water. They are in food and on other objects. You have germs inside you and on your skin all the time.

Germs can get into your body through a cut on your skin. You might breathe germs from the air. You might take in germs on food or touch an object that has germs. Sometimes disease germs grow inside your body. Then you feel sick.

You get different diseases from different kinds of disease germs. You learned in Chapter 3 that some bacteria cause diseases. For example, bacteria germs can cause strep throat and other infections. **Viruses** are germs that are smaller in size than bacteria. Flu, chicken pox, and measles are caused by viruses.

The pictures show some ways you can help keep germs from spreading. Keeping your skin clean is important. Washing with soap and water can get rid of many germs on your skin. Proper food, exercise, and sleep can help keep your body strong enough to fight off many diseases.

Medicines called antibiotics can kill many kinds of bacteria that cause diseases. Taking antibiotics for a disease caused by certain bacteria can help a sick person get well.

virus (vī′rəs), a kind of disease germ that causes diseases such as colds and flu.

Use your own glass.

Don't Get too Much Sun

Don't Smoke

diabetes (dī′ə bē′tis), a disease in which the body cannot use sugar properly.

cancer, a disease in which cells that are not normal destroy healthy body cells.

Diseases That Do Not Spread

Some diseases are not passed from person to person. These diseases are caused by changes that happen inside a person's body.

Diabetes is one kind of disease that you cannot catch from another person. Diabetes is a disease in which the body cannot use sugar properly. Children with this disease need to take medicine every day. People with diabetes also must eat carefully. They can help control their disease by eating fewer sweets and fats, and exercising regularly.

Cancer is a disease that cannot spread from person to person. In this disease, cells that are not normal destroy healthy body cells. Operations, medicines, and other treatments can control some kinds of cancers. Doctors are trying to find better ways to treat cancer.

People can help reduce their chances of getting some kinds of cancer. Not smoking can help keep people from getting lung cancer. Not spending long periods of time in the sun can help keep people from getting skin cancer.

Heart disease can keep the heart from working properly. Heart disease does not spread from person to person. Following good health habits can help keep a person's heart healthy. What ways to keep your body strong and healthy are shown on these posters?

Lesson Review

1. How can diseases spread from person to person?
2. What are some diseases that do not spread from person to person?
3. **Challenge!** Why should you cover your nose when you sneeze?

Study on your own, pages 342–343.

Some people have allergies to certain plants. Find out what an allergy is. What are some plants that people have allergies toward?

L I F E   S C I E N C E

**FIND OUT
ON YOUR OWN**

C O N N E C T I O N

Making a Model of Bacteria Growth

Purpose
Observe how bacteria increase in their number.

Gather These Materials
• package of popcorn kernels
• glue • 8 file cards

Follow This Procedure
1. Use a chart like the one shown to record your observations.
2. Label your first file card 12:00. Label the second file card 12:30. Continue labeling the file cards with the times of every half hour. Label the last file card 3:30.
3. Pretend the popcorn kernels are bacteria. On the 12:00 card, glue 1 popcorn kernel as shown in the picture.
4. At 12:30, your bacteria cell divides to form 2 cells. Glue 2 kernels on the 12:30 card.
5. At 1:00, the two bacteria divide to make 4 bacteria cells. Glue 4 kernels on the 1:00 card.
6. At 1:30, the 4 bacteria divide again. Glue the right number of kernels on the 1:30 card. Keep going until you have finished the 3:30 card.
7. Count the number of popcorn kernels on each card.

Record Your Results

Time	Number of Bacteria
12:00	
12:30	
1:00	
1:30	
2:00	
2:30	
3:00	
3:30	

State Your Conclusion
1. How many bacteria did you have at 3:30?
2. How many bacteria would you have at 4:00?

Use What You Learned
How many hours do you think it would take to go from one bacteria cell to a thousand cells?

Becoming a Doctor

When José Sandoval was your age, he was already a farm worker. He traveled with his family, and they found jobs wherever they could. They picked cotton, chilies, and other crops. José was so busy working, he could not go to school regularly.

When José was twelve years old, his father made an important decision. He decided that his family would not travel and be farm workers anymore. His children would go to school full-time. José studied science because he was interested in spiders and bugs. He became a very good student even though he spoke very little English until he went to school.

José went to college in California. Then, he got a job as a United States Peace Corps volunteer in a faraway country. There, he became interested in medicine. He wanted to help people get well and stay healthy. He returned to California to go to medical school and became a doctor.

Dr. Sandoval especially likes taking care of people who cannot easily afford care. He teaches his patients how important it is to take care of themselves. He reminds them to see a doctor

Dr. José Sandoval

when they show early signs of illness.

Dr. Sandoval also works with other doctors to help encourage young people to become doctors. He feels that if young people see that he worked hard and became a doctor, they will feel like they could do it too.

What Do You Think?
1. Why do you think Dr. Sandoval tells people to see a doctor when they first feel ill?
2. If you were a doctor, what would you tell your patients about how to stay healthy?

3 How Can Alcohol, Tobacco, and Drugs Affect the Body?

You will learn
- how alcohol can harm the body.
- how tobacco is harmful to a person's health.
- how using harmful drugs can be dangerous to a person's health.

alcohol (al′kə hôl), a drug that can be harmful and is found in beer, wine, and liquor.

Medicines can help sick people.

This boy is taking medicine because he is ill. Medicines can help sick people get better. Some medicines can keep people from getting ill. You need to be careful with medicines. They can be dangerous if taken in the wrong way. Medicines are a kind of drug. All drugs cause changes in the body. Many drugs can harm a person's health. Some drugs can change the way a person thinks, feels, or acts.

Alcohol

Some drinks have a drug called **alcohol.** This drug is found in beer, wine, and liquor. Drinking too much alcohol can harm the body. Alcohol changes the way a person's brain works. A person who drinks alcohol might have trouble thinking clearly.

People who drink too much alcohol can become quarrelsome. Alcohol can cause a person to get a stomachache or a bad headache. Alcohol also affects the way a person moves. A person who drinks too much alcohol can have trouble walking. Drinking too much alcohol can change the way a person talks. The person might forget the correct words or not be able to speak clearly.

Alcohol can keep a person from acting quickly. A person who drinks too much alcohol might feel dizzy and have trouble seeing clearly. Alcohol also can make a person feel tired and go to sleep. A person who has been drinking alcohol should not ride a bicycle or drive a car.

Some drugs that doctors use to help people are placed in patches that a person wears like a bandage. These patches can be placed on the skin so that the medicine goes into the body through the skin.

Tobacco

nicotine (nik′ə tēn′), a drug in tobacco that can harm a person's body.

Cigarettes and cigars are made from the leaves of the tobacco plant. Tobacco contains a drug called **nicotine.** This drug can be harmful to the health. Nicotine makes the heart beat faster than normal. A person who smokes is more likely to get heart disease than a person who never smokes.

Cigarette smoke also can be harmful. Some of the materials in cigarette smoke can damage the lungs. A person who smokes is more likely to get lung cancer and other lung diseases than a person who never smokes. Cigarette smoke can harm the health of people who are around smokers. Many buildings have signs like the one in the picture. How can this sign help protect people's health?

Find the sign that warns people not to smoke.

Other Harmful Drugs

Sometimes people use drugs that are against the law. These **illegal drugs** include marijuana and cocaine. These drugs can damage body organs and change the way the brain works. They can change the way a person thinks or acts.

A person should always say *no* to illegal drugs. The boy in the picture enjoys doing activities that make him feel good. He knows that staying away from harmful drugs will help keep him healthy.

illegal (i lē′gəl) **drug,** a drug that is against the law to use or have.

Lesson Review

1. How can alcohol harm a person?
2. How can tobacco harm the body?
3. How are illegal drugs harmful?
4. **Challenge!** What are some ways a person can say no to illegal drugs?

Study on your own, pages 342–343.

Exercising can help a person feel good.

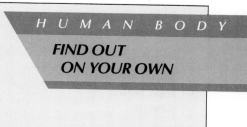

Caffeine is a drug found in many drinks. Caffeine speeds up the heartbeat and can make some people very nervous. Use library books to find out about caffeine. Make a list of drinks with caffeine. Also make a list of healthy drinks people can choose.

H U M A N   B O D Y

FIND OUT ON YOUR OWN

Skills for Solving Problems

Using Diagrams and Bar Graphs

Problem: How are the servings a child needs from the four food groups different from the servings an adolescent needs?

Part A. Using Diagrams to Collect Information

1. The diagram shows the four basic food groups. Eating the right amounts of foods from each group helps you get all the nutrients you need. What are the four food groups?

2. The diagram shows how many servings from each group children, teenagers, and adults need each day. A child needs four servings a day from the bread-cereal group. How many servings does a teenager need? an adult?

3. How many servings from the fruit-vegetable group does a child need? a teenager? an adult?

4. How many servings from the meat-poultry-fish-bean group does a child need? a teenager? an adult?

5. How many servings from the milk group does a child need? a teenager? an adult?

Food group	Total number of servings		
	Child	Teenager	Adult
Milk group 	3	4	2
Meat poultry fish bean group 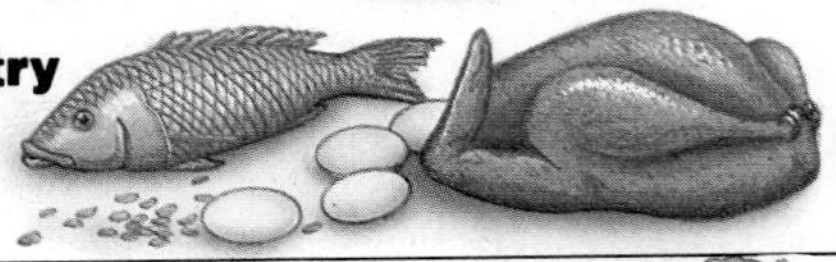	2	2	2
Fruit vegetable group 	4	4	4
Bread cereal group 	4	4	4

Part B. Using a Bar Graph to Organize and Interpret Information

6. The bar graph contains information you collected about the servings needed of the four food groups. The bars show how many daily servings of the four food groups a child and a teenager need. Compare the two bars shown for each food group. For which groups do a child and a teenager need the same number of servings? a different number of servings?

7. Why might a teenager need a different number of servings of a food group than a child does?

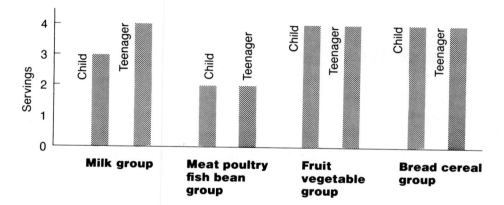

Part C. Using Diagrams and Bar Graphs to Solve a Problem

Problem: How are the numbers of servings a child needs from the four food groups different from the numbers of servings an adult needs?

8. Use the diagram in Part A to collect the information you need to solve the problem. Make a bar graph similar to the one shown in Part B to organize your information.

9. Look at your bar graph. For which food groups does an adult need a different number of servings than a child does? Why might an adult need a different number of servings of a food group than a child does?

Chapter 14 Review

☑ Chapter Main Ideas

Lesson 1 • Eating the right amounts of foods from each of the four food groups helps a person get all the needed nutrients. • Exercising properly helps all the parts of the body work well. • Getting the right amount of sleep also helps a person stay healthy.

Lesson 2 • People can help keep themselves well by following good health habits. Germs such as bacteria and viruses can cause diseases that spread from person to person. • Some diseases do not spread from person to person.

Lesson 3 • Drinking too much alcohol can harm the body. • Smoking is harmful to the health. • Illegal drugs can be harmful to the body.

☑ Reviewing Science Words

alcohol	disease	physical fitness
cancer	illegal drugs	virus
diabetes	nicotine	

Copy each sentence. Fill in the blank with the correct word from the list.

1. The ability to exercise, work, and play without getting tired easily is ▨.
2. ▨ is a disease in which the body cannot use sugar properly.
3. ▨ is a drug that is contained in beer, wine, and liquor.
4. An illness is called a ▨.
5. Marijuana and cocaine are two kinds of ▨ that can harm a person's health.
6. Tobacco contains a drug called ▨ that makes the heart beat faster and can be harmful to health.
7. ▨ is a disease in which cells that are not normal destroy healthy body cells.
8. A ▨ is a kind of germ that can cause flu, chicken pox, and measles.

✓ Reviewing What You Learned

Write the letter of the best answer.

1. Materials in food that help the body grow and stay healthy are
   (a) bread.   (b) nutrients.   (c) viruses.   (d) fruit.
2. One way to help the heart get stronger is to
   (a) read.   (c) watch television.
   (b) sleep.   (d) play active games.
3. How many servings do you need each day from the milk-cheese group?
   (a) one   (b) none   (c) three   (d) six
4. Which disease can be passed from person to person?
   (a) flu   (b) cancer   (c) diabetes   (d) heart disease
5. Cocaine is a drug that is
   (a) legal.   (b) illegal.   (c) not harmful.   (d) weak.
6. A disease that cannot spread from person to person is
   (a) flu.   (b) measles.   (c) cancer.   (d) a cold.
7. How many servings do you need each day from the meat-poultry-fish-bean group?
   (a) one   (b) two   (c) six   (d) five

✓ Interpreting What You Learned

Write a short answer for each question or statement.

1. What are some ways a person can stay healthy?
2. Explain how a person can get the nutrients he or she needs for good health.
3. Why should a person never drink alcohol and drive?
4. Explain how a person with diabetes can help control his or her disease.

✓ Extending Your Thinking

Write a paragraph to answer each question or statement.

1. Why is it important for people to wash their hands before they cook food or eat a meal?
2. What advice would you give to someone who is thinking of smoking a cigarette?

 To explore scientific methods, see Experiment Skills on pages 374–375.

311

Careers

How do you help your body stay healthy? You can eat healthy foods and exercise regularly. Many people work to keep other people healthy.

When you think of a doctor, perhaps your family doctor comes to mind. Family doctors treat all kinds of health problems. Some doctors only treat certain health problems. **Sports medicine physicians** help athletes get back into top physical condition after injuries. They also help athletes keep in good physical shape. To become a sports medicine doctor, you must go to medical school after college. Then you must work with experienced doctors for several years.

Some athletes and others might lose the use of one or more body parts from injuries. **Physical therapists** help these people recover the use of their body parts. A physical therapist works out a treatment plan for each patient. This plan might include exercise, massage, and whirlpool baths. If a patient will remain partly disabled, the therapist will show him or her how to do everyday tasks. To become a physical therapist, you must go to college for at least four years.

Registered nurses care for hospital patients in many ways. They observe and record a patient's progress in getting well. They teach patients how to care for themselves when they get home. Many registered nurses work in hospitals. Registered nurses also work in doctors' offices, nursing homes, schools, homes, and industry. Nurses who work in hospitals or nursing homes might have to work nights and weekends. Registered nurses go to school for two to five years after high school.

Sometimes a nurse takes a sample of your blood. A **medical laboratory technician** then looks at the sample under a microscope. He or she can find out more about your illness by seeing this sample. Medical laboratory technicians might also look at samples from other body tissues. Medical laboratory technicians take classes for two years after high school.

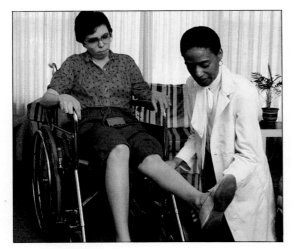

Physical therapist

Canning of Food

Food spoils when germs grow in it. Germs grow best when food is warm and moist. Air also helps most germs to grow.

Food can be stored for a long time if germs and air are kept away from it. Some foods can be dried or frozen to keep them safe from germs. Canning is another way to keep food from spoiling. The picture shows how food is packed in cans.

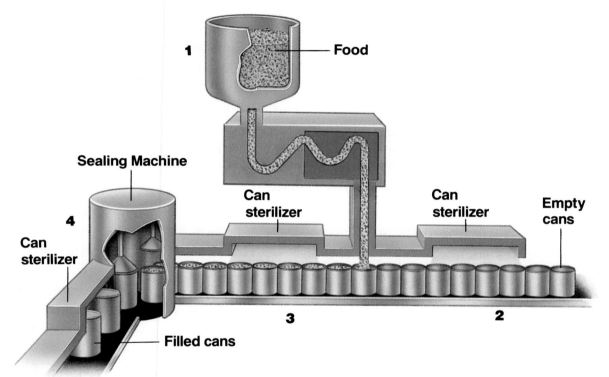

1

Food

Sealing Machine

4

Can sterilizer

Can sterilizer

Can sterilizer

Empty cans

Filled cans

3

2

1 First, the food is washed and prepared. Fruits and vegetables might be peeled or cut up. Some foods, such as soup, are cooked just like you cook soup at home. Cooking helps kill germs in the food.

2 Next, the food is sent to the canning machine. The machine contains empty cans with no tops. The cans are heated to a very high temperature, or sterilized, to kill germs in them. Then the machine fills the cans with food.

3 The filled cans are then sterilized. This kills germs that might be left in the cans. Also, heating pushes air out of the cans. The hot food expands and fills the can to the top.

4 Finally, a machine puts a top tightly on each can. Then, the can is sterilized again to make sure all the germs have been killed.

Unit 4 Review

Complete the Sentence

Fill in the blank with the correct word or words from the list.

alcohol   nicotine
cancer   organ
contracts   physical fitness
diabetes   tendon
illegal   virus
joints

1. When a person has the disease of ___, the body cannot use sugar properly.
2. Tissues in an ___ work together to do a job in your body.
3. A muscle ___ when it becomes shorter.
4. A kind of germ that causes diseases such as colds and flu is a ___.
5. A disease in which cells that are not normal destroy healthy body cells is ___.
6. The drug ___ is found in beer and wine.
7. A place where two bones join together is a ___.
8. A ___ holds a muscle to a bone.
9. Tobacco has a drug called ___ that can harm a person's heart.
10. Cocaine and marijuana are ___ drugs.
11. Being able to exercise, work, and play without getting tired easily is ___.

Short Answer

Write a short answer for each question or statement.

1. Why does your body need many different kinds of cells?
2. Compare the ways a shoulder joint and a knee joint help a person move.
3. What happens to upper arm muscles when you bend your arm at the elbow?
4. Name three ways to keep your body healthy.
5. In what ways can a person build physical fitness?
6. How can germs on the skin get inside the body and make a person sick?
7. How is diabetes different from measles, flu, or a cold?
8. Name two ways that people can help reduce their chances of getting cancer.
9. In what ways can drinking alcohol make people feel sick?
10. How can cigarette smoke harm the health of people who don't smoke?

Essay

Write a paragraph for each question or statement.

1. Describe what the muscles and bones do when a person throws a ball.
2. How does smoking cigarettes harm a person's health?

Science Projects

1. Some bones are not covered by very many muscles. These bones can be felt easily. Feel your face, your sides, your arms, and your legs. Make a list of the bones you can feel.

2. One kind of joint allows you to bring one part of your body closer to another part of your body. For example, if you bend your elbow, you bring your lower arm closer to your upper arm. What happens when you bend your fingers and your knees. How does the movement of these joints differ from the movement of your hip joint?

3. Make a poster with a slogan that says no to drinking, smoking, or using harmful drugs.

Books About Science

Cells and Tissues by Leslie Jean LeMaster. Children's Press, 1985. Learn about cells and what they are made of. Also find out how cells form tissues.

Muscles and Movement by Gwynne Vevers. Lothrop, 1984. Find out about different kinds of muscles and what they help you do.

Germs Make Me Sick! by Melvin Berger. T.Y. Crowell, 1985. Learn about germs and how your body fights them.

Science and Society

Smokeless Flights People on a flight from San Francisco to Los Angeles are talking about smoking. A recent law banned smoking on all airline flights within California. Some people like the ban on smoking. "This new policy has really cleared the air," they say. "Smokers do not have the right to harm our health." The smokers are not happy with the law. "We have rights too," they say. "We do not tell others what to eat or drink. How can they tell us not to smoke?" The nonsmokers reply, "We have the right to clean air. In a crowded airplane, we get sick when other people smoke." The smokers answer that they can smoke on flights in other parts of the country. What are reasons for banning smoking on airplane flights? What are reasons for allowing smoking in one section of an airplane?

Independent Study Guide

Use the *Independent Study Guide* to review the lessons in each chapter.

Chapter 1 Study Guide

On a separate sheet of paper, write the word or words that best complete the sentence or answer the question.

LESSON 1

pages 10–13

1. How are the roots of weeds and grasses different?
2. What two things do roots do for a plant?
3. Materials in the soil that were never alive are ▨ .
4. The ▨ of most plants hold up the leaves and other plant parts that grow above the ground.
5. How do water and minerals get from the roots of a plant to its leaves?
6. The ▨ of green plants make most of the food for the plant.
7. How does a plant take in carbon dioxide?
8. Most plants store some ▨ in their roots and stems.

LESSON 2

pages 16–19

1. The ▨ from flowers grow into new plants.
2. What part of the plant in each of the pictures below makes seeds?

3. What must happen before a flower can form seeds?
4. When the center part of a flower changes into a fruit, the flower ▦ dry up and fall off.
5. What does the fruit of a plant do for the seeds?
6. How do bees move pollen between flowers?
7. Name two other animals that help pollinate flowers.
8. Animals and ▦ can scatter pollen.
9. How are corn and other grasses pollinated?
10. The ▦ on some trees have pollen inside.
11. Most trees with cones have needle-shaped ▦ .
12. What is one kind of tree that has cones?

LESSON 3

pages 20–22

1. What does a seed coat do for the seed?
2. Water, wind, and ▦ help scatter seeds.
3. A seed needs enough air and water and the proper ▦ to germinate.
4. A young plant that has just pushed through the ground is called a ▦ .
5. The time during which a plant grows from a seed until it makes its own seeds is the plant's ▦ .
6. How would you put the following pictures in the order that they happen?

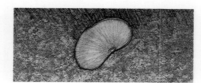

Chapter 2 Study Guide

On a separate sheet of paper, write the word or words that best complete the sentence or answer the question.

LESSON 1

pages 30–31

1. One way that scientists classify animals is by whether or not they have a ▨ .
2. What does your backbone help you do?
3. Why would bees and birds not be classified into the same group?

LESSON 2

pages 32–36

1. How do birds breathe?
2. How do baby birds get food?
3. Snakes are ▨ because their body temperatures change with the temperature of the air around them.
4. Young reptiles come from ▨ .
5. A fish's ▨ help it swim.
6. How do fish breathe?
7. How are fish and reptiles the same?
8. What happens to young fish after they hatch?
9. Which of the animals in the pictures is warm-blooded and which are cold-blooded?

10. Animals with backbones and hair or fur are ▨ .

11. What are two kinds of mammals that live on land?

12. What is one kind of mammal that lives in water?

13. Mammals breathe with ▨ .

14. How are the ways mammals and birds are born different from one another?

15. People belong in the group of ▨ .

16. What food do young mammals eat?

LESSON 3

pages 38–41

1. A ▨ has a thin, soft body and no legs.

2. Earthworms make ▨ in the soil.

3. A ▨ has a soft body and a hard shell.

4. A spider has two main body parts and ▨ legs.

5. A spider spins a ▨ from silk that it makes inside its body.

6. The largest group of animals without backbones are the ▨ .

7. How are insects different from spiders?

8. The butterfly has ▨ stages in its life cycle.

9. Describe the larva of the butterfly.

10. These pictures show the way a butterfly changes. Describe how you would put the pictures in the correct order.

Chapter 3 Study Guide

On a separate sheet of paper, write the word or words that best complete the sentence or answer the question.

LESSON 1

pages 50–52

1. Living things are called ▨.
2. Organisms are made of one or more ▨.
3. How can you see cells?
4. Scientists have divided organisms into ▨ different groups.
5. Some ▨ move by whipping their tails back and forth.
6. A plant's ▨ keep it attached to the soil.
7. Name the kind of organism in each picture.

LESSON 2

pages 54–56

1. A group of sheep living in one place together form a ▨.
2. The ▨ of a population often changes because of the number of births and deaths in the group.
3. What happens to the size of a population when it has plenty of food?
4. The organisms in a ▨ depend on each other for food and shelter.

5. Why do the squirrels in a forest community need the trees?
6. What do insects do for a forest community?
7. What organisms live in the community you see in the picture below?

8. An organism gets everything it needs from its ▨.
9. How is a habitat different from a community?

LESSON 3

pages 58–60

1. Why are green plants producers?
2. Mice, deer, and rabbits are ▨ because they eat other organisms for food.
3. Snakes and lions are ▨ because they hunt for their food.
4. Lions hunt for antelope, so antelope are the lion's ▨ .
5. Grass growing in a meadow and then a mouse eating the grass is an example of a part of a ▨ .
6. Where are food chains found?

Chapter 4 Study Guide

On a separate sheet of paper, write the word or words that best complete the sentence or answer the question.

LESSON 1

pages 68–71

1. What are three things organisms get from their habitats?
2. Air, water, and land habitats are often destroyed by ▦.
3. How do factories cause air pollution?
4. How do factories cause water pollution?
5. Litter can change the ▦ of plants and animals.
6. When many organisms of the same kind die, that kind of organism can become ▦.
7. Look at the pictures below. Tell whether each organism is endangered or extinct.

LESSON 2

pages 72–74

1. People cannot hunt animals or collect plants in ▦.
2. What is one way factories can keep water from becoming polluted?

3. What is one way factories can keep the air from becoming polluted?
4. How do scientists help protect endangered plants?
5. Some endangered animals are kept in ▨ to keep them from becoming extinct.

LESSON 3

pages 76–79

1. What are two things you get from plants and animals?
2. Fruits, grains, and ▨ come from plants.
3. Name three different kinds of grains.
4. What part of the celery plant do people eat?
5. What part of a plant is an apple?
6. Cheese, butter, yogurt, and ice cream come from ▨ .

7. Look at the pictures above. Tell whether each food comes from a plant or an animal.
8. People use ▨ from trees to make paper.
9. Where does linen come from?
10. Leather comes from the ▨ of animals.
11. Name a plant that can cause some people to get an itchy rash.

Chapter 5   Study Guide

On a separate sheet of paper, write the word or words that best complete the sentence or answer the question.

LESSON 1

pages 94–98

1. The objects on your desk are alike because they all take up ▨ .
2. The amount of space an object fills is its ▨ .
3. A car has a ▨ volume than a bicycle does.
4. How can you measure how much mass an object has?
5. An apple has ▨ mass than an eraser.
6. How are people like objects in a room?
7. When you describe an object, you tell about its ▨ .
8. What are five properties you can use to describe an object?
9. What state of matter is a rock?
10. What state of matter is the air you breathe?
11. How are solid objects and liquid objects different from one another?
12. What happens to the air in a balloon when the balloon breaks?
13. Using a chart like the one below, list some of the properties of three objects you have at your desk.

Object	Properties

LESSON 2

pages
100–102

1. Two or more ▨ join to form larger particles of matter.
2. A solid has particles that are ▨ than the particles in liquids.
3. How do liquids change their shape?
4. In which of the states of matter do the particles have the weakest pull?
5. A ▨ can spread to fill any space.

LESSON 3

pages
104–108

1. Changes in the shape of an object made of clay are ▨ changes.
2. What are three kinds of physical changes?
3. How can liquid water be changed to a solid?
4. 0° Celsius is the ▨ of water.
5. What does heat do to the particles in ice?
6. Over time, water in a puddle changes into a ▨.
7. Liquid water ▨ to form water vapor.
8. What happens to liquid water when it is heated to a temperature of 100° Celsius?
9. Water vapor ▨ when it cools.
10. Burning wood causes a ▨ to take place.
11. How does rust form on a can?
12. Rusting is a ▨ change.
13. A change in the color of silver is a ▨ change.
14. What kind of change has taken place below?

Chapter 6   Study Guide

On a separate sheet of paper, write the word or words that best complete the sentence or answer the question.

LESSON 1

pages
116–120

1. A ▧ changes the way an object moves.
2. Would you need more force to move a chair or a pencil?
3. A ball thrown in the air is pulled down by the force of ▧.
4. The more ▧ an object has, the more gravity pulls on it.
5. If you weigh 85 pounds the pull of the earth's gravity on you is ▧ pounds.
6. What is one reason a ball stops when it is rolled across the floor?
7. You do ▧ when you move a book across the room.
8. You are able to do work because you have ▧.

LESSON 2

pages
122–127

1. What is a simple machine?
2. What kind of simple machines are each of the objects in the pictures?

3. If you use a board to lift a heavy object, you use the board as a ▨ .
4. Pushing down on a lever makes it move back and forth on its ▨ .
5. What kind of simple machine is a seesaw?
6. An ▨ is a simple machine with a flat surface that is higher at one end.
7. How do inclined planes help a person do work?
8. What are two examples of inclined planes?
9. How does a wedge help do work?
10. What simple machine is like an inclined plane wrapped around a rod?
11. The axle turns when you put force on the ▨ .
12. A ▨ can be used to move a load up, down, or sideways.
13. What kind of simple machine would you use to move an object to a hard-to-reach place?

LESSON 3

pages
130–131

1. What makes a paddle boat a compound machine?
2. The ▨ in a pencil sharpener sharpen the pencil.
3. Following ▨ can help keep you safe when using machines.
4. How is the person in this picture using a machine safely?

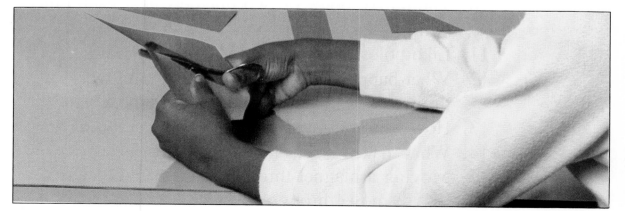

Chapter 7 Study Guide

On a separate sheet of paper, write the word or words that best complete the sentence or answer the question.

LESSON 1

pages
138–139

1. You use ___ when you move objects from one place to another.
2. What is energy of motion?
3. What happens to the energy from electricity when you turn on an electric lamp?
4. Plants get energy from the ___.

LESSON 2

pages
140–145

1. What happens when you rub two objects together?
2. Unlike charges ___ each other.
3. Like charges ___ each other.
4. A ___ pushes electric charges from place to place.
5. What is electric current?
6. A bulb lights when the ___ is complete.
7. Name two kinds of materials that do not carry electric current well.
8. What does the rubber on an electric cord do?
9. Magnetism is strongest at a magnet's ___.
10. The unlike poles of two magnets near each other will ___ each other.
11. Like poles of magnets will ___ each other.
12. What happens when electric current moves through loops of wire wrapped around a nail?
13. How can you make an electromagnet stronger?
14. What makes electromagnets useful?
15. Moving a magnet through loops of wire causes ___ to move through the wire.

1. What is a source?
2. ▨ is the flow of energy from warmer places and objects to cooler ones.
3. Tell why the ice cube in the picture below is melting.

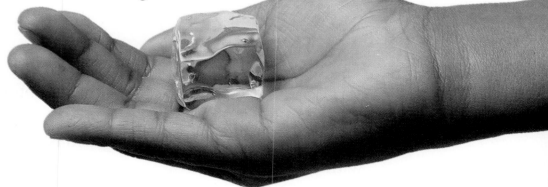

4. Why do many cooking pans have wooden handles?
5. Most liquids and gases are ▨ energy conductors.
6. ▨ is a measure of how fast particles of matter are moving.
7. The faster the particles of matter move, the ▨ the temperature of the matter.
8. Some thermometers measure temperature in degrees ▨.
9. What are thermostats used for?
10. Lining a building's roof and walls with an ▨ helps keeps heat from moving into the outside air.

1. What happens when light strikes an object?
2. Most of the light you see is ▨ light.
3. Light energy travels in ▨.
4. Light waves ▨ when they pass through a lens.
5. What are two uses of lenses?
6. Muscles in the iris of the eye control the size of the ▨.

Chapter 8 Study Guide

On a separate sheet of paper, write the word or words that best complete the sentence or answer the question.

LESSON 1

pages
164–166

1. When you hit a drum, parts of the drum ▧.
2. What is volume?
3. The more an object vibrates, the ▧ the sound.
4. A soft sound has ▧ volume than a loud sound.
5. What is pitch?
6. When an object vibrates ▧, it makes a sound with a high pitch.
7. An object that vibrates ▧ makes a sound with a low pitch.
8. How can you make a string vibrate more quickly?
9. Look at the rubber bands in the picture below. Tell which rubber band would have the sound with the highest pitch.

LESSON 2

pages
168–170

1. How does sound travel?
2. When a bell rings, it causes the ▧ around it to vibrate.
3. Sound waves get ▧ as they move away from the object that made them.
4. You can only hear sounds when they travel through ▧.

5. Sound moves more ▦ through liquids than it does through solids.
6. When sound bounces back from an object, you hear an ▦.
7. What kind of surfaces produce echoes best?

LESSON 3

pages
172–174

1. What happens to your vocal cords when you speak?
2. Vocal cords are thin flaps at the top of your ▦.
3. When you talk, air comes from your ▦ and passes between your vocal cords.
4. What does the outer part of the ear do?
5. What do sound waves do to the eardrum?
6. The eardrum makes the ▦ in the middle of your ear vibrate.
7. What part inside the ear tells your brain about sounds you hear?
8. Name the parts of the ear shown in the picture below.

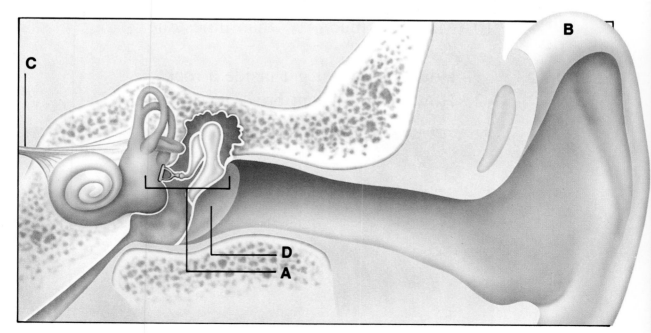

Chapter 9   Study Guide

On a separate sheet of paper, write the word or words that best complete the sentence or answer the question.

LESSON 1

pages
188–191

1. Each mineral has its own special .
2. What are some properties a mineral might have?
3. What makes the different colors you might see in a rock?
4. Why do minerals melt when they are deep inside the earth?
5. What happens when melted rocks reach the earth's surface?
6. What happens as layers of rocks and shells harden at the bottom of lakes and oceans?
7. Pressure can change igneous or sedimentary rock to ___.
8. Limestone is a ___ rock.
9. What happens to limestone when it is heated and squeezed inside the earth?
10. Marble is much ___ than limestone.

LESSON 2

pages
194–196

1. How does water get inside a rock?
2. How can this plant break apart the rock?

3. How can water break apart a rock?
4. Over many years, rock is broken down and forms ▨.
5. What materials make up soil?
6. What gives soil its dark color?
7. Soil can have pieces of different sizes and ▨.
8. Tiny grains in ▨ make it feel smooth.
9. Why might plants be unable to grow in clay soil?
10. ▨ is loose and easy to dig.
11. Why might plants not grow well in sandy soil?
12. Loam is a mixture of clay, sand, and ▨.
13. Which soil type would be best for growing plants?

LESSON 3

pages
198–201

1. The glass you drink from is made of ▨ that come from rock.
2. People need soil to get ▨ to make clothing.
3. What object do you use each day in school that was made from trees?
4. People use the mineral ▨ to make coins, electric wires, and pots and pans.
5. A rock with large amounts of copper would be copper ▨.
6. People who dig deep tunnels to search for minerals are ▨.
7. A ▨ is something people use that comes from the earth.
8. What is one way people can prevent wasting natural resources?
9. Why should farmers change the kinds of plants they grow from year to year?

Chapter 10 Study Guide

On a separate sheet of paper, write the word or words that best complete the sentence or answer the question.

LESSON 1

pages
208–210

1. Name the three layers of Earth shown below.

2. The land under the oceans makes up part of the earth's ▨.
3. Some of the rock inside the earth's mantle is solid and some of it is ▨.
4. What is the earth's core made of?
5. The ▨ part of the core has liquid iron.
6. The ▨ part of the core has solid iron.
7. ▨ of the earth's crust give scientists information about the inner layers of the earth.

LESSON 2

pages
212–215

1. What happens when rocks weather?
2. Water that ▓ and melts weathers rocks.
3. What parts of plants help weather rocks?
4. A material made from the ▓ in the air and water helps weather rocks.
5. Underground ▓ often form in weathered rock.
6. What has happened in the picture below?

LESSON 3

pages
218–221

1. What makes earthquakes dangerous?
2. Scientists try to ▓ earthquakes to help save lives.
3. What should you do if you are indoors during an earthquake?
4. What should you do if you are outdoors during an earthquake?
5. What is magma?
6. How does lava form new crust?
7. Why are volcano eruptions dangerous?

LESSON 4

pages
222–223

1. How does building roads and buildings change the earth's crust?
2. What can happen to the land when people cut down plants and trees?
3. How do people change the earth's crust when they search for ores?
4. How do earthworms change the earth's crust?
5. How do plants protect the land from erosion?

Chapter 11   Study Guide

On a separate sheet of paper, write the word or words that best complete the sentence or answer the question.

LESSON 1

pages
230–232

1. After you swim, water on your skin ▦ and becomes water vapor.
2. Water vapor in the air at night ▦ into drops of dew.
3. Why can you see your breath on a cold day?
4. As warm air rises, it ▦ .
5. When air condenses into tiny droplets of water high in the sky, a ▦ forms.
6. How is fog different from a cloud?
7. What kinds of clouds might you see in good weather?
8. What are cirrus clouds made of?
9. The weather can become ▦ when cumulus clouds become large.
10. You might see ▦ clouds during a light rain.
11. What has happened to the air in this picture?

1. Why can the tiny drops of water in clouds float in the air?
2. When drops of water become larger they might fall as ___.
3. Snow is one kind of ___.
4. Explain how the pictures below show the steps in the water cycle.

1. Thunderstorms occur when ___ air moves in to replace warm air that is quickly rising.
2. You see ___ when electric charges jump between clouds.
3. What do you often hear after lightning flashes?
4. Where do hurricanes form?
5. What two things make hurricanes dangerous?
6. What do tornados look like?
7. Why might a tornado be dangerous when it touches ground?
8. Where should people go when there is a hurricane or a tornado?

Chapter 12   Study Guide

On a separate sheet of paper, write the word or words that best complete the sentence or answer the question.

LESSON 1

pages
248–252

1. The earth is like a spinning top in the way that it ▨.
2. What is the earth's axis?
3. How long does it take the earth to complete one rotation?
4. Why does the earth have daylight and darkness each day?
5. What is the earth's orbit?
6. The earth's orbit is shaped like a ▨.
7. How long does it take the earth to complete one revolution around the sun?
8. What is one way in which the earth and the moon are different?
9. The moon is a satellite of the earth because it ▨ around the earth.
10. How long does it take for the moon to complete one revolution around the earth?
11. The moon's light comes from the ▨ light reflecting off the moon.
12. What are phases of the moon?

LESSON 2

pages
254–257

1. Stars are made of hot, glowing ▨.
2. The closer an object is to you, the ▨ it looks.
3. Why does the sun look larger than other stars?
4. The surface temperature of the sun is ▨ than the temperature in the center of the sun.
5. What is a planet?

6. Name the nine planets that revolve around the sun.
7. Why are the temperatures on Mercury and Venus very hot?
8. The temperatures on Earth are close to those on ▦.
9. Saturn is ▦ in size than Earth.
10. Jupiter is made mostly of ▦.
11. The rings around Saturn are made of ▦.
12. Look at the picture below. Which planet has the coolest temperatures.

LESSON 3

pages
260–263

1. What did the telescope help scientists learn about the earth?
2. What are astronauts?
3. What do scientists think caused the craters on the moon?
4. Venus is always covered by ▦.

Chapter 13   Study Guide

On a separate sheet of paper, write the word or words that best complete the sentence or answer the question.

LESSON 1

pages
276–278

1. What is the basic unit of an organism?
2. About how many cells make up your body?
3. What kind of cells cover and protect your body?
4. A group of nerve cells forms a nerve ▨.
5. Name four body organs.
6. Your heart and the other organs that work together to move blood through your body form a ▨.

LESSON 2

pages
280–282

1. Your bones and ▨ work together to help you move.
2. Your bones help ▨ organs in your body.
3. What kind of bones would the long parts of your body, like your legs, have?
4. Your shoulder and arm come together at the ▨.
5. What do the joints below do for the body?

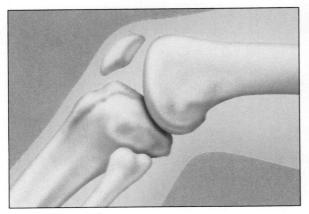
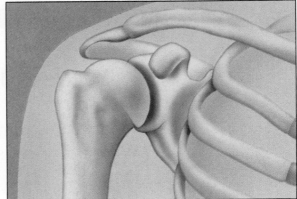

LESSON 3

pages
284–286

1. What helps give your body its shape?
2. When you move your arms or your legs you are using ___ muscles.
3. The ___ muscles of your body help you breathe and keep your heart working.
4. What kind of muscles work without you thinking about them?
5. When you move your body, your muscles ___ or become shorter and thicker.
6. When a muscle contracts, the ___ causes a bone to move.
7. Look at the boy in the picture. Tell what kind of muscles he is using to exercise.

Chapter 14 Study Guide

On a separate sheet of paper, write the word or words that best complete the sentence or answer the question.

LESSON 1

pages
294–296

1. What do you get from foods that help you grow and stay healthy?
2. How many servings from each food group are needed each day?
3. Look at the meal in the picture below. Tell why this is a healthy meal.

4. Why is it important to build physical fitness?
5. What are three types of exercise you can do to build physical fitness?
6. Your heart is a ▨ .
7. How does exercising help your heart?
8. How does sleeping help your body grow properly?

1. What is a disease that can spread from person to person?
2. Germs that might be on your skin can get into your body through a ___ .
3. What makes you feel sick?
4. What are two diseases caused by viruses?
5. Why is it important to keep your skin clean?
6. People who have diabetes cannot use ___ properly.
7. What are two ways in which people with diabetes can control their disease.
8. How does cancer hurt the body?
9. What are two ways doctors can treat some kinds of cancer?
10. What is one way people can help keep from getting lung cancer?
11. People protect themselves from ___ cancer by not spending long periods of time in the sun.
12. Cancer and ___ disease do not spread from person to person.

1. What is one way medicines help people?
2. Medicines are a kind of ___ .
3. Alcohol changes the way a person's ___ works.
4. What are two skills people might have trouble doing after they have drunk too much alcohol?
5. What drug is contained in tobacco?
6. What disease are people who smoke more likely to get than those who do not smoke?
7. Drugs that are against the law to use are ___ drugs.
8. What are two drugs that are against the law?
9. How can people protect themselves from the harmful effects of drugs?

Using Scientific Methods

Scientists ask many questions. No one may know the answers. Then scientists use scientific methods to find answers. Scientific methods include steps like the ones on the next page. Sometimes scientists use the steps in different order. You can use these steps to do the experiments in this section.

Identify Problem
The problem is usually a question such as, "Does sound travel faster through water than through air?"

Make Observations
Notice many things about an object such as its size, color, or shape.

State Hypothesis
Try to answer the problem.

Test Hypothesis
If possible, do an experiment to see if your hypothesis is correct. Then you should do the experiment again to be sure.

Collect Data
Your observations from the experiment are your data.

Study Data
You can understand your data better if you put it in charts and graphs.

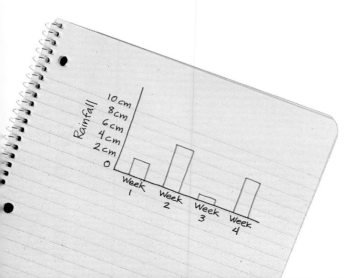

Make Conclusions
Decide if your hypothesis is correct.

Safety in Science

Scientists are careful when they do experiments. You need to be careful too. The next page shows some rules to remember.

- Never taste or smell unknown things.

- Handle thermometers carefully.

- Read each experiment carefully.

- Wear cover goggles when needed.

- Clean up spills right away.

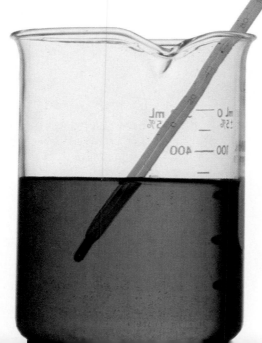

- Put things away when you finish an experiment.

- Wash your hands after each experiment.

347

Chapter 1 Experiment Skills

Setting Up a Control

Marianne wanted to have colored glass put in her bedroom window. She had several plants in her room. She wondered if colored light coming in through the window would change how the plants grew. She decided to do an experiment with plants and light to find out. In her experiment, Marianne found out that plants grow better in regular light than in colored light.

Read Marianne's experiment on the next page. Then answer the questions on this page.

Thinking About the Experiment

1. How many cups did Marianne use for her experiment?

Anything in an experiment that could change is called a variable. Only one variable should change during an experiment.

2. What variable did Marianne change between the two cups using cellophane?

3. Why was it important for the two cups to have all the same things except for the kind of cellophane?

The cup with a clear cellophane cone was the control in Marianne's experiment. It let in all light, just as clear glass would. Marianne could compare the plant from the control cup with the plant from the other cup.

4. Suppose Marianne did not have a control cup. Could she tell if the plant with red cellophane was growing any differently? Why or why not?

See pages 344-347 to review scientific methods and safety.

Experimenting with Plants

Problem
How does red light affect bean seed growth?

Hypothesis
A bean plant will not grow as well in red light as in regular sunlight.

Materials
2 bean seeds
cellophane, clear
    and red squares
metric ruler
2 plastic cups
potting soil
stapler
tape
water

Procedure
1. Fill one of the cups with water. Soak 2 bean seeds in it overnight.
2. Empty the water from the cup. Fill both cups more than half full with potting soil.
3. Put a seed in each. Add a little soil on top of the seeds.
4. Water both cups well.
5. Make cones out of the two squares of cellophane. Use a staple to keep their shapes.
6. Tape a cone onto each cup.
7. Place the cups in a sunny spot.
8. After a week, measure the height of the plants. Count the number of leaves on each.

Data and Observations

	Red wrap	Clear wrap
Plant height		
Number of leaves		

Conclusions
You might do Marianne's experiment to find your own data and make observations. Draw conclusions based on your data.

Practice Setting Up a Control
Plants need minerals to grow. Suppose you want to find out if plants grow better when minerals are added to the soil.
1. How would you change Marianne's experiment to find out how well plants grow with added minerals?
2. What would the control in your experiment be?

349

Chapter 2 Experiment Skills

Making Observations

Tom liked visiting his uncle's farm. One day he noticed some tiny animals called mealworms. They were living in a damp sack of grain that an animal had spilled. Tom wondered if the mealworms like to live in a damp place or a dry place. He decided to do an experiment with ten mealworms to find out.

At the end of his experiment, Tom observed that only two of the ten mealworms crawled to a dry place. All the rest crawled to a wet place.

Read Tom's experiment on the next page. Then answer the questions on this page.

Thinking About the Experiment

1. Where did Tom first observe the mealworms?
2. What was Tom trying to find out in his experiment?
3. What materials did Tom use in his experiment?

Making observations means watching closely. Tom used his observations to make a conclusion.

4. How many mealworms did Tom observe at the dry sponge?
5. How many mealworms did Tom observe at the wet sponge?
6. What conclusion do you think Tom made?

Experimenting with Mealworms

Problem
Do mealworms prefer to live in a damp place or a dry place?

Hypothesis
Mealworms prefer to live in a damp place.

Materials
small cake pan   2 sponges
10 mealworms   water
cardboard   sand

Procedure
1. Fill the bottom of the pan with sand.
2. Wet 1 sponge. Then squeeze it.
3. Place the wet sponge in the sand on one side of the pan.
4. Place the dry sponge opposite the wet sponge.
5. Use a piece of cardboard to put the mealworms on the sand in the middle of the pan.
6. Observe the mealworms after 30 minutes. Write down how many are at each sponge.

Data and Observations

	Number of mealworms
Wet sponge	
Dry sponge	

Conclusions
You might do Tom's experiment to find your own data and make observations. Draw conclusions based on your data.

Practice Making Observations

1. Suppose you observed the mealworms for five days. Set up the data table that you would use.
2. Suppose you wanted to see if the mealworms grew. How could you make observations about growth?
3. What would you use to measure how much they grew?

351

Chapter 3 Experiment Skills

Stating a Hypothesis

When Robert started to make a peanut butter sandwich, he saw that mold was growing on the bread. He also noticed water on the bread wrapper. Robert wondered if water helped the mold to grow. He thought mold would grow faster on wet bread than on dry bread. He did an experiment with dry and wet bread to see if he was right. In his experiment, Robert observed that more mold grew on the wet bread than on the dry bread.

Read Robert's experiment on the next page. Then answer the questions on this page.

Thinking About the Experiment

1. What question did Robert have about how fast bread mold grows?
2. How would Robert finish this sentence? "Mold grows faster on . . ."

Robert's sentence is his hypothesis. A good hypothesis is one that can be tested with an experiment.

3. What materials did Robert use to test the hypothesis he made?
4. What procedure did Robert follow to test his hypothesis?

Suppose Robert wanted to show that mold grow better in the dark than in light.

5. What would be his new hypothesis?

See pages 344-347 to review scientific methods and safety.

Experimenting with Mold

Problem
Will mold grow faster on wet bread than on dry bread?

Hypothesis
Give your own hypothesis for this experiment.

Materials
2 slices bread   2 plastic
marker   sandwich bags
masking tape   water

Procedure
1. Leave 2 slices of bread out overnight. This will allow mold to start growing on the bread.
2. The next day, place 1 of the slices in a plastic sandwich bag.
3. Wet the second slice. Let several drops of water fall from your finger onto the bread in several places. Place the slice in a plastic sandwich bag.
4. Tape both bags shut. Label them by writing on the tape.
5. Place the bags in a warm, dark place.
6. Observe the bread slices through the plastic every other day for 1 week. Write your observations in a data table.
7. After the experiment, throw the closed bags away.

Data and Observations

	Day			
	1	3	5	7
Wet bread				
Dry bread				

Conclusions
You might do Robert's experiment to find your own data and make observations. Draw conclusions based on your data.

Practice Stating a Hypothesis

Some breads have chemicals called preservatives that keep the bread from getting moldy. Other breads do not have preservatives. Do preservatives keep mold from growing on bread?
1. Write a hypothesis to answer this question.
2. How could you test this hypothesis?

353

Chapter 4 Experiment Skills

Setting Up an Experiment

Lori's grandmother lived on a farm with a big pond. A garden was near the pond. Lori noticed that the water nearest the garden looked greener than the rest of the pond. This water was covered with many tiny floating duckweed plants. Her grandmother said she used fertilizer in the garden. Lori wondered if the fertilizer had washed into the pond and made the duckweed near the garden grow quickly.

She set up an experiment using pond water, duckweed, and fertilizer to find out. In her experiment, Lori found out that duckweed with fertilizer grows faster than duckweed without fertilizer.

Read Lori's experiment on the next page. Then answer the questions on this page.

Thinking About the Experiment

1. What was Lori's hypothesis?
2. How many cups did Lori use to set up her experiment?

When Lori set up her experiment, she made sure the cups were the same size. She put the same amount of pond water with duckweed in each cup. Then she put the cups in the sun. Lori changed one variable. This was the variable she was testing.

3. What variable did Lori change?

The cup without fertilizer was Lori's control.

4. How did the control help Lori with her observations?

See pages 344-347 to review scientific methods and safety.

Experimenting with Fertilizer on Plants

Problem
Does fertilizer change how fast duckweed grows?

Hypothesis
Fertilizer helps duckweed grow quickly in water.

Materials
gloves
2 large
  plastic cups
marker
phosphate fertilizer
water with
  duckweed
medicine dropper

Procedure
1. Fill each cup half full with pond water.
2. Put on the gloves. Add 10 drops of fertilizer to one of the cups. Stir the fertilizer in the water.
3. Place 20 duckweed plants in each cup.
4. Record the number of plants in your data table beside "At start."
5. Label the cups. Put them in a sunny place.
6. Observe the cups once a week for two weeks. Count the duckweed plants in each cup each time. Record the numbers on your data table.

Data and Observations
Number of Duckweed

	With fertilizer	Without fertilizer
At start		
After 1 week		
After 2 weeks		

Conclusions
You might do Lori's experiment to find your own data and make observations. Draw conclusions based on your data.

Practice Setting Up an Experiment

Does the temperature of water affect how fast duckweed plants grow? Suppose you wanted to set up an experiment to find out. You could use two cups of pond water with duckweed.
1. What would be the same about each cup?
2. What would be the variable?
3. What would be the control?

Identifying Variables

Mario was making a snack. His father had given him a cup of warm water. Mario was mixing a packet of instant tomato soup in the water. He noticed that the instant soup mixed quickly in the warm water. He wondered if the temperature of water changes how fast something will mix. Mario decided to do an experiment to find out. In his experiment, he mixed sugar in water of different temperatures.

Read Mario's experiment on the next page. Then answer the questions on this page.

Thinking About the Experiment

In his experiment, Mario used jars that were the same size. He put the same amount of water and of sugar in each jar.

1. What else was the same for all the jars?
2. What was different in the three jars?

A variable is anything in the experiment that can be changed. An experiment should test only one variable at a time.

3. What variable did Mario want to test?
4. Would it have been a mistake for Mario to stir the liquid in only one of the jars? Explain your answer.

Experimenting with Mixtures

Problem
Does the temperature of water change how fast something will mix in it?

Hypothesis
A substance will mix faster in warm water than in cold water.

Materials
warm water	sugar
room temperature water	spoon
cold water	clock
3 jars of the same size	tape
graduated cylinder	marker

Procedure
1. Label the jars *Warm*, *Cold*, and *Room temperature.*
2. Put 25 mL of sugar in each jar.
3. Measure 100 mL of warm water. Pour it into the jar marked *Warm.* Observe the time.
4. Stir the sugar and water until the sugar crystals disappear.
5. Observe how much time the sugar took to disappear. Write the time on a chart like this one.

6. Follow the same procedure again. Add cold water to the jar marked *Cold.* Add room temperature water to the jar marked *Room temperature.*

Data and Observations

Water temperature	Time for sugar to disappear
Warm	
Room temperature	
Cold	

Conclusions
You might do Mario's experiment to find your own data and make observations. Draw conclusions based on your data.

Practice Identifying Variables

Suppose you wanted to do an experiment to find out if the amount of water changes how fast sugar will dissolve.
1. How would you set up the experiment?
2. What would have to be the same in your experiment?
3. What variable changes?

357

Setting Up an Experiment

Jeff's father used a wedge to split wood. The hammer pushed the wedge into the wood and the wood split or cracked. Jeff wondered if the sharpness of a wedge makes a difference in how well it works. He decided to set up an experiment to find out. Jeff knew it was not safe to use his father's sharp wedge. He used wedges made out of chalk.

Read Jeff's experiment on the next page. Then answer the questions on this page.

Thinking About the Experiment

Jeff set up his experiment carefully. He kept every part of the setup the same except for one variable. That was the variable he wanted to test.

1. What variable is Jeff testing?
2. What variables did Jeff keep the same in the experiment?
3. What kind of data did Jeff get from the experiment?

Experimenting with Wedges

Problem
Does the sharpness of a wedge make a difference in how easily it can be pushed into something?

Hypothesis
A wedge is most useful if it has a sharp edge.

Materials
3 pieces of chalk
large ball of modeling clay
rough surface

Procedure
1. Rub one end of each piece of chalk on the rough surface to make a wedge shape. Make the ends of the wedges sharp, rounded, and flat.
2. Push each chalk wedge into the ball of clay.
3. Record how hard or easy it is to push each wedge.

Data and Observations

Wedge shape	Force needed
Rounded	
Flat-ended	
Sharp	

Conclusions
You might do Jeff's experiment to find your own data and make observations. Draw conclusions based on your data.

Practice Setting Up an Experiment

Suppose you wanted to know if the material a wedge is made of affects how well it works.
1. What might be your hypothesis?
2. What variable would you test?
3. How would you set up your experiment?

Chapter 7 Experiment Skills

Making Conclusions

Kelly was studying magnets at school. Her teacher said there were ways you could make your own magnet. He said that to do this you would need only a paper clip and a bar magnet. These were the only directions her teacher would give.

Kelly decided she would do an experiment to find out how to make a magnet. She tried to make a magnet in three different ways.

Read Kelly's experiment on the next page. Then answer the questions on this page.

Thinking About the Experiment

Kelly tested the paper clip that the laid next to the magnet. It did not pick up any small paper clips.
1. What is Kelly's conclusion about making a magnet this way?

Kelly tested the paper clip that she rubbed back and forth with a magnet. The paper clip picked up another paper clip.
2. What is Kelly's conclusion?

Next, Kelly tested the paper clip that she rubbed in one direction with the magnet. The paper clip picked up four other paper clips.
3. What is Kelly's conclusion about the best way to make a magnet?

Experimenting with Magnets

Problem
How can you make a magnet?

Hypothesis
Rubbing a paper clip with one end of a bar magnet can turn the paper clip into a magnet.

Materials
three large paper clips
bar magnet
several small paper clips

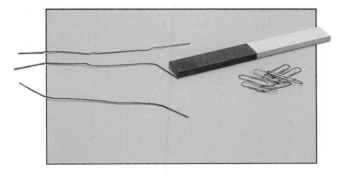

Procedure
1. Straighten out the large clips.
2. Set one end of the magnet next to one end of a straightened clip for 30 minutes.
3. Rub one end of the magnet back and forth over the end of another paper clip. Do this at least 20 times.
4. Rub one end of the magnet over the end of the third paper clip. But this time rub the clip in only one direction. Do this at least 20 times.

5. Test each of your straightened clips to see how well they are magnetized. Write down how many small paper clips are attracted to each of your homemade magnets.

Data and Observations

Straightened paper clips	Number of paper clips picked up
Laid next to magnet	
Rubbed back and forth	
Rubbed in only one direction	

Conclusions
You might do Kelly's experiment to find your own data and make observations. Draw conclusions based on your data.

Practice Making Conclusions

1. Suppose the paper clip laid next to the magnet was able to pick up the most paper clips. What would be your conclusion to this experiment?
2. Suppose a conclusion does not agree with a hypothesis. Explain why the experiment is still useful.

361

Chapter 8 Experiment Skills

Collecting Data

Ann tapped gently with a spoon on her glass of fruit juice. She was keeping time with music on the radio. Then she drank most of the juice. When she tapped the glass again she noticed that the sound was different. The sound was higher with less juice in the glass.

Ann wondered if this would be true if she tapped bottles. She thought of this hypothesis to answer her question. *The more liquid in a bottle, the lower the sound made when you tap on the bottle.* She decided to set up an experiment to test her hypothesis.

Read Ann's experiment on the next page. Then answer the questions on this page.

Thinking About the Experiment

In an experiment, you collect data about the problem you want to solve.

1. What is the problem in Ann's experiment?
2. What did Ann collect data about?
3. How did Ann organize the data she collected?
4. After looking at her data, what do you think Ann's conclusions were?

Experimenting with Sound

Problem
Does the amount of liquid in a bottle make a difference in the sound made by tapping on the bottle?

Hypothesis
The more liquid in a bottle, the lower the sound made when you tap on the bottle.

Materials
4 bottles of the same size
water
spoon

Procedure
1. Put four bottles on a desk or table.
2. Leave the first bottle empty. Put a little water in the second bottle. Fill the third bottle about halfway. Fill the fourth bottle almost full.
3. Tap the first and second bottles gently with a spoon. Compare the sounds. Record which is higher.

4. Tap the third bottle. Compare the sound with the sounds of the first and second bottles. Record your observations.
5. Tap the fourth bottle and compare the sounds. Record your observations.

Data and Observations

Amount of water in bottle	Sound from tapping
Empty	
A little water	
Half full	
Full	

Conclusions
You might do Ann's experiment to collect your own data and make observations. Make conclusions based on your data.

Practice Collecting Data

Suppose you wanted to do an experiment to find out if the size of the bottle makes a difference in the sound produced.
1. What might your hypothesis be?
2. How could you set up an experiment to test the hypothesis?
3. What data is important to collect in your experiment?

Chapter 9 Experiment Skills

Making Observations

Alice helped her father get the soil in the garden ready for new plants. They mixed decaying leaves and grass clippings into the soil. Alice wondered if plants grow better in mixed soil than in sandy soil or in gravel. Alice did an experiment to find out.

She planted bean seeds in different kinds of soil and in gravel. She observed and measured the growing plants. In the experiment, Alice found out that plants grow best in mixed soil.

Read Alice's experiment on the next page. Then answer the questions on this page.

Thinking About the Experiment

The first step in solving a problem is to make observations.
1. What observations did Alice make about the plants?
2. What units of measurement did Alice use?
3. Where did Alice record her observations and measurements?

Alice treated the bean seeds alike except for one thing.
4. What variable did Alice change?
5. What was Alice trying to find out about the plants?

See pages 344-347 to review scientific methods and safety.

Experimenting with Soil

Problem
Do plants grow better in some substances than in others?

Hypothesis
Plants grow better in some substances than in others.

Materials
9 bean seeds soaked
   in water overnight
3 paper or plastic cups
loam, sand, and fine gravel
large plastic or metal tray
measuring cup   water
metric ruler   pencil
masking tape   marker

Procedure
1. Label the cups *1, 2,* and *3.*
2. Poke a hole in the bottom of each cup with a pencil.
3. Put soil in cup *1,* gravel in cup *2,* and sand in cup *3.*
4. Plant 3 seeds in each cup. Plant the seeds about 2 cm deep.
5. Put the tray of cups on a windowsill.
6. Every 3 days, add 15 mL of water to each cup.
7. On days you water the cups, observe each plant. Measure the height of the plants in centimeters. Record your observations and measurements on a chart like the one shown.

Data and Observations

Cup	Substance	Height and appearance
1		
2		
3		

Conclusions
You might do Alice's experiment to find your own data and make observations. Draw conclusions based on your data.

Practice Making Observations

Suppose you wanted to find out if the amount of water makes a difference in how a plant grows.
1. What hypothesis could you make?
2. How would you set up an experiment to test your hypothesis?
3. What observations would you make?

365

Chapter 10 Experiment Skills

Identifying Variables

Bob was digging in his garden when it started to rain. He ran inside and left a pile of dirt out in the rain. Then he watched the pouring rain wash away the dirt. He wondered if a lot of rain washed away more dirt than only a little bit of rain could. He decided to do an experiment using sand and water to find out.

In his experiment Bob found out that a lot of water washes away more sand than a small amount of water. Read Bob's experiment on the next page. Then answer the questions on this page.

Thinking About the Experiment

Bob made three mounds of sand all the same size. He poured a different amount of water over each mound.

1. Why was it important for Bob to make all three mounds of sand the same size?
2. What did Bob use to shape the mounds?

Only one variable should change in an experiment. That is the variable you want to test.

3. What variable did Bob want to test?
4. How did he test this variable?

See pages 344-347 to review scientific methods and safety.

Experimenting with Sand and Water

Problem
Does a large amount of water wash away more sand than a small amount of water does?

Hypothesis
A large amount of water washes away more sand than a small amount does.

Materials
1 plastic cup	sand
3 pans of the same size	marker
measuring cup	water
3 plastic straws	

Procedure
1. Fill the plastic cup with sand. Pack sand firmly in the cup.
2. Turn the cup over into a pan. Remove the cup so that the sand forms a mound.
3. Repeat step 2 to form the same size sand mounds in each of the other pans.
4. Stand a straw up in the center of each mound. Mark how high the sand comes on each straw.
5. Pour 50 mL of water over the first mound. Observe what happens to the sand. Record how the height of the sand changes.
6. Pour 250 mL of water over the second mound. Pour 500 mL of water over the third mound. Record your observations.

Data and Observations
Effect of Water on Mounds

	How mounds look after using water
Mound 1	
Mound 2	
Mound 3	

Conclusions
You might do Bob's experiment to find your own data and make observations. Make conclusions based on your data.

Practice Identifying Variables

Suppose you wanted to do an experiment to find out how much sand is washed away when the same amount of water is poured onto different amounts of sand.
1. What should be the variable in this experiment?
2. How would this experiment be different from Bob's experiment?

367

Chapter 11 Experiment Skills

Testing a Hypothesis

Nathan was keeping a weather chart as part of his science project. He noticed that the air seemed to get colder on clear nights than on cloudy nights. He wondered if clouds really affected the temperature of the air below them. He thought of this hypothesis as a possible answer to his question: *Covering air in some way helps keep it warm.*

Nathan did an experiment to test his hypothesis. He placed thermometers in two boxes. Then he covered both boxes and placed them in the sun for twenty minutes.

Read Nathan's experiment on the next page. Decide if Nathan's hypothesis was correct. Then answer the questions on this page.

Thinking About the Experiment

Usually in an experiment, parts of the experiment take the place of things in nature. For example, the bottom of Nathan's shoe boxes act like the ground.

1. What does the plastic cover on the boxes take the place of?
2. Why did Nathan remove the cover from one of his boxes?
3. To test his hypothesis, did Nathan really need to remove the cover from one box? Why?
4. What do you think happened to the temperature of the air in each of the boxes?

Experimenting with Heating Air

Problem
Do clouds help keep air warm?

Hypothesis
Covering air in some way helps keep it warm.

Materials
2 shoe boxes
   the same size
2 thermometers

plastic wrap
masking tape
60-watt bulb

Procedure
1. Place a thermometer in the bottom of 2 shoe boxes. Cover both with a double thickness of clear plastic wrap.
3. Set the boxes under a lighted bulb, about 10 cm from the bulb. Be careful, light bulbs can cause burns!
4. After 20 minutes, remove the plastic wrap from one of the boxes.

5. Record the temperature in each box every minute for the next 5 minutes. Do not remove the thermometers.

Data and Observations
Temperature of Air in Each Box

Time	Uncovered Box	Covered Box
0		
1		
2		
3		
4		
5		

Conclusions
You might do Nathan's experiment to find your own data and make observations. Draw conclusions based on your data.

Practice Testing a Hypothesis
1. Suppose you wanted to do an experiment to find out if the color of the ground affects how fast air heats up. What would be your hypothesis?
2. How could you change Nathan's experiment to test your hypothesis?
3. What variable would change in testing this hypothesis?

369

Chapter 12 Experiment Skills

Using Models

Lupe observed an eclipse of the moon one evening. She watched the shape of the full moon change as though something was covering it. She knew that the shadow of the earth is important in an eclipse. She wondered what the positions of the moon, sun, and earth are during an eclipse. She made this hypothesis to answer her question. *The earth blocks the sun's light from shining on the moon during an eclipse of the moon.* Lupe decided to experiment with a model to understand how an eclipse takes place.

Read Lupe's experiment on the next page. Then answer the questions on this page.

Thinking About the Experiment

Models stand for the real thing.
1. In Lupe's model what do the flashlight, the globe, and the plastic ball stand for?
2. How did Lupe's model help her test her hypothesis?
3. After reading Lupe's experiment, draw sketches of where you think the earth, moon, and sun would be during an eclipse of the moon.

See pages 344-347 to review scientific methods and safety.

Experimenting with Models

Problem
What causes an eclipse of the moon?

Hypothesis
The earth blocks the sun's light from shining on the moon during an eclipse of the moon.

Materials
globe   dowel rod
flashlight   modeling clay
plastic foam ball meter stick

Procedure
1. Push one end of the dowel rod halfway into the ball.
2. Push the other end of the rod into the clay. Use the clay to hold the rod and ball upright.
3. Place the globe on the floor or on a table. Place the rod and ball 50 cm from the globe.
4. Darken the room. Shine the light on the globe from a distance of 1 m.
5. Move the light around the globe until the shadow of the globe covers the ball. Observe the positions of the light, globe, and ball.
6. Draw three circles in the data table to show the positions in Step 5. Your table shows a model of an eclipse.

Data and Observations

Sun	Earth	Moon

Conclusions
You might do Lupe's experiment to collect your own data and make observations. Draw conclusions based on your data.

Practice Using Models
Suppose you wanted to find the positions of the earth, moon, and sun during the moon's phases.
1. What would you use to make models to experiment with the moon's phases?
2. How could you find the moon's positions at different phases?

Chapter 13 Experiment Skills

Testing a Hypothesis

Andy helped his father rake leaves. The muscles in his arms got tired and sore. He had learned at school that he had two kinds of muscles, voluntary and involuntary. He knew that involuntary muscles work all the time. He wondered if they got tired and sore like voluntary muscles. He thought of this hypothesis to answer his question. *Involuntary muscles can work longer without getting sore than voluntary muscles can.*

Andy set up an experiment to test his hypothesis. He compared how voluntary muscles and involuntary muscles felt after they each worked for a minute.

Read Andy's experiment on the next page. Then answer the questions on this page.

Thinking About the Experiment

1. What muscles did Andy test in his experiment?
2. How long did Andy test each muscle?

A variable is anything in the experiment that changes. An experiment should have only one variable that changes. The variable is the one you are testing.

3. What variable is being tested in this experiment?
4. What things stayed the same in the experiment?

See pages 344-347 to review scientific methods and safety.

Experimenting with Muscles

Problem
Do involuntary muscles get tired and sore as easily as voluntary muscles?

Hypothesis
Involuntary muscles can work longer without getting sore than voluntary muscles can.

Materials
clock or watch with a second hand

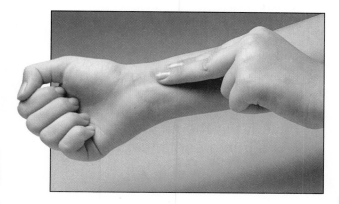

Procedure
1. Make a fist. Squeeze and open your fist for 1 minute. Try to squeeze 90 times in a minute.
2. Record how many times you squeezed your hand. Record how your hand muscles feel.
3. Count the number of times your heart beats in a minute. Feel your heartbeat by putting your hand on your chest. You can count the beats by feeling the pulse on your wrist.

4. Record the number of heartbeats in a minute. Record how your heart muscle feels.

Data and Observations

Kind of muscle muscle	Number of beats	How the muscles feel
Hand (voluntary)		
Heart (involuntary)		

Conclusions
You might do Andy's experiment to find your own data and make observations. Draw conclusions based on your data.

Practice Testing a Hypothesis

Suppose you wonder if one kind of voluntary muscle can work faster than another kind.
1. What hypothesis might you make?
2. How could you set up an experiment to test your hypothesis?
3. What variable would you change in your experiment?

Chapter 14 Experiment Skills

Making Conclusions

Sarah had some pizza in a box. She noticed a shiny grease spot on the box. It came from the fat in the pizza. She knew that eating too much fat was not good for a person's health. Sarah wondered what foods she ate had fat in them. She decided to do an experiment to find out.

In Sarah's experiment, she put several kinds of foods into paper bags. The next day, she looked at the bags. The foods that made grease spots had fat in them.

Read Sarah's experiment on the next page. Then answer the questions on this page.

Thinking About the Experiment

1. What was Sarah trying to find out in her experiment?

Sarah tested an apple, a potato, some oatmeal, and peanut butter.
2. Which of these foods do you think have fat? Write your answer in a sentence. This sentence is your hypothesis.

When Sarah looked at the bags the next day, she saw only one grease spot.
3. Which of the foods had fat in it? Write your answer in a sentence.

Your answer to question 3 is a conclusion. You can also make another conclusion from this experiment.
4. Which of the foods did not have fat in them? Write your answer in a sentence.

See pages 344-347 to review scientific methods and safety.

Experimenting with Fat

Problem

What are some foods that have fat in them?

Hypothesis

Write your own hypothesis for this experiment.

Materials

1 slice of apple
dry oatmeal
peanut butter
newspaper

1 slice of raw potato
4 small paper bags

Procedure

1. Place the potato slice and apple slice into different paper bags.
2. Put a tablespoon of oatmeal and tablespoon of peanut butter into different bags.

3. Fold the bags over so the food does not spill out. Place the bags on the newspaper.
4. Let the bags sit overnight.
5. The next day, look on the outside of each bag. A fatty food will leave a grease spot.

Data and Observations

Food	Grease spot	No grease spot
Apple		
Oatmeal		
Potato		
Peanut butter		

Conclusions

You might do Sarah's experiment to find your own data and make observations. Draw conclusions based on your data.

Practice Making Conclusions

Matt put peanuts, almonds, cashews, walnuts, and pecans in five different paper bags. All the nuts made greasy spots in the bags.

1. What conclusion did he make about the nuts he tested?
2. Should he make the same conclusion about all nuts? Explain.

Glossary

A

alcohol (al′kə hôl), a drug that can be harmful and is found in beer, wine, and liquor.

amphibian (am fib′ē ən), an animal that has a backbone and lives some of the time in water and some of the time on land.

astronaut (as′trə nôt), a person who travels in space.

atom (at′əm), a small particle that makes up matter.

axis (ak′sis), imaginary line through the center of the earth around which the earth rotates.

B

bacteria (bak tir′ē ə), organisms made of one cell that can be seen through a microscope.

C

cancer, a disease in which cells that are not normal destroy healthy body cells.

carbon dioxide (kär′bən dī ok′sīd), a gas in the air that plants use to make food.

cell (sel), the basic unit of an organism.

chemical (kem′ə kəl) **change,** a change that causes matter to become a new kind of matter.

376

circuit (sėr/kit), the path along which electric current moves.

cirrus (sir/əs) **clouds,** feathery white clouds made of ice.

clay soil, tightly packed soil with tiny grains.

cold-blooded (kōld/ blud/id), an animal with a body temperature that changes with the temperature of the air or water around it.

community (kə myū/nə tē), all organisms that live in a place.

compound machine (kom/pound mə shēn/), a machine made of two or more simple machines.

condense (kən dens/), to change from a gas to a liquid.

conductor (kən duk/tər), a material that carries energy.

consumer (kən sü/mər), an organism that eats food.

contract (kən trakt/), the action of a muscle becoming shorter.

control (kən trōl/), the part of an experiment that does not change.

core (kôr), Earth's center part.

crater (krā/tər), a large hole in the ground shaped like a bowl.

crust (krust), the outer layer of the earth.

cumulus (kyü/myə ləs) **clouds,** clouds that look like cotton.

D

data (dā/tə), information gathered from an experiment.

decay (di kā/), to slowly rot.

degrees Celsius (di grēz/ sel/sē əs), metric unit for measuring temperature.

dew (dü), water vapor that condenses on cool surfaces, usually during the night.

diabetes (dī/ə bē/tis), a disease in which the body cannot use sugar properly.

dinosaur (dī/nə sôr), one of a group of extinct reptiles that lived millions of years ago.

disease (də zēz/), an illness.

E

eardrum, thin skin that covers the middle ear.

earthquake (ėrth/kwāk/), a shaking of the earth's crust.

echo (ek/ō), a sound that bounces back from an object.

electric charges (i lek/tric chärjəz), tiny bits of electricity in all matter.

electric current (kėr/ənt), the smooth flow of electric charges from one place to another.

electromagnet (i lek/trō mag/nit), a wire coil that is a magnet when electric current moves through it.

endangered (en dān′jərd) **organisms,** kinds of organisms that are very few in number and might someday no longer be found on the earth.

energy (en′ər jē), the ability to do work.

energy of motion (mō′shən), energy of moving objects.

erosion (i rō′zhən), the movement of soil or rocks by wind or water.

erupt (i rupt′), to burst out.

evaporate (i vap′ə rāt′), to change from a liquid to a gas.

extinct (ek stingkt′) **organisms,** organisms that no longer are found on the earth.

F

fibers (fī′bərz), strong thin threads in plants that can be used to make cloth.

fog, a cloud that forms just above the surface of the earth.

food chain, the way food passes from one organism to another organism in a community.

force (fôrs), a push or pull.

fossil (fos′əl), the hardened remains or traces of an animal or plant of a former age.

friction (frik′shən), force caused by objects rubbing together that slows moving objects.

fuel (fyü′əl), coal, wood, oil, or any other material that can be burned to produce useful heat or power.

fulcrum (ful′krəm), point on which a lever is supported and turns.

fungus (fung′gəs), an organism, such as a mold or mushroom, that gets food from dead material or by growing on food or a living thing. [Plural: **fungi** (fun′jī)]

G

gear (gir), a wheel with jagged edges like teeth.

germinate (jėr′mə nāt), begin to grow and develop.

gills (gils), the parts of fish that are used to take in oxygen from the water.

gravity (grav′ə tē), the force that makes objects pull toward each other.

H

habitat (hab′ə tat), the place where an organism lives.

humus (hyü′məs), the decayed matter in soil.

hurricane (hėr′ə kān), a huge storm that forms over a warm ocean and has strong winds and heavy rains.

hypothesis (hī poth′ə sis), a possible answer to a problem.

I

igneous (ig′nē əs) **rock,** a rock formed from melted minerals.

illegal (i lē′gəl) **drug,** a drug that is against the law to use or have.

image (im′ij), a copy.

inclined (in klīnd′) **plane,** a simple machine that is a flat surface with one end higher than the other.

insect (in′sekt), an animal with three main body parts, six legs, and no backbone.

insulator (in′sə lā′tər), a material through which energy cannot easily flow.

involuntary (in vol′ən ter′ē) **muscle,** a muscle that works without a person's control.

iris (ī′ris), colored part of the eye.

J

joint, a place where bones join together; different joints allow different movement.

L

larva (lär′və), the young of an animal that is different from the adult. [Plural: **larvae** (lär′vē)]

lava (lä′və), hot, melted rock that flows from a volcano.

lens (lenz), a piece of clear material that bends light waves that pass through it.

lever (lev′ər), a simple machine made of a bar that is supported underneath at some point.

life cycle (sī′kəl), the stages in the life of a plant or animal.

load (lōd), an object that is being moved.

loam (lōm), soil that is a mixture of clay, sand, and humus.

M

machine (mə shēn), a tool that makes work easier.

magma (mag′ma), hot, melted rock deep inside the earth.

magnet (mag′nit), object that attracts objects with iron in them.

magnetism (mag′nə tiz′əm), the force around a magnet.

mammal (mam′əl), an animal with a backbone and hair.

mantle (man′tl), the middle layer of the earth.

mass (mas), how much matter an object contains.

matter (mat′ər), a substance of which all objects are made.

medicine (med′ə sən), a drug that can help protect people from sickness, or treat or cure a disease.

metamorphic (met′ə môr′fik) **rock,** an igneous or sedimentary rock that was changed by heat or pressure.

mineral (min′ər əl), material that was never alive and that can be found in soil.

N

natural resource (nach′ər əl ri′sôrs), something people use that comes from the earth.

nerve (nėrv), a body part that carries messages to the brain.

nicotine (nik′ə tēn′), a drug in tobacco that can harm the body.

nutrient (nü′trē ənt), a material that plants and animals need to live and grow.

O

orbit (ôr′bit), a closed, curved path an object follows as it moves around another object.

ore (ôr), rock with useful minerals.

organ (ôr′gən), a group of tissues that work together to do a job in the body.

organism (ôr′gə niz′əm), a living thing.

oxygen (ok′sə jən), a gas in air that living things need to stay alive.

P

particle (pär′tə kəl), a little bit.

petal (pet′l), the outside, colored part of a flower.

phase (fāz), the shape of the lighted part of the moon as it is seen from the earth.

physical (fiz′ə kel) **change,** a change in the size, shape, state, or appearance of matter.

physical (fiz′ə kəl) **fitness,** the ability to work, play, and exercise without getting tired or injured easily.

pitch (pich), how high or low a sound is.

planet (plan′it), a large body of matter revolving around the sun.

pollen (pol′ən), a fine yellowish powder in a flower.

pollinate (pol′ə nāt), to carry pollen to the center part of a flower.

pollution (pə lü′shən), anything harmful added to the air, water, or land.

population (pop′yə lā′shən), organisms of the same kind that live in the same place.

precipitation (pri sip′ə tā′shən), moisture that falls to the ground.

predator (pred′ə tər), organism that captures and eats other organisms.

prey (prā), organism that is captured and eaten by another organism.

prism (priz′əm), a clear piece of glass or plastic that is used for separating white light.

producer (prə dü′sər), an organism that makes food.

property (prop′ər tē), something about an object that can be observed, such as size or shape.

protist (prō′tist), an organism that lives in a wet place and has one or more cells.

pulley (pul′ē), a simple machine made of a wheel and a rope.

pupa (pyü′pə), stage in the insect life cycle between larva and adult. [Plural: **pupae** (pyü′pē)]

pupil (pyü′pəl), the opening in the eye that lets in light.

R

recycle (rē sī′kəl), to change something so it can be reused.

reflect (ri flekt′), to turn back.

reptile (rep′təl), a cold-blooded animal with a backbone, scales, and lungs.

revolution (rev′ə lü′shən), movement of an object in an orbit around another object.

rotation (rō tā′shən), the act of spinning on an axis.

S

sandy soil, loose soil with large grains.

satellite (sat′l īt), object that revolves around another object.

scale, one of the thin, hard plates that cover fish and reptiles.

scientific methods, organized ways of solving problems.

screw (skrü), a simple machine used to hold objects together.

sedimentary (sed′ə men′tər ē) **rock,** rock that forms when layers of material are pressed together.

seed coat (sēd kōt), the outside covering of a seed.

seed leaf (sēd lēf), a part that looks like a leaf and is inside each seed.

seedling (sēd′ling), a young plant that grows from a seed.

simple machine (sim′pəl mə shēn′), one of six kinds of tools with few or no moving parts that makes work easier.

skeleton (skel′ə tən), the bones of a body, fitted together in their natural places.

solar system (sō′lər sis′təm), the sun, the planets and their moons, and other objects that revolve around the sun.

source (sôrs), a place from which something comes.

star, a ball of hot, glowing gases.

states of matter, the three forms of matter—solid, liquid, and gas.

stratus (strā′təs) **clouds,** clouds that form in sheets or layers.

system (sis′təm), a group of organs that work together to do a job in the body.

T

tadpole (tad′pōl′), young frog.

temperature (tem′pər ə chər), a measurement of the speed at which particles of matter are moving.

tendon (ten′dən), a tissue that holds a muscle to a bone.

thermometer (thər mom′ə tər), tool for measuring temperature.

thermostat (thėr′mə stat), a tool that controls temperature in a home or building.

tissue (tish′ü), a group of cells that look alike and do the same job.

tornado (tôr nā′dō), a funnel cloud that has very strong winds and moves along a narrow path.

V

variable (ver′ē ə bəl), anything in an experiment that can be changed.

vibrate (vī′brāt), move quickly back and forth.

virus (vī′rəs), a kind of disease germ that causes diseases such as colds and flu.

visible spectrum (viz′ə bəl spek′trəm), the band of colors formed when a wave of white light is bent.

vocal cords (vō′kəl kôrdz), thin flaps at the top of the windpipe.

volcano (vol kā′nō), a mountain with an opening through which lava, ashes, rocks, and other materials come out.

volume (vol′yəm), (1) amount of space an object takes up; (2) loudness or softness of a sound.

voluntary (vol′ən ter′ē) **muscle,** a muscle a person can control.

W

warm-blooded (wôrm′ blud′id), animals that usually keep about the same body temperature.

water cycle (sī′kəl), the movement of water by evaporation, condensation, and precipitation.

water vapor (wô′tər vā′pər), water in the form of gas.

weather (weŧh′ər), to wear down or break apart rocks.

wedge (wej), a simple machine used to cut or split an object.

wheel and axle (hwēl ənd ak′səl), a simple machine with a center rod attached to a wheel.

work (wėrk), something done when a force moves an object through a distance.

Index

A **bold-faced** number indicates a page with a picture about the topic

Acknowledgments

Unless otherwise acknowledged, all photos are the property of Scott, Foresman and Company. Page positions are as follows: (T)top, (C)center, (B)bottom, (L)left, (R)right, (INS)inset.

iv: Biophoto Associates/Photo Researchers **viii(1):** Stuart Cohen **viii(c):** FPG **x(tl):** Ed Reschke **x(tc):** Centre National de Recherches Iconographiques **x(tr):** Eric V. Grave/Phototake **x(bl):** Manfred Kage/Peter Arnold, Inc. **x(br):** Ed Reschke **xii:** Jim Steers/Chicago Symphony Orchestra **4T:** David Burnett/Woodfin Camp & Associates **4B:** Courtesy Moog Music, Inc. **5B:** Roger Ressmeyer/Starlight **6:** Mitch Reardon/Tony Stone Worldwide/Masterfile **8:** Lynn M. Stone **13ALL:** Walter Chandoha **15:** Anitra Thorhaug **16:** Robert E. Lyons/Color Advantage **17T:** Dan Suzio **18(BOTH):** Dwight R. Kuhn **19T:** Ruth Dixon **19BL:** William E. Ferguson Photography **19BR:** Ed Cooper **21L:** Robert E. Lyons/Color Advantage **21R:** Lynn M. Stone **28:** Wolfgang Bayer Productions **30L:** Jim Brandenburg **30BR:** Jim Brandenburg **30TR:** Gwen Fidler **31TL:** D. Wilder **31R:** Marty Snyderman **31BL:** Dwight R. Kuhn **32:** Don and Pat Valenti **33L:** Lynn M. Stone **33R:** Carl Roessler **34L:** G.I.Bernard/ANIMALS ANIMALS **34R:** Zig Leszczynski/ANIMALS ANIMALS **35TL:** Dr. Merlin D. Tuttle **35BL:** C.Allan Morgan/Peter Arnold, Inc. **35R:** Loren McIntyre **36:** G.Ziesler/Peter Arnold, Inc. **38:** Dwight R. Kuhn **39L:** Doug Wechsler **39R:** Dwight R. Kuhn **41:** Bill Ivy **43B:** Transactions of the Academy of Science of St. Louis, Vol.XXIV, No. 9, December 1923/Academy of Science of St. Louis **43T:** Don and Pat Valenti **48:** Bob & Clara Calhoun/Bruce Coleman Inc. **50T:** Manfred Kage/Peter Arnold, Inc. **50BL:** CNRI/Science Photo Library/Photo Researchers **50BR:** Biophoto Assoc./Photo Researchers **51L:** Leonard LaRue III/Bruce Coleman Inc. **56T:** Johnny Johnson/DRK Photo **56BL:** Dr. M.P.Kahl/DRK Photo **56BC:** Alex Kerstitch/Sea of Cortez Enterprises **56BR:** Don and Pat Valenti **59:** Stephen J. Krasemann/DRK Photo **61:** WWF/Timm Rautert/Bruce Coleman Ltd. **66:** Bill Ivy **68:** C.C.Lockwood/Cactus Clyde Productions **69:** Milt & Joan Mann/Cameramann International, Ltd. **70L:** Larry West **70R:** Fred Bavendam/Peter Arnold, Inc. **71T:** Jane Burton/Bruce Coleman Inc. **72:** Lynn M. Stone **74:** Jose Azel/Contact Press Images **79L:** J. Serrao **79R:** Lynn M. Stone **81T:** Sierra Club/William E. Colby Memorial Library **81B:** Harald Sund **90:** Michael Melford/The Image Bank **92:** Harald Sund **97:** Jeffrey L. Rotman **103:** Fermilab Photo Dept. **118:** (c) Mickey Plefeger 1987 **123R:** Jeanne Trombly **124L:** Tom Bean/DRK Photo **124BR:**

Yoav/Phototake **126:** Greg Pease **129:** Milt & Joan Mann/Cameramann International, Ltd. **130R:** Milt & Joan Mann/Cameramann International, Ltd. **136:** Greg Pease **144T:** Harald Sund **147T:** UPI/Acme/Bettmann Newsphotos **147B:** Peter Menzel **151:** Courtesy Owens-Corning **153:** David R. Frazier Photolibrary **162:** Howard Hall **175:** Brown Brothers **180B:** Bob Daemmrich **184:** Luis Padilla/The Image Bank **186:** Tom Algire **188ALL:** Stuart Cohen **189L:** Harald Sund **189R:** David R. Frazier Photolibrary **190:** Gary Braasch **191L:** FPG **191R:** Stuart Cohen **193:** G. Marche/FPG **194-195:** Harald Sund **195INS:** Lawrence Hudetz **196(ALL):** Barry L. Runk/Grant Heilman Photography **199:** Milt & Joan Mann/Cameramann International, Ltd. **200:** L.L.T.Rhodes/Taurus Photos, Inc. **200(ALL):** L.L.T.Rhodes/Taurus Photos, Inc. **201:** Charlton Photos **206:** Tom Algire **210:** U.S. Geological Survey **212:** Harald Sund **213:** Chip Clark **214:** Steven C. Wilson/Entheos **215:** Lawrence Hudetz **217:** Rob Lewine Photography **218:** James Balog/Black Star **219:** Guillermo Aldana **220:** Greg Vaughn/Black Star **222:** Don and Pat Valenti **228:** John Foster/Masterfile **230:** Ewing Galloway **232L:** Gary Braasch **232C:** David R. Frazier Photolibrary **232R:** David R. Frazier Photolibrary **236L:** Tom Branch/Photo Researchers **236TR:** Gary Braasch **236BR:** Tom Algire **239:** Howie Bluestern/Science Source/Photo Researchers **241:** Dan McCoy/Rainbow **246:** NASA **251L:** NASA **251R:** Dennis Milon **252:** NASA **255:** NASA **259:** NASA **261ALL:** NASA **262:** James Sugar/Black Star **263:** NASA **268:** NASA **274:** David Black **277BC:** Centre National de Recherches Iconographiques **277BR:** Ed Reschke **277TL:** Ed Reschke **277TR:** Manfred Kage/Peter Arnold, Inc. **277BL:** Eric V. Grave/Phototake **279:** Medichrome/Tsiaras/The Stock Shop **303:** Courtesy Dr.Jose Sandoval **307:** (c) Mickey Pfleger 1987 **312:** Brent Jones **316L:** Lynn M. Stone **316R:** Ruth Dixon **318L:** Carl Roessler **318C:** Bob & Clara Calhoun/Bruce Coleman Inc. **318R:** Lynn M. Stone **320CL:** Leonard LaRue III/Bruce Coleman Inc. **320L:** CNRI/Science Photo Library/Photo Researchers **322L:** The Bettmann Archive **322R:** Fred Bavendam/Peter Arnold, Inc. **335: ALL** Lawrence Hudetz **337L:** Tom Branch/Photo Researchers **337TR:** Gary Braasch **337BR:** Tom Algire

Using Metric

About 1 centimeter

About 1 meter

About 1 millimeter

Water boils (100°C)

Normal body temperature (37°C)

Water freezes (0°C)

Degrees Celsius

1 cm
1 cm
1 square centimeter

1 cm
1 cm
1 cm
1 cm
1 cubic centimeter

About 1 kilogram

11 football fields end to end is about 1 kilometer

1 liter of milk

TAAS Practice Tests

Practice reading skills.
Practice writing skills.
Learn about science.
Answer the questions on your own paper.

Reading ■ Read the story. Then answer the questions.

Most new plants grow from seeds. A seed has a tiny plant in it. A seed also has food for the plant. As the tiny plant grows, it uses food from the inside of the seed. The seed breaks open and the roots begin to grow down into the soil. The stem and leaves begin to grow up.

A new plant can start from other parts of a plant. New plants can grow from stems, roots, and leaves. A potato is an underground stem. A new potato plant can grow from a piece of potato with a *bud*.

Have you ever seen potatoes with buds? If you plant these potatoes in soil, new stems, leaves, and roots would grow. Finally, a new potato plant would grow from each potato.

You can also grow a plant from a leaf. If you keep the leaf in water, it will grow roots. A new plant will grow from the leaf and its roots.

1. The word *bud* in this story means
   A. part of a root.
   B. a new potato plant.
   C. part of a potato that can start new potato plants.
   D. a seed.

2. Which group of words best tells how a plant grows from a seed?
   A. roots grow into soil, stem and leaves grow up, seed breaks open, tiny plant uses food
   B. tiny plant uses food, seed breaks open, roots grow into soil, stem and leaves grow up
   C. seed breaks open, stem and leaves grow up, roots grow into soil, tiny plant uses food
   D. stem and leaves grow up, roots grow into soil, tiny plant uses food, seed opens

3. What is this story mostly about?
  A. Plants can grow from seeds or start up from other parts of a plant.
  B. Gardening is a fun hobby.
  C. Potatoes are easy to grow.
  D. Plants need sun and water.

4. If you placed a leaf from a plant in water, what might happen?
  A. The leaf would turn brown.
  B. Nothing.
  C. A new plant would grow.
  D. A potato would form.

Writing ■ Read the story and choose the word or group of words that belongs in each space.

Some scientists _(5)_ for new ways to grow plants. They _(6)_ seeds in a spacecraft far away from earth! These plants _(7)_ in holes in large tubes. Special lights help the plants grow. Machines _(8)_ water and food on the plants.

5. A. searching
  B. were searching
  C. is searching
  D. am searching

6. A. has planted
  B. is planting
  C. am planting
  D. planted

7. A. grow
  B. grown
  C. have growed
  D. is growing

8. A. has sprayed
  B. will have sprayed
  C. spray
  D. spraying

Reading ■ Read the story. Then answer the questions.

Where Do Animals Live?

Animals live in different *habitats.* Some mammals, insects, and birds can live in water. Some live in oceans. Others live in rivers, lakes, and ponds.

Snakes, insects, and some small mammals can live in the desert. Animals that live in a dry habitat must work hard to find food and water.

Many kinds of animals live in the forest. Some live in trees. Some live on the ground. What forest animals can you think of?

A few animals can live in places that always have ice and snow. Most of these animals have thick fur to keep them warm.

Some animals live in one place during the summer and another place during the winter. The winter habitat usually has a warmer climate. Sometimes these animals must travel many miles to their winter and summer homes.

9. In this story, the word *habitat* means
   A. the desert.
   B. a forest.
   C. a place where an animal lives.
   D. a place with ice and snow.

10. Which animals must work hard to find water?
   A. animals that live in snowy places and caves
   B. animals that live in dry habitats
   C. animals that live in lakes
   D. animals that live in the forest

11. What is this story mostly about?
   A. the different habitats where animals live
   B. animals that live in the desert
   C. animals that live in water
   D. animals that live in trees

12. Why do animals that live in cold places have thick fur?

A. to help them swim

B. to help them find food

C. to help them stay cool

D. to keep the heat in their bodies

13. What could be real in this story?

A. Different kinds of mammals live in different habitats.

B. Desert animals need thick fur.

C. Food and water are easy for desert animals to find.

D. Desert mammals live in water.

14. What animals live in the desert?

A. fish, birds, and some small mammals

B. snakes, insects, and some small mammals

C. insects, birds, and fish

D. snakes, fish, and some small mammals

15. What might happen to a mammal that moves from a warm place to a cold one?

A. Its fur might become thinner.

B. It would keep the same amount of fur.

C. Its fur might become thicker.

D. It would not be able to stay warm.

Writing ■ Follow the instructions below.

16. Imagine that you are a polar bear like the one in the picture. Write a story for your class. Describe yourself and the place you live.

What Tells About Life Long Ago?

Fossils tell about plants and animals of long ago. Fossils can be parts or marks of plants and animals. The parts or marks were often left in mud. The mud got hard and turned into rock after many years.

Fossils show what kinds of plants and animals used to live on earth. Fossils show the size and shapes of plants and animals.

Fossils also can tell about what the climate was like long ago. The climate is the kind of weather a place has over a very long time. In a warm, wet climate, large plants with large leaves often grow.

Fossils of animals can give clues about what the animal was like. Fossils of pointed teeth tell that the animal ate meat. Fossils of an animal with flat teeth tell us that the animal ate mostly plants. A fossil of an animal with claws might show that the animal had been able to dig, climb, or hang from trees.

17. Which sentence best tells how a fossil of a plant is formed?
    A. Mud hardens to rock, the plant's parts or marks are left in the mud, and a fossil forms.
    B. The plant leaves parts or marks in the mud, the mud hardens to rock, and a fossil is formed.
    C. Mud hardens to rock, the plant leaves parts or marks in the mud, a fossil is formed, and people study the fossils.
    D. The plant leaves parts or marks in the mud, a fossil forms, and the mud hardens to rock.

18. What might a fossil of an animal with sharp teeth and claws tell you about the animal?
A. It was a bird.
B. It probably ate meat, and used the claws to grasp its food.
C. It ate plants.
D. The animal was old.

19. What might be true in this story?
A. Fossils tell people about the plants and animals that lived on earth long ago.
B. Fossils form quickly.
C. Fossils do not tell people anything.
D. Plants did not live on earth long ago.

20. What kinds of plants often grow in warm, wet climates?
A. ones with no leaves
B. tall trees and grasses
C. plants that do not need much water
D. large plants with large leaves

21. Many years from now, what might people use to learn about the plants and animals of today?
A. the radio
B. the newspaper
C. fossils left by the plants and animals that live on earth today
D. movies about dinosaurs

Writing ■ Follow the instructions below.

22. Look at the pictures of the fossils. Write a report telling what you think these animals were like.

Writing ■ Read the story and choose the best way to write each underlined part. If the passage is written correctly, mark "D. No Mistake."

Some people care. About African giraffes. They
23

know that giraffes need a safe place to live. They
24

made a park. For giraffes. The giraffes are

protected. No one may hunt giraffes in the park.
25

There is plenty of food the giraffes live well.
26

23. A. Some people care, about African giraffes.
    B. Some people care about African giraffes.
    C. Some people, care about African giraffes.
    D. No Mistake

24. A. They made a park for giraffes.
    B. They made a park, for giraffes.
    C. They made, a park for giraffes.
    D. No Mistake

25. A. No one. May hunt giraffes in the park.
    B. No one may hunt. Giraffes in the park.
    C. No one may hunt giraffes. In the park.
    D. No Mistake

26. A. There is plenty of food, the giraffes live well.
    B. There is plenty of food, The giraffes live well.
    C. There is plenty of food. The giraffes live well.
    D. No Mistake

Writing ■ Read the story and decide which type of mistake is in each underlined part. If the underlined part is correctly written, mark "D. No Mistake."

Feathers cover most animals <u>in the Bird</u>
                                                 27
<u>Group.</u> Most birds can fly. <u>Birds have wing's.</u>
                                                        28
Geese are birds that can fly and swim. <u>Thier</u>
                                                                29
<u>webbed feet help</u> them <u>swim, A special oil</u> keeps
29   30
their feathers from getting wet. Geese live in the

north <u>in the summer. when the weather gets</u> <u>cold,</u>
            31   32
<u>geese fly south.</u>

27. A. Spelling
    B. Capitalization
    C. Punctuation
    D. No Mistake

28. A. Spelling
    B. Capitalization
    C. Punctuation
    D. No Mistake

29. A. Spelling
    B. Capitalization
    C. Punctuation
    D. No Mistake

30. A. Spelling
    B. Capitalization
    C. Punctuation
    D. No Mistake

31. A. Spelling
    B. Capitalization
    C. Punctuation
    D. No Mistake

32. A. Spelling
    B. Capitalization
    C. Punctuation
    D. No Mistake

Reading ■ Read the story. Then answer the questions.

How Can Matter Change?

Matter can change from one kind to another. A solid can change to a liquid. Heat makes this change. Heat changes ice into water. Solid butter can become a liquid. Heat from a stove can change the butter.

Liquids can change to solids. A liquid can change to a solid when it cools. Liquid butter *returns* to a solid when it cools. Freezing changes liquids to solids. Water that freezes is ice.

1. What can make a solid become a liquid?
   A. freezing
   B. a machine
   C. cooling
   D. heat

2. In this story, the word *returns* means
   A. freezes
   B. is heated
   C. changes back again
   D. melts

3. Pretend you worked hard to build a snow fort. The snow fort melted right away. How would you feel?
   A. afraid
   B. happy
   C. sad
   D. excited

4. What is this story mostly about?
   A. Butter can become a liquid.
   B. Matter can change from one form to another.
   C. Liquids can change to gases.
   D. Cold can make solids become liquids.

5. In which setting would ice cubes most likely melt quickly?
   A. the freezer
   B. an ice chest
   C. outside on a very cold day
   D. outside on a hot day

6. Suppose an ice cube is melting. Which is the correct order of the steps?

A. ice, water vapor, water

B. ice, water, water vapor

C. liquid, ice, water vapor

D. water vapor, ice, liquid

7. What might happen if you ate a frozen juice bar on a very hot day?

A. The juice would become a liquid.

B. Nothing

C. The juice would stay solid.

D. Heat would make the bar become solid.

Writing ■ Follow the instructions below.

9. Write a story about the snow figure in the picture. Tell how you might build this figure. Tell what you would do first. Tell what you would do next.

8. Suppose you need to melt one cup of butter for a cookie recipe. How can you make the butter melt?

A. Freeze it.

B. Put it in the refrigerator.

C. Heat it on the stove.

D. Cover it tightly.

Reading ■ Read the story. Then answer the questions.

What Can Electricity Do?

Electricity is a kind of energy. Most of the electricity people use is made in special places. It travels through wires from these places to your home. People also get electric energy from batteries. What machines that use energy can you think of?

Energy from electricity is used to light lamps. It heats many kinds of buildings. It runs different kinds of machines.

Suppose someone plugs in a lamp. Then the person turns it on. The lamp wire carries electricity. It makes the light go on. When the lamp is turned off, the wire no longer carries electricity. Then the light goes out.

People use electric energy from batteries in many ways. The electricity moves to toys, radios, and flashlights. Can you think of some machines that use batteries?

10. What is electricity used for?
    A. to travel through wires to a special place
    B. to make batteries for toys and flashlights
    C. to light lamps, heat homes, and run machines
    D. to plug in a lamp

11. Which sentence best describes how people get electricity?
    A. Electricity is made in a special place, it travels through wires, and then people use it.
    B. Electricity is made in a special place, people use it, and then it travels through wires.
    C. Electricity travels through wires to a special place, and then it lights lamps.
    D. People use electricity, then it travels through wires to a special place.

12. What is this story about?
 A. Machines use electricity.
 B. Electricity is a gas.
 C. Batteries make toys work.
 D. Electricity can be used in many ways.

13. What could be real?
 A. Electricity from batteries makes a radio work.
 B. Lamps make electricity.
 C. Wires make electricity.
 D. Electricity is a gas.

Writing ■ Read the story and decide which word or group of words belongs in each space.

George (14) a new robot. He was very excited, and decided to (15) it right away. When he pushed the button, the robot (16) not work. I (17) so disappointed!" cried George.

14. A. had got
 B. got
 C. have gotten
 D. get

16. A. does
 B. do
 C. did
 D. doing

15. A. trying
 B. tried
 C. will try
 D. try

17. A. am
 B. is
 C. are
 D. was

Writing ■ Follow the instructions below.

18. How did George feel when his robot did not work? Imagine that you are George. Write a letter to the toy company telling what happened. Then tell how you feel.

How Can Machines and Electricity Be Used Safely?

Using machines safely is important. People need to keep their hair and clothes away from the machines to be safe.

Always ask an adult for help before using any tools. Tools and machines belong in special places. Be sure to put tools in their special places after you use them. This can help keep you and others safe.

Never use a machine or tool if you do not know how to use it properly. Ask an adult for help when using an *electric appliance.* Do not use an appliance that has a broken cord.

Electricity moves through water. Only use electric appliances if your hands are dry and you are in a dry place.

When you finish using a small appliance that heats up, turn it off. Then unplug the appliance. This can help keep fires from happening.

19. In this story, the term *electric appliance* means
    A. a place for tools
    B. an electric cord
    C. a safety rule
    D. an electric machine

20. What could not be true in this story?
    A. People need to keep their hair and clothes away from machines.
    B. You should never use appliances that have broken cords.
    C. You should never use appliances when you have wet hands.
    D. All electric appliances are safe to use.

21. What is this story mostly about?
    A. how to store tools safely
    B. how to safely use machines and electricity
    C. how machines help people
    D. how machines can hurt people

22. What might happen if a person follows the directions in this story?
  A. He or she might get hurt.
  B. He or she would break the machine.
  C. He or she would be using machines and electricity safely.
  D. His or her work area would be neat.

23. How can people use machines and tools safely?
  A. by using them with adults, keeping hair and clothes away from machines, and keeping machines in their places.
  B. by using them near water.
  C. by leaving them out after using them.
  D. by wearing loose clothing.

Writing ■ Follow the instructions below.

24. Imagine that you have invented a new tool or machine. Write an advertisement for a magazine telling what your tool or machine looks like and what it does. Then write directions for using it safely.

25. Write a report for your teacher about the machines in the pictures. Describe how they are alike. Then tell how they are different.

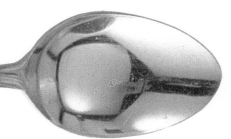

Writing ■ Read the story and choose the best way to write each underlined part. If the underlined part is correctly written, mark "D. No Mistake."

Sasha is going to do a project. to find out how
26

electricity lights a bulb. She will use a battery,

a flashlight bulb, and some wire. Sasha will try to
27

light the bulb She will attach the wire to the

battery and bulb. She will record what she sees.

She will show her teacher the project.

26. A. Sasha is going to do a project, it is an experiment to find out how electricity lights a bulb.
   B. Sasha is going to do a project. To find out how electricity lights a bulb.
   C. Sasha is going to do a project to find out how electricity lights a bulb.
   D. No Mistake

27. A. Sasha will try to light the bulb, she will attach the wire to the battery and also to the bulb.
   B. Sasha will try to light the bulb. She will attach the wire to the battery and attach the wire to the bulb.
   C. Sasha will try to light the bulb. She will attach the wire to the battery and the bulb.
   D. No Mistake

Writing ■ Read the story and decide which type of mistake is in each underlined part. If the underlined part is correctly written, mark "D. No Mistake."

Mr. Lee is a heating technician. Mr. Lee puts

heating machenes in buildings. He checks the
28

machines and fixes them. Mr. Lee makes sure
29

that, all rooms in a building get the right amount

of heat. Large pipes often carry heat through
30

buildings. Mr. lee checks the air temperature
31

inside the pipes. Mr. Lee works hard. He likes

his job.

28. A. Spelling
    B. Capitalization
    C. Punctuation
    D. No Mistake

29. A. Spelling
    B. Capitalization
    C. Punctuation
    D. No Mistake

30. A. Spelling
    B. Capitalization
    C. Punctuation
    D. No Mistake

31. A. Spelling
    B. Capitalization
    C. Punctuation
    D. No Mistake

Reading ■ Read the story. Then answer the questions.

What Is Inside an Empty Glass?

Last week, Mrs. Casey walked into science class and said, "Today, we are going to talk about something you need to stay alive. You can't see it. But, it is all around you. It is outside the school, and inside the classroom—even inside this glass," she said, holding up an empty glass.

Then Mrs. Casey did something strange. She took the glass and stuffed a paper towel into it. She filled a large bowl with water. Next, holding the glass upside down, she pushed it into the water. "What do you think will happen to the paper towel?" she asked.

"It will get wet!" the class answered all together.

Mrs. Casey took the glass out of the water, and pulled out the paper towel. The towel was dry!

Mrs. Casey asked, "Do you know why the towel is dry?" No one answered. She asked, "What else do you think was in the glass with the paper towel?"

"Air!" a student called.

"That's right!" answered Mrs. Casey. "The air in the glass keeps the water from going into the glass. So, the air keeps the towel from getting wet.

"Watch what happens if I tilt the glass. You can see little bubbles of air rise from under the glass. The air is leaving the glass, and the water is going into the glass." Then, pulling the glass from the water, she said, "See. The towel is wet!" Mrs. Casey held up the soggy paper towel.

"When the glass was full of air," she said, "there was no room for water. When the air went out, the water went into the glass and made the towel wet."

1. The towel stayed dry the first time Mrs. Casey put the glass into the water because
   A. air filled the glass.
   B. the paper towel kept the water out.
   C. water was in the glass already.
   D. the glass was empty.

2. This story takes place in
   A. a science class.
   B. a schoolyard.
   C. a playground.
   D. Mrs. Casey's house.

3. How do you think the students felt when Mrs. Casey pulled out the dry towel from the glass?
   A. angry
   B. surprised
   C. frightened
   D. sad

4. After Mrs. Casey filled the bowl with water, she
   A. wet the paper towel.
   B. pulled the paper towel out.
   C. pushed the glass into the water.
   D. cleaned the glass.

Writing ■ Follow the instructions below.

5. Look at the pictures. Decide which season is shown in each picture. Write a report for your class, telling how the two seasons are different. Describe how the weather might feel during each season. Tell which season you like better and explain your reasons. Use colorful details to make your report interesting.

How Can Weather Change?

What did the air feel like when you left your home this morning? Do you think the weather has changed since then? Weather can change all through the day. It can change from hot to cool and from sunny to cloudy.

Air temperature can change. You use a thermometer to measure changes in air temperature. The temperature goes up as the air gets warmer.

Wind can change. It can blow hard. It can blow gently. Wind can also change direction. A wind vane points in the direction the wind comes from.

The weather changes through the year. In many places, the four *seasons* have different weather.

Spring often has rain and warm temperatures. Summer can have very hot temperatures. The air can be wet or dry.

Fall often has cool air. Rain might turn to snow in late fall. Winter often has cold and snowy weather.

In many places, the weather does not change much in different seasons. Some places stay warm most of the year. Other places usually stay cool.

6. What is this story mostly about?
   A. Weather changes through the day and through the year.
   B. Wind vanes tell which way the wind is blowing.
   C. The four seasons have different weather.
   D. Winter has cold and snowy weather.

7. What could be real in this story?
   A. Rain might turn to snow in late fall.
   B. Winter never has snow.
   C. Summer never has wet weather.
   D. Fall always has snow.

8. In this story, the word *seasons* means
A. weather changes that happen through the day.
B. changes in wind direction.
C. four times of the year that often have different weather.
D. changes in air temperature.

9. What helps measure changes in air temperature?
A. a wind vane
B. the way air feels on a person's skin
C. the direction the wind is blowing
D. a thermometer

10. What might happen if the air temperature got very cold on a rainy day?
A. The sun would come out.
B. The rain would turn to snow.
C. The wind would stop blowing.
D. The temperature would go up.

11. How can you tell which direction the wind is blowing?
A. by checking a thermometer
B. by looking at the sky
C. by checking the temperature
D. by checking a wind vane

Writing ■ Follow the instructions below.

12. Write a paragraph for your teacher describing this picture of the earth. Explain why part of the earth is dark and part of it is light. Tell what happens as the earth turns.

Reading ■ Read the story. Then answer the questions.

What Moves Around the Sun?

Earth is a planet. The earth takes about 365 days, or one year, to move in an orbit around the sun. Nine planets move around the sun. The planets' names are Mercury, Venus, Earth, Mars, Jupiter, Saturn, Uranus, Neptune, and Pluto.

Each planet is a different size. Each is a different distance from the sun. Mercury is the planet closest to the sun. Earth is the third planet from the sun. Pluto is the planet farthest from the sun.

The moon *orbits* the earth. While the moon orbits the earth, the earth is moving around the sun. The earth and moon orbit the sun together.

Moonlight comes from the sun. The sun shines on the moon like it shines on the earth. We can see this light in the night sky.

13. What makes the moon appear lighted?
    A. light from the moon
    B. light from the earth
    C. light from the sun
    D. light from stars

14. In this story, the word *orbits* means
    A. the light that shines on the moon.
    B. to move around a planet, moon, or the sun.
    C. the size of a planet.
    D. the distance of each planet from the sun.

15. What could be true in this story?
    A. The moon moves in an orbit around the earth.
    B. The earth moves in an orbit around the moon.
    C. The sun moves in an orbit around the earth.
    D. The earth and moon orbit other planets.

16. Which planets are in the correct order—from closest to the sun to the farthest from the sun.
    A. Pluto, Mercury, Earth
    B. Pluto, Earth, Mercury
    C. Mercury, Pluto, Earth
    D. Mercury, Earth, Pluto

17. The earth's trip around the sun takes
    A. one day.
    B. one week.
    C. one month.
    D. one year.

Writing ■ Read the story and choose the words that belong in each space.

Linda Morabito (18) pictures taken from space. One picture (19) a moon of Jupiter. The moon (20) a cloud that no one had ever seen. Linda Morabito studied the picture carefully. She (21) that the cloud came from a volcano. She was the first person to discover a volcano on a moon.

18. A. did studied
    B. studied
    C. have studied
    D. has study

19. A. will show
    B. have shown
    C. has showed
    D. showed

20. A. have had
    B. have
    C. had
    D. will have

21. A. found
    B. find
    C. finded
    D. will find

Writing ■ Read the story and choose the best way to write each underlined part of the story. If the underlined part is correct as it is written, mark "D. No Mistake."

Astronomers study the moon, the sun. And the planets.
22

They measure the size. Of stars. They measure
23   **24**

how far away objects are. They draw maps they
                                    25

also study pictures from space.

22. A. Astronomers study the moon. The sun. And the planets.
B. Astronomers study the moon, the sun, and the planets.
C. Astronomers study the moon the sun and the planets.
D. No Mistake

23. A. They measure the size of stars.
B. They measure, the size of stars.
C. They measure. The size of stars.
D. No Mistake

24. A. They measure. How far away are objects.
B. How far away objects are, they measure.
C. They measure how far objects are away.
D. No Mistake.

25. A. They draw maps. Also study pictures from space.
B. They draw maps. They also study. Pictures from space.
C. They draw maps. They also study pictures from space.
D. No Mistake

Writing ■ Read the story and decide which type of mistake is in each underlined part. If the underlined part is correctly written in the story, mark "D. No Mistake."

A Thermometer is a glass tube that holds a liquid.
26

When the temperature gets warmer, the liquid

expands, or getts bigger. The liquid then
27

moves up the tube, The numbers and marks
28

along the thermometer show degrees. Read the

temperature by checking the level of the liquid.
29

26. A. Spelling
   B. Capitalization
   C. Punctuation
   D. No Mistake

28. A. Spelling
   B. Capitalization
   C. Punctuation
   D. No Mistake

27. A. Spelling
   B. Capitalization
   C. Punctuation
   D. No Mistake

29. A. Spelling
   B. Capitalization
   C. Punctuation
   D. No Mistake

Writing ■ Follow the instructions below.

30. Imagine that a lake in your town is in danger of becoming polluted. Write a report for your class about why it is important to have clean water. Then tell how the people in your town can help keep the water in the lake clean.

Reading ■ Read the story. Then answer the questions.

What Happens to the Food You Eat?

You must eat food to stay alive. Food helps you grow. It helps you stay healthy. Food gives you energy. You need energy to work and play.

The food you eat must be *digested* before your body can use it. When your body digests food, it changes the form of food.

Food starts to be digested in your mouth. Your teeth break food into small pieces when you chew it. Special juices in your mouth help make the food soft before you swallow it.

The food goes down a long food tube to the stomach. Muscles in the food tube move the food.

Special juices in the stomach mix with the food. Stomach muscles turn the food around and round.

After a while, the food looks like a thick liquid. Then the food moves out of the stomach into your small intestine. The small intestine is a long tube curled up inside you.

Juices in your small intestine finish digesting the food. The food is changed to a thin liquid. Substances from the liquid move into the blood. Then the blood carries these substances to all the parts of your body.

1. What is the first paragraph mostly about?
   A. Food helps keep you healthy and gives you energy.
   B. Without energy, you would not be able to play every day.
   C. Food can help you grow tall and strong.
   D. Your health depends on the foods you eat.

2. What could NOT be real in this story?

   A. Your teeth help break food into small bits.

   B. Blood carries the changed food to all parts of your body.

   C. Food cannot give you energy.

   D. Juices in your mouth help soften food.

3. In this story, the word *digested* means

   A. understood.

   B. moved in the stomach.

   C. became thicker.

   D. changed the form of food.

4. What happens first?

   A. Blood carries changed food to all body parts.

   B. Food moves through a tube to the stomach.

   C. Juices in your stomach help break up food.

   D. Your teeth break food into small pieces.

5. When it leaves the stomach, food is

   A. a thin liquid.

   B. a thick liquid.

   C. a soft solid.

   D. a part of the blood.

Writing ■ Follow the instructions below.

6. Imagine that you learned to play the trombone in the picture. Write a story about how you learned to play. Tell what happened first. Tell what happened next. Tell how your lungs help you play the trombone.

Reading ■ Read the story. Then answer the questions.

What Helps Protect You?

Germs are tiny living things. You cannot see them. They can get inside your body through your nose and mouth and through cuts in your skin. Some kinds of germs can make you sick.

Dirt can have germs in it. Keeping clean can protect you from some germs that could make you sick. Washing your hands with soap and warm water can help get rid of germs.

Objects can have germs on them. You can help protect yourself from sickness by keeping objects out of your mouth.

Some medicines can protect you from sickness. Sometimes you get these medicines in shots. You take some medicines by mouth. The medicine that helps protect people from a sickness called polio is given by mouth.

If you do get sick from germs, your body works hard to help you *recover*. Special parts of your body work to get rid of the germs that made you sick. You can help your body get healthy by getting extra rest and eating healthy foods.

7. What is the story mostly about?
   A. Washing your hands is important.
   B. You need to keep objects like pencils out of your mouth.
   C. You get some medicines in shots. You get other medicines by mouth.
   D. You can help protect yourself from germs that cause sickness.

8. In this story, the word *recover* means
   A. cover again.
   B. get healthy again.
   C. build muscles.
   D. protect.

9. Washing your hands with soap and water is important because
  A. it can help get rid of germs on your hands.
  B. it can protect you from all sicknesses.
  C. it kills all germs.
  D. it makes you strong.

10. If you get sick from germs, you need to
  A. eat extra food.
  B. get extra rest.
  C. stop eating many foods.
  D. get extra exercise.

11. What might happen if a person with a cold sneezes into the air?
  A. The person will lose all the germs.
  B. No germs will pass to other people.
  C. Germs might spread to others.
  D. All germs will die.

12. A sick person usually feels
  A. happy.
  B. excited.
  C. pleased.
  D. unhappy.

Writing ■ Read the story and choose the word or words that belong in each group.

Abby and Jim (13) two safety signs. They (14) one sign yellow. They (15) dark paper for the other. The yellow sign (16) easier to see.

13. A. drawed
  B. have drawed
  C. drew
  D. drawn

14. A. maked
  B. will make
  C. made
  D. make

15. A. use
  B. used
  C. will use
  D. uses

16. A. was
  B. were
  C. will become
  D. been

Writing ■ Read the story and choose the best way to write each underlined part.

Doctors have jobs they are different kinds of
17

jobs. Some doctors take. Care of children. They
18   19

make sure children are healthy. They ask
20

children how they feel they help them stay well.

17. A. Doctors have
   different kinds of
   jobs.
   B. Doctors have jobs.
   Different kinds.
   C. Doctors have.
   Different kinds of
   jobs.
   D. No Mistake

18. A. Some doctors. Take
   care of children.
   B. Some doctors take
   care. Of children.
   C. Some doctors take
   care of children.
   D. No Mistake

19. A. They make sure.
   Healthy children.
   B. They make sure of.
   Healthy children.
   C. They check children
   they make sure they
   are healthy.
   D. No Mistake

20. A. They ask children,
   how they feel, they
   help them stay well.
   B. They ask. Children
   if they are well.
   C. They ask children
   how they feel. They
   help them stay well.
   D. No Mistake

Writing ■ Follow the instructions below.

21. Write a letter to a younger child explaining
   how to cross a street safely. Tell what he or
   she should do first, second, and so on.

Writing ■ Read the story and decide which type of mistake is in each underlined part. If the underlined part is correctly written, mark "D. No Mistake."

George Washington Carver taught people about

farming. <u>He began to study penuts.</u> <u>He found</u>
       22   **23**

<u>that peanuts, were a good food.</u> He found <u>ways</u>
                                                    24

<u>to make chese, milk, and flour from peanuts.</u>

<u>carver found new ways to use foods.</u>
25

22. A. Spelling
    B. Capitalization
    C. Punctuation
    D. No Mistake

23. A. Spelling
    B. Capitalization
    C. Punctuation
    D. No Mistake

24. A. Spelling
    B. Capitalization
    C. Punctuation
    D. No Mistake

25. A. Spelling
    B. Capitalization
    C. Punctuation
    D. No Mistake

Writing ■ Follow the instructions below.

26. Pretend that you made this sandwich. Write a story for your classmates explaining how you made it. Also tell why healthy foods are important.